# MORE PRAISE
## FOR THE JOBBANK SERIES...

"If you are looking for a job ... before you go to the newspapers and the help-wanted ads, listen to Bob Adams, publisher of *The Metropolitan New York JobBank*."
### -Tom Brokaw, *NBC*

"Help on the job hunt ... Anyone who is job-hunting in the New York area can find a lot of useful ideas in a new paperback called *The Metropolitan New York JobBank* ..."
### -Angela Taylor, *New York Times*

"One of the better publishers of employment almanacs is Adams Media Corporation ... publisher of *The Metropolitan New York JobBank* and similarly named directories of employers in Texas, Boston, Chicago, Northern and Southern California, and Washington DC. A good buy ..."
### -*Wall Street Journal's*
### *National Business Employment Weekly*

"For those graduates whose parents are pacing the floor, conspicuously placing circled want ads around the house and typing up resumes, [*The Carolina JobBank*] answers job-search questions."
### -*Greensboro News and Record*

"A timely book for Chicago job hunters follows books from the same publisher that were well received in New York and Boston ... [*The Chicago JobBank* is] a fine tool for job hunters ..."
### -Clarence Peterson, *Chicago Tribune*

"Because our listing is seen by people across the nation, it generates lots of resumes for us. We encourage unsolicited resumes. We'll always be listed [in *The Chicago JobBank*] as long as I'm in this career."
### -Tom Fitzpatrick, Director of Human Resources
### Merchandise Mart Properties, Inc.

"Job-hunting is never fun, but this book can ease the ordeal ... [*The Los Angeles JobBank*] will help allay fears, build confidence, and avoid wheel-spinning."
### -Robert W. Ross, *Los Angeles Times*

"*The Seattle JobBank* is an essential resource for job hunters."
### -Gil Lopez, Staffing Team Manager
### Battelle Pacific Northwest Laboratories

"*The Phoenix JobBank* is a first-class publication. The information provided is useful and current."

**-Lyndon Denton**
**Director of Human Resources and Materials Management**
**Apache Nitrogen Products, Inc.**

"Job hunters can't afford to waste time. *The Minneapolis-St. Paul JobBank* contains information that used to require hours of research in the library."

**-Carmella Zagone**
**Minneapolis-based Human Resources Administrator**

"*The Florida JobBank* is an invaluable job-search reference tool. It provides the most up-to-date information and contact names available for companies in Florida. I should know -- it worked for me!"

**-Rhonda Cody, Human Resources Consultant**
**Aetna Life and Casualty**

"I read through the 'Basics of Job Winning' and 'Resumes' sections [in *The Dallas-Fort Worth JobBank*] and found them to be very informative, with some positive tips for the job searcher. I believe the strategies outlined will bring success to any determined candidate."

**-Camilla Norder, Professional Recruiter**
**Presbyterian Hospital of Dallas**

"Through *The Dallas-Fort Worth JobBank,* we've been able to attract high-quality candidates for several positions."

**-Rob Bertino, Southern States Sales Manager**
**CompuServe**

"Packed with helpful contacts, *The Houston JobBank* empowers its reader to launch an effective, strategic job search in the Houston metropolitan area."

**-Andrew Ceperley, Director**
**College of Communication Career Services**
**The University of Texas at Austin**

"*The San Francisco Bay Area JobBank* ... is a highly useful guide, with plenty of how-to's ranging from resume tips to interview dress codes and research shortcuts."

**-A.S. Ross, *San Francisco Examiner***

"[*The Atlanta JobBank* is] one of the best sources for finding a job in Atlanta!"

**-Luann Miller, Human Resources Manager**
**Prudential Preferred Financial Services**

# What makes the
# JobBank series
# the nation's premier
# line of employment guides?

With vital employment information on thousands of employers across the nation, the JobBank series is the most comprehensive and authoritative set of career directories available today.

Each book in the series provides information on **dozens of different industries** in a given city or area, with the primary employer listings providing contact information, telephone and fax numbers, e-mail addresses, Websites, a summary of the firm's business, internships, and in many cases descriptions of the firm's typical professional job categories.

All of the reference information in the JobBank series is as up-to-date and accurate as possible. Every year, the entire database is thoroughly researched and verified by mail and by telephone. Adams Media Corporation publishes **more local employment guides more often** than any other publisher of career directories.

The JobBank series offers **28 regional titles**, from Minneapolis to Houston, and from Boston to San Francisco as well as **two industry-specific titles**. All of the information is organized geographically, because most people look for jobs in specific areas of the country.

A condensed, but thorough, review of the entire job search process is presented in the chapter **The Basics of Job Winning**, a feature which has received many compliments from career counselors. In addition, each JobBank directory includes a section on **resumes and cover letters** the *New York Times* has acclaimed as "excellent."

The JobBank series gives job hunters the most comprehensive, timely, and accurate career information, organized and indexed to facilitate your job search. An entire career reference library, JobBank books are designed to help you find optimal employment in any market.

# Top career publications from Adams Media Corporation

## The JobBank Series:
*each JobBank book is $17.95*

The Atlanta JobBank, 14th Ed.
The Boston JobBank, 19th Ed.
The Carolina JobBank, 6th Ed.
The Chicago JobBank, 18th Ed.
The Colorado JobBank, 13th Ed.
The Connecticut JobBank, 2nd Ed.
The Dallas-Fort Worth JobBank, 13th Ed.
The Florida JobBank, 15th Ed.
The Houston JobBank, 11th Ed.
The Los Angeles JobBank, 17th Ed.
The Metropolitan New York JobBank, 18th Ed.
The Greater Philadelphia JobBank, 14th Ed.
The Phoenix JobBank, 8th Ed.
The Portland JobBank, 3rd Ed.
The Seattle JobBank, 12th Ed.
The Virginia JobBank, 3rd Ed.
The Metropolitan Washington DC JobBank, 15th Ed.

The National JobBank, 2004 (Covers the entire U.S.: $450.00 hc)

## Other Career Titles:
The Adams Cover Letter Almanac ($12.95)
The Adams Internet Job Search Almanac, 6th Ed. ($12.95)
The Adams Executive Recruiters Almanac, 2nd Ed. ($17.95)
The Adams Job Interview Almanac ($12.95)
The Adams Jobs Almanac, 8th Ed. ($16.95)
The Adams Resume Almanac ($10.95)
Business Etiquette in Brief ($7.95)
Campus Free College Degrees, 8th Ed. ($16.95)
Career Tests ($12.95)
Closing Techniques, 2nd Ed. ($8.95)
Cold Calling Techniques, 4th Ed. ($8.95)
College Grad Job Hunter, 4th Ed. ($14.95)
The Complete Resume & Job Search Book for College Students, 2nd Ed. ($12.95)
Cover Letters That Knock 'em Dead, 5th Ed. ($12.95)
Every Woman's Essential Job Hunting & Resume Book ($11.95)
The Everything Cover Letter Book ($12.95)
The Everything Get-A-Job Book ($12.95)
The Everything Hot Careers Book ($12.95)
The Everything Job Interview Book ($12.95)
The Everything Online Business Book ($12.95)
The Everything Online Job Search Book ($12.95)
The Everything Resume Book ($12.95)
The Everything Selling Book ($12.95)
First Time Resume ($7.95)
How to Start and Operate a Successful Business ($9.95)
Knock 'em Dead, 2003 ($14.95)
Knock 'em Dead Business Presentations ($12.95)
Market Yourself and Your Career, 2nd Ed. ($12.95)
The New Professional Image ($12.95)
The 150 Most Profitable Home Businesses for Women ($9.95)
The Resume Handbook, 3rd Ed. ($7.95)
Resumes That Knock 'em Dead, 5th Ed. ($12.95)
The Road to CEO ($20.00 hc)
The 250 Job Interview Questions You'll Most Likely Be Asked ($9.95)
Your Executive Image ($10.95)

If you cannot find these titles at your favorite book outlet, you may order them directly from the publisher. **BY PHONE:** Call 800/872-5627 (in Massachusetts 508/427-7100). We accept Visa, Mastercard, and American Express. $4.95 will be added to your total for shipping and handling. **BY MAIL:** Write out the full titles of the books you'd like to order and send payment, including $4.95 for shipping and handling to: Adams Media Corporation, 57 Littlefield Street, Avon MA 02322. 30-day money back guarantee.
**BY FAX:** 800/872-5628.
*Discounts available for standing orders.*

# 17th Edition
## THE San Francisco Bay Area
# JobBank

|  |  |
|---|---|
| *Editor:* | Erik L. Herman |
| *Assistant Editor:* | Sarah Rocha |
| *Researchers:* | Maurice Curran |
|  | Megan Danahy |
|  | Emily Mozzone |

Adams Media

AVON, MASSACHUSETTS

Published by Adams Media, an F+W Publications Company
57 Littlefield Street, Avon, MA 02322 U.S.A.
www.adamsmedia.com

ISBN: 1-58062-862-1
ISSN: 1089-9889
Manufactured in the United States of America.

*This book is available on standing order and at quantity discounts for bulk purchases. For information, call 800/872-5627 (in Massachusetts, 508/427-7100) or email at jobbank@adamsmedia.com*

# TABLE OF CONTENTS

- *Automotive Repair Shops*
- *Automotive Stampings*
- *Industrial Vehicles and Moving Equipment*
- *Motor Vehicles and Equipment*
- *Travel Trailers and Campers*

### Banking/Savings and Loans/77

### Biotechnology, Pharmaceuticals, and Scientific R&D/83
- *Clinical Labs*
- *Lab Equipment Manufacturers*
- *Pharmaceutical Manufacturers and Distributors*

### Business Services and Non-Scientific Research/93
- *Adjustment and Collection Services*
- *Cleaning, Maintenance, and Pest Control Services*
- *Credit Reporting Services*
- *Detective, Guard, and Armored Car Services/Security Systems Services*
- *Miscellaneous Equipment Rental and Leasing*
- *Secretarial and Court Reporting Services*

### Charities and Social Services/96
- *Job Training and Vocational Rehabilitation Services*

### Chemicals/Rubber and Plastics/99
- *Adhesives, Detergents, Inks, Paints, Soaps, Varnishes*
- *Agricultural Chemicals and Fertilizers*
- *Carbon and Graphite Products*
- *Chemical Engineering Firms*
- *Industrial Gases*

### Communications: Telecommunications and Broadcasting/102
- *Cable/Pay Television Services*
- *Communications Equipment*
- *Radio and Television Broadcasting Stations*
- *Telephone, Telegraph, and Other Message Communications*

### Computer Hardware, Software, and Services/110
- *Computer Components and Hardware Manufacturers*
- *Consultants and Computer Training Companies*
- *Internet and Online Service Providers*
- *Networking and Systems Services*
- *Repair Services/Rental and Leasing*
- *Resellers, Wholesalers, and Distributors*
- *Software Developers/Programming Services*

### Educational Services/157
- *Business/Secretarial/Data Processing Schools*
- *Colleges/Universities/Professional Schools*
- *Community Colleges/Technical Schools/Vocational Schools*
- *Elementary and Secondary Schools*
- *Preschool and Child Daycare Services*

### Electronic/Industrial Electrical Equipment/163
- *Electronic Machines and Systems*
- *Semiconductor Manufacturers*

### Environmental and Waste Management Services/187
- *Environmental Engineering Firms*
- *Sanitary Services*

### Fabricated/Primary Metals and Products/191
- *Aluminum and Copper Foundries*
- *Die-Castings*
- *Iron and Steel Foundries/Steel Works, Blast Furnaces, and Rolling Mills*

### Financial Services/193
- *Consumer Financing and Credit Agencies*
- *Investment Specialists*

- *Mortgage Bankers and Loan Brokers*
- *Security and Commodity Brokers, Dealers, and Exchanges*

### Food and Beverages/Agriculture/201

- *Crop Services and Farm Supplies*
- *Dairy Farms*
- *Food Manufacturers/Processors and Agricultural Producers*
- *Tobacco Products*

### Government/207

- *Courts*
- *Executive, Legislative, and General Government*
- *Public Agencies (Firefighters, Military, Police)*
- *United States Postal Service*

### Health Care: Services, Equipment, and Products/209

- *Dental Labs and Equipment*
- *Home Health Care Agencies*
- *Hospitals and Medical Centers*
- *Medical Equipment Manufacturers and Wholesalers*
- *Offices and Clinics of Health Practitioners*
- *Residential Treatment Centers/Nursing Homes*
- *Veterinary Services*

### Hotels and Restaurants/221

### Insurance/225

### Legal Services/233

### Manufacturing: Miscellaneous Consumer/235

- *Art Supplies*
- *Batteries*
- *Cosmetics and Related Products*
- *Household Appliances and Audio/Video Equipment*
- *Jewelry, Silverware, and Plated Ware*
- *Miscellaneous Household Furniture and Fixtures*
- *Musical Instruments*
- *Tools*
- *Toys and Sporting Goods*

### Manufacturing: Miscellaneous Industrial/237

- *Ball and Roller Bearings*
- *Commercial Furniture and Fixtures*
- *Fans, Blowers, and Purification Equipment*
- *Industrial Machinery and Equipment*
- *Motors and Generators/Compressors and Engine Parts*
- *Vending Machines*

### Mining/Gas/Petroleum/Energy Related/245

- *Anthracite, Coal, and Ore Mining*
- *Mining Machinery and Equipment*
- *Oil and Gas Field Services*
- *Petroleum and Natural Gas*

### Paper and Wood Products/247

- *Forest and Wood Products and Services*
- *Lumber and Wood Wholesale*
- *Millwork, Plywood, and Structural Members*
- *Paper and Wood Mills*

### Printing and Publishing/249

- *Book, Newspaper, and Periodical Publishers*
- *Commercial Photographers*
- *Commercial Printing Services*
- *Graphic Designers*

### Real Estate/256

- *Land Subdividers and Developers*

## SECTION FOUR: INDEX

# Index of Primary Employers by Industry/277

# INTRODUCTION

# HOW TO USE THIS BOOK

Right now, you hold in your hands one of the most effective job-hunting tools available anywhere. In *The San Francisco JobBank*, you will find valuable information to help you launch or continue a rewarding career. But before you open to the book's employer listings and start calling about current job openings, take a few minutes to learn how best to use the resources presented in *The San Francisco JobBank*.

*The San Francisco JobBank* will help you to stand out from other jobseekers. While many people looking for a new job rely solely on newspaper help-wanted ads, this book offers you a much more effective job-search method – direct contact. The direct contact method has been proven twice as effective as scanning the help-wanted ads. Instead of waiting for employers to come looking for you, you'll be far more effective going to them. While many of your competitors will use trial and error methods in trying to set up interviews, you'll learn not only how to get interviews, but what to expect once you've got them.

In the next few pages, we'll take you through each section of the book so you'll be prepared to get a jump-start on your competition.

## Basics of Job Winning

Preparation. Strategy. Time management. These are three of the most important elements of a successful job search. *Basics of Job Winning* helps you address these and all the other elements needed to find the right job.

One of your first priorities should be to define your personal career objectives. What qualities make a job desirable to you? Creativity? High pay? Prestige? Use *Basics of Job Winning* to weigh these questions. Then use the rest of the chapter to design a strategy to find a job that matches your criteria.

In *Basics of Job Winning*, you'll learn which job-hunting techniques work, and which don't. We've reviewed the pros and cons of mass mailings, help-wanted ads, and direct contact. We'll show you how to develop and approach contacts in your field; how to research a prospective employer; and how to use that information to get an interview and the job.

Also included in *Basics of Job Winning*: interview dress code and etiquette, the "do's and don'ts" of interviewing, sample interview questions, and more. We also deal with some of the unique problems faced by those jobseekers who are currently employed, those who have lost a job, and college students conducting their first job search.

## Resumes and Cover Letters

The approach you take to writing your resume and cover letter can often mean the difference between getting an interview and never being noticed. In this section, we discuss different formats, as well as what to put on (and what to leave off) your resume. We review the benefits and drawbacks of professional resume writers, and the importance of a follow-up letter. Also included in this section are sample resumes and cover letters which you can use as models.

## The Employer Listings

Employers are listed alphabetically by industry. When a company does business under a person's name, like "John Smith & Co.," the company is usually listed by the surname's spelling (in this case "S"). Exceptions occur when a company's name is widely recognized, like "JCPenney" or "Howard Johnson Motor Lodge." In those cases, the company's first name is the key ("J" and "H" respectively).

*The San Francisco JobBank* covers a very wide range of industries. Each company profile is assigned to one of the industry chapters listed below.

| | |
|---|---|
| Accounting and Management Consulting | Fabricated/Primary Metals and Products |
| Advertising, Marketing, and Public Relations | Financial Services |
| Aerospace | Food and Beverages/Agriculture |
| Apparel, Fashion, and Textiles | Government |
| Architecture, Construction, and Engineering | Health Care: Services, Equipment, and |
| Arts, Entertainment, Sports, and Recreation | Products |
| Automotive | Hotels and Restaurants |
| Banking/Savings and Loans | Insurance |
| Biotechnology, Pharmaceuticals, and | Legal Services |
| Scientific R&D | Manufacturing: Miscellaneous Consumer |
| Business Services and Non-Scientific | Manufacturing: Miscellaneous Industrial |
| Research | Mining/Gas/Petroleum/Energy Related |
| Charities and Social Services | Paper and Wood Products |
| Chemicals/Rubber and Plastics | Printing and Publishing |
| Communications: Telecommunications and | Real Estate |
| Broadcasting | Retail |
| Computer Hardware, Software, and Services | Stone, Clay, Glass, and Concrete Products |
| Educational Services | Transportation/Travel |
| Electronic/Industrial Electrical Equipment | Utilities: Electric/Gas/Water |
| Environmental and Waste Management | Miscellaneous Wholesaling |
| Services | |

Many of the company listings offer detailed company profiles. In addition to company names, addresses, and phone numbers, these listings also include contact names or hiring departments, and descriptions of each company's products and/or services. Many of these listings also feature a variety of additional information including:

**Positions advertised** - A list of open positions the company was advertising at the time our research was conducted. Note: Keep in mind that *The San Francisco JobBank* is a directory of major employers in the area, not a directory of openings currently available. Positions listed in this book that were advertised at the time research was conducted may no longer be open. Many of the companies listed will be hiring, others will not. However, since most professional job openings are filled without the placement of help-wanted ads, contacting the employers in this book directly is still a more effective method than browsing the Sunday papers.

**Special programs -** Does the company offer training programs, internships, or apprenticeships? These programs can be important to first time jobseekers and college students looking for practical work experience. Many employer profiles will include information on these programs.

**Parent company -** If an employer is a subsidiary of a larger company, the name of that parent company will often be listed here. Use this information to supplement your company research before contacting the employer.

**Number of employees -** The number of workers a company employs.

Company listings may also include information on other U.S. locations and any stock exchanges the firm may be listed on.

A note on all employer listings that appear in *The Shell JobBank*: This book is intended as a starting point. It is not intended to replace any effort that you, the jobseeker, should devote to your job hunt. Keep in mind that while a great deal of effort has been put into collecting and verifying the company profiles provided in this book, addresses and contact names change regularly. Inevitably, some contact names listed herein have changed even before you read this. We recommend you contact a company before mailing your resume to ensure nothing has changed.

### Index

*The San Francisco JobBank* index is listed alphabetically by industry.

# THE JOB SEARCH

# THE BASICS OF JOB WINNING: A CONDENSED REVIEW

This chapter is divided into four sections. The first section explains the fundamentals that every jobseeker should know, especially first-time jobseekers. The next three sections deal with special situations faced by specific types of jobseekers: those who are currently employed, those who have lost a job, and college students.

## THE BASICS:
### Things Everyone Needs to Know

### Career Planning

The first step to finding your ideal job is to clearly define your objectives. This is better known as career planning (or life planning if you wish to emphasize the importance of combining the two). Career planning has become a field of study in and of itself.

If you are thinking of choosing or switching careers, we particularly emphasize two things. First, choose a career where you will enjoy most of the day-to-day tasks. This sounds obvious, but most of us have at some point found the idea of a glamour industry or prestigious job title attractive without thinking of the key consideration: Would we enjoy performing the *everyday* tasks the position entails?

The second key consideration is that you are not merely choosing a career, but also a lifestyle. Career counselors indicate that one of the most common problems people encounter in jobseeking is that they fail to consider how well-suited they are for a particular position or career. For example, some people, attracted to management consulting by good salaries, early responsibility, and high-level corporate exposure, do not adapt well to the long hours, heavy travel demands, and constant pressure to produce. Be sure to ask yourself how you might adapt to the day-to-day duties and working environment that a specific position entails. Then ask yourself how you might adapt to the demands of that career or industry as a whole.

### Choosing Your Strategy

Assuming that you've established your career objectives, the next step of the job search is to develop a strategy. If you don't take the time to develop a plan, you may find yourself going in circles after several weeks of randomly searching for opportunities that always seem just beyond your reach.

The most common jobseeking techniques are:

- following up on help-wanted advertisements (in the newspaper or online)
- using employment services
- relying on personal contacts
- contacting employers directly (the Direct Contact method)

Each of these approaches can lead to better jobs. However, the Direct Contact method boasts twice the success rate of the others. So unless you have specific reasons to employ other strategies, Direct Contact should form the foundation of your job search.

If you choose to use other methods as well, try to expend at least half your energy on Direct Contact. Millions of other jobseekers have already proven that Direct Contact has been twice as effective in obtaining employment, so why not follow in their footsteps?

## Setting Your Schedule

Okay, so now that you've targeted a strategy it's time to work out the details of your job search. The most important detail is setting up a schedule. Of course, since job searches aren't something most people do regularly, it may be hard to estimate how long each step will take. Nonetheless, it is important to have a plan so that you can monitor your progress.

When outlining your job search schedule, have a realistic time frame in mind. If you will be job-searching full-time, your search could take at least two months or more. If you can only devote part-time effort, it will probably take at least four months.

You probably know a few people who seem to spend their whole lives searching for a better job in their spare time. Don't be one of them. If you are presently working and don't feel like devoting a lot of energy to jobseeking right now, then wait. Focus on enjoying your present position, performing your best on the job, and storing up energy for when you are really ready to begin your job search.

> **The first step in beginning your job search is to clearly define your objectives.**

Those of you who are currently unemployed should remember that *job-hunting is tough work, both physically and emotionally.* It is also intellectually demanding work that requires you to be at your best. So don't tire yourself out by working on your job campaign around the clock. At the same time, be sure to discipline yourself. The most logical way to manage your time while looking for a job is to keep your regular working hours.

If you are searching full-time and have decided to choose several different strategies, we recommend that you divide up each week, designating some time for each method. By trying several approaches at once, you can evaluate how promising each seems and alter your schedule accordingly. Keep in mind that the *majority of openings are filled without being advertised.* Remember also that positions advertised on the Internet are just as likely to already be filled as those found in the newspaper!

If you are searching part-time and decide to try several different contact methods, we recommend that you try them sequentially. You simply won't have enough time to put a meaningful amount of effort into more than one method at once. Estimate the length of your job search, and then allocate so many weeks or months for each contact method, beginning with Direct Contact. The purpose of setting this schedule is not to rush you to your goal but to help you periodically evaluate your progress.

## The Direct Contact Method

Once you have scheduled your time, you are ready to begin your search in earnest. Beginning with the Direct Contact method, the first step is to develop a checklist for categorizing the types of firms for which you'd like to work. You might categorize firms by product line, size, customer type (such as industrial or consumer), growth prospects, or geographical location. Keep in mind, the shorter the list the easier it will be to locate a company that is right for you.

Next you will want to use this *JobBank* book to assemble your list of potential employers. Choose firms where *you* are most likely to be able to find a job. Try matching your skills with those that a specific job demands. Consider where your skills might be in demand, the degree of competition for employment, and the employment outlook at each company.

Separate your prospect list into three groups. The first 25 percent will be your primary target group, the next 25 percent will be your secondary group, and the remaining names will be your reserve group.

After you form your prospect list, begin working on your resume. Refer to the Resumes and Cover Letters section following this chapter for more information.

Once your resume is complete, begin researching your first batch of prospective employers. You will want to determine whether you would be happy working at the firms you are researching and to get a better idea of what their employment needs might be. You also need to obtain enough information to sound highly informed about the company during phone conversations and in mail correspondence. But don't go all out on your research yet! You probably won't be able to arrange interviews with some of these firms, so save your big research effort until you start to arrange interviews. Nevertheless, you should plan to spend several hours researching each firm. Do your research in batches to save time and energy. Start with this book, and find out what you can about each of the firms in your primary target group. For answers to specific questions, contact any pertinent professional associations that may be able to help you learn more about an employer. Read industry publications looking for articles on the firm. (Addresses of associations and names of important publications are listed after each section of employer listings in this book.) Then look up the company on the Internet or try additional resources at your local library. Keep organized, and maintain a folder on each firm.

**The more you know about a company, the more likely you are to catch an interviewer's eye. (You'll also face fewer surprises once you get the job!)**

Information to look for includes: company size; president, CEO, or owner's name; when the company was established; what each division does; and benefits that are important to you. An abundance of company information can now be found electronically, through the World Wide Web or commercial online services. Researching companies online is a convenient means of obtaining information quickly and easily. If you have access to the Internet, you can search from your home at any time of day.

You may search a particular company's Website for current information that may be otherwise unavailable in print. In fact, many companies that maintain a site update their information daily. In addition, you may also search articles written about the company online. Today, most of the nation's largest newspapers, magazines, trade publications, and regional business periodicals have online versions of their publications. To find additional resources, use a search engine like Yahoo! or Alta Vista and type in the keyword "companies" or "employers."

If you discover something that really disturbs you about the firm (they are about to close their only local office), or if you discover that your chances of getting a job there are practically nil (they have just instituted a hiring freeze), then cross them off your prospect list. If possible, supplement your research efforts by contacting individuals who know the firm well. Ideally you should make an informal contact with someone at that particular firm, but often a direct competitor or a major customer will be able to supply you with just as much information. At the very least, try to obtain whatever printed information the company has available – not just annual reports, but product brochures, company profiles, or catalogs. This information is often available on the Internet.

## Getting the Interview

Now it is time to make Direct Contact with the goal of arranging interviews. If you have read any books on job-searching, you may have noticed that most of these books tell you to avoid the human resources office like the plague. It is said that the human resources office never hires people; they screen candidates. Unfortunately, this is often the case. If you can identify the appropriate manager with the authority to hire you, you should try to contact that person directly.

The obvious means of initiating Direct Contact are:

- Mail (postal or electronic)
- Phone calls

Mail contact is a good choice if you have not been in the job market for a while. You can take your time to prepare a letter, say exactly what you want, and of course include your resume. Remember that employers receive many resumes every day. Don't be surprised if you do not get a response to your inquiry, *and don't spend weeks waiting for responses that may never come.* If you do send a letter, follow it up (or precede it) with a phone call. This will increase your impact, and because of the initial research you did, will underscore both your familiarity with and your interest in the firm. Bear in mind that your goal is to make your name a familiar one with prospective employers, so that when a position becomes available, your resume will be one of the first the hiring manager seeks out.

### DEVELOPING YOUR CONTACTS: NETWORKING

Some career counselors feel that the best route to a better job is through somebody you already know or through somebody to whom you can be introduced. These counselors recommend that you build your contact base beyond your current acquaintances by asking each one to introduce you, or refer you, to additional people in your field of interest.

The theory goes like this: You might start with 15 personal contacts, each of whom introduces you to three additional people, for a total of 45 additional contacts. Then each of these people introduces you to three additional people, which adds 135 additional contacts. Theoretically, you will soon know every person in the industry.

Of course, developing your personal contacts does not work quite as smoothly as the theory suggests because some people will not be able to introduce you to anyone. The further you stray from your initial contact base, the weaker your references may be. So, if you do try developing your own contacts, try to begin with as many people that you know personally as you can. Dig into your personal phone book and your holiday greeting card list and locate old classmates from school. Be particularly sure to approach people who perform your personal business such as your lawyer, accountant, banker, doctor, stockbroker, and insurance agent. These people develop a very broad contact base due to the nature of their professions.

If you send a fax, always follow with a hard copy of your resume and cover letter in the mail. Often, through no fault of your own, a fax will come through illegibly and employers do not often have time to let candidates know.

Another alternative is to make a "cover call." Your cover call should be just like your cover letter: concise. Your first statement should interest the employer in you. Then try to subtly mention your familiarity with the firm. Don't be overbearing; keep your introduction to three sentences or less. Be pleasant, self-confident, and relaxed. This will greatly increase the chances of the person at the other end of the line developing the conversation. But don't press. If you are asked to follow up with "something in the mail," this signals the conversation's natural end. Don't try to prolong the conversation once it has ended, and don't ask what they want to receive in the mail. Always send your resume and a highly personalized follow-up letter, reminding the addressee of the phone conversation. *Always* include a cover letter if you are asked to send a resume, and treat your resume and cover letter as a total package. Gear your letter toward the specific position you are applying for and prove why you would be a "good match" for the position.

> **Always include a cover letter if you are asked to send a resume.**

Unless you are in telephone sales, making smooth and relaxed cover calls will probably not come easily. Practice them on your own, and then with your friends or relatives.

---

### DON'T BOTHER WITH MASS MAILINGS OR BARRAGES OF PHONE CALLS

Direct Contact does not mean burying every firm within a hundred miles with mail and phone calls. Mass mailings rarely work in the job hunt. This also applies to those letters that are personalized -- but dehumanized -- on an automatic typewriter or computer. Don't waste your time or money on such a project; you will fool no one but yourself.

The worst part of sending out mass mailings, or making unplanned phone calls to companies you have not researched, is that you are likely to be remembered as someone with little genuine interest in the firm, who lacks sincerity -- somebody that nobody wants to hire.

---

If you obtain an interview as a result of a telephone conversation, be sure to send a thank-you note reiterating the points you made during the conversation. You will appear more professional and increase your impact. However, unless specifically requested, don't mail your resume once an interview has been arranged. Take it with you to the interview instead.

You should never show up to seek a professional position without an appointment. Even if you are somehow lucky enough to obtain an interview, you will appear so unprofessional that you will not be seriously considered.

## HELP WANTED ADVERTISEMENTS

Only a small fraction of professional job openings are advertised. Yet the majority of jobseekers -- and quite a few people not in the job market -- spend a lot of time studying the help wanted ads. As a result, the competition for advertised openings is often very severe.

A moderate-sized employer told us about their experience advertising in the help wanted section of a major Sunday newspaper:

*It was a disaster. We had over 500 responses from this relatively small ad in just one week. We have only two phone lines in this office and one was totally knocked out. We'll never advertise for professional help again.*

If you insist on following up on help wanted ads, then research a firm before you reply to an ad. Preliminary research might help to separate you from all of the other professionals responding to that ad, many of whom will have only a passing interest in the opportunity. It will also give you insight about a particular firm, to help you determine if it is potentially a good match. That said, your chances of obtaining a job through the want ads are still much smaller than they are with the Direct Contact method.

### Preparing for the Interview

As each interview is arranged, begin your in-depth research. You should arrive at an interview knowing the company upside-down and inside-out. You need to know the company's products, types of customers, subsidiaries, parent company, principal locations, rank in the industry, sales and profit trends, type of ownership, size, current plans, and much more. By this time you have probably narrowed your job search to one industry. Even if you haven't, you should still be familiar with common industry terms, the trends in the firm's industry, the firm's principal competitors and their relative performance, and the direction in which the industry leaders are headed.

Dig into every resource you can! Surf the Internet. Read the company literature, the trade press, the business press, and if the company is public, call your stockbroker (if you have one) and ask for additional information. If possible, speak to someone at the firm before the interview, or if not, speak to someone at a competing firm. The more time you spend, the better. Even if you feel extremely pressed for time, you should set aside several hours for pre-interview research.

> **You should arrive at an interview knowing the company upside-down and inside-out.**

If you have been out of the job market for some time, don't be surprised if you find yourself tense during your first few interviews. It will probably happen every time you re-enter the market, not just when you seek your first job after getting out of school.

Tension is natural during an interview, but knowing you have done a thorough research job should put you more at ease. Make a list of questions that you think might be asked in each interview. Think out your answers carefully and practice them with a friend. Tape record your responses to the problem questions. (*See also in this chapter: Informational Interviews.*) If you feel particularly unsure of your interviewing skills, arrange your first interviews at firms you are not as interested in. (But remember it is common courtesy to seem enthusiastic about the possibility of working for any firm at which you interview.) Practice again on your own after these first few interviews. Go over the difficult questions that you were asked.

Take some time to really think about how you will convey your work history. Present "bad experiences" as "learning experiences." Instead of saying "I hated my position as a salesperson because I had to bother people on the phone," say "I realized that cold-calling was not my strong suit. Though I love working with people, I decided my talents would be best used in a more face-to-face atmosphere." Always find some sort of lesson from previous jobs, as they all have one.

## Interview Attire

How important is the proper dress for a job interview? Buying a complete wardrobe, donning new shoes, and having your hair styled every morning are not enough to guarantee you a career position as an investment banker. But on the other hand, if you can't find a clean, conservative suit or won't take the time to wash your hair, then you are just wasting your time by interviewing at all.

Personal grooming is as important as finding appropriate clothes for a job interview. Careful grooming indicates both a sense of thoroughness and self-confidence. This is not the time to make a statement -- take out the extra earrings and avoid any garish hair colors not found in nature. Women should not wear excessive makeup, and both men and women should refrain from wearing any perfume or cologne (it only takes a small spritz to leave an allergic interviewer with a fit of sneezing and a bad impression of your meeting). Men should be freshly shaven, even if the interview is late in the day, and men with long hair should have it pulled back and neat.

Men applying for any professional position should wear a suit, preferably in a conservative color such as navy or charcoal gray. It is easy to get away with wearing the same dark suit to consecutive interviews at the same company; just be sure to wear a different shirt and tie for each interview.

Women should also wear a business suit. Professionalism still dictates a suit with a skirt, rather than slacks, as proper interview garb for women. This is usually true even at companies where pants are acceptable attire for female employees. As much as you may disagree with this guideline, the more prudent time to fight this standard is after you land the job.

The final selection of candidates for a job opening won't be determined by dress, of course. However, inappropriate dress can quickly eliminate a first-round candidate. So while you shouldn't spend a fortune on a new wardrobe, you should be sure that your clothes are adequate. The key is to dress at least as formally or slightly more formally and more conservatively than the position would suggest.

## What to Bring

Be complete. Everyone needs a watch, a pen, and a notepad. Finally, a briefcase or a leather-bound folder (containing extra, *unfolded*, copies of your resume) will help complete the look of professionalism.

Sometimes the interviewer will be running behind schedule. Don't be upset, be sympathetic. There is often pressure to interview a lot of candidates and to quickly fill a demanding position. So be sure to come to your interview with good reading material to keep yourself occupied and relaxed.

## The Interview

The very beginning of the interview is the most important part because it determines the tone for the rest of it. Those first few moments are especially crucial. Do you smile when you meet? Do you establish enough eye contact, but not too much? Do you walk into the office with a self-assured and confident stride? Do you shake hands firmly? Do you make small talk easily without being garrulous? It is

---

**BE PREPARED:**
**Some Common Interview Questions**

Tell me about yourself.

Why did you leave your last job?

What excites you in your current job?

Where would you like to be in five years?

How much overtime are you willing to work?

What would your previous/present employer tell me about you?

Tell me about a difficult situation that you
faced at your previous/present job.

What are your greatest strengths?

What are your weaknesses?

Describe a work situation where you took initiative
and went beyond your normal responsibilities.

Why should we hire you?

---

human nature to judge people by that first impression, so make sure it is a good one. But most of all, try to be yourself.

Often the interviewer will begin, after the small talk, by telling you about the company, the division, the department, or perhaps, the position. Because of your detailed research, the information about the company should be repetitive for you, and the interviewer would probably like nothing better than to avoid this regurgitation of the company biography. So if you can do so tactfully, indicate to the interviewer that you are very familiar with the firm. If he or she seems intent on providing you with background information, despite your hints, then acquiesce.

But be sure to remain attentive. If you can manage to generate a brief discussion of the company or the industry at this point, without being forceful, great. It will help to further build rapport, underscore your interest, and increase your impact.

> ## The interviewer's job is to find a reason to turn you down; your job is to not provide that reason.
>
> -John L. LaFevre, author,
> *How You Really Get Hired*
>
> Reprinted from the 1989/90 *CPC Annual,* with permission of the National Association of Colleges and Employers (formerly College Placement Council, Inc.), copyright holder.

Soon (if it didn't begin that way) the interviewer will begin the questions, many of which you will have already practiced. This period of the interview usually falls into one of two categories (or somewhere in between): either a structured interview, where the interviewer has a prescribed set of questions to ask; or an unstructured interview, where the interviewer will ask only leading questions to get you to talk about yourself, your experiences, and your goals. Try to sense as quickly as possible in which direction the interviewer wishes to proceed. This will make the interviewer feel more relaxed and in control of the situation.

Remember to keep attuned to the interviewer and make the length of your answers appropriate to the situation. If you are really unsure as to how detailed a response the interviewer is seeking, then ask.

As the interview progresses, the interviewer will probably mention some of the most important responsibilities of the position. If applicable, draw parallels between your experience and the demands of the position as detailed by the interviewer. Describe your past experience in the same manner that you do on your resume: emphasizing results and achievements and not merely describing activities. But don't exaggerate. Be on the level about your abilities.

The first interview is often the toughest, where many candidates are screened out. If you are interviewing for a very competitive position, you will have to make an impression that will last. Focus on a few of your greatest strengths that are relevant to the position. Develop these points carefully, state them again in different words, and then try to summarize them briefly at the end of the interview.

Often the interviewer will pause toward the end and ask if you have any questions. Particularly in a structured interview, this might be the one chance to really show your knowledge of and interest in the firm. Have a list prepared of specific questions that are of real interest to you. Let your questions subtly show your research and your knowledge of the firm's activities. It is wise to have an extensive list of questions, as several of them may be answered during the interview.

Do not turn your opportunity to ask questions into an interrogation. Avoid reading directly from your list of questions, and ask questions that you are fairly certain the interviewer can answer (remember how you feel when you cannot answer a question during an interview).

Even if you are unable to determine the salary range beforehand, do not ask about it during the first interview. You can always ask later. Above all, don't ask about fringe benefits until you have been offered a position. (Then be sure to get all the details.)

Try not to be negative about anything during the interview, particularly any past employer or any previous job. Be cheerful. Everyone likes to work with someone who seems to be happy. Even if you detest your current/former job or manager, do not make disparaging comments. The interviewer may construe this as a sign of a potential attitude problem and not consider you a strong candidate.

Don't let a tough question throw you off base. If you don't know the answer to a question, simply say so -- do not apologize. Just smile. Nobody can answer every question -- particularly some of the questions that are asked in job interviews.

Before your first interview, you may be able to determine how many rounds of interviews there usually are for positions at your level. (Of course it may differ quite a bit even within the different levels of one firm.) Usually you can count on attending at least two or three interviews, although some firms are known to give a minimum of six interviews for all professional positions. While you should be more relaxed as you return for subsequent interviews, the pressure will be on. The more prepared you are, the better.

Depending on what information you are able to obtain, you might want to vary your strategy quite a bit from interview to interview. For instance, if the first interview is a screening interview, then be sure a few of your strengths really stand out. On the other hand, if later interviews are primarily with people who are in a position to veto your hiring, but not to push it forward, then you should primarily focus on building rapport as opposed to reiterating and developing your key strengths.

If it looks as though your skills and background do not match the position the interviewer was hoping to fill, ask him or her if there is another division or subsidiary that perhaps could profit from your talents.

## After the Interview

Write a follow-up letter immediately after the interview, while it is still fresh in the interviewer's mind (see the sample follow-up letter format found in the Resumes and Cover Letters chapter). Not only is this a thank-you, but it also gives you the chance to provide the interviewer with any details you may have forgotten (as long as they can be tactfully added in). If you haven't heard back from the interviewer within a week of sending your thank-you letter, call to stress your continued interest in the firm and the position. If you lost any points during the interview for any reason, this letter can help you regain footing. Be polite and make sure to stress your continued interest and competency to fill the position. Just don't forget to proofread it thoroughly. If you are unsure of the spelling of the interviewer's name, call the receptionist and ask.

# THE BALANCING ACT:
## Looking for a New Job While Currently Employed

For those of you who are still employed, job-searching will be particularly tiring because it must be done in addition to your normal work responsibilities. So don't overwork yourself to the point where you show up to interviews looking exhausted or start to slip behind at your current job. On the other hand, don't be tempted to quit your present job! The long hours are worth it. Searching for a job while you have one puts you in a position of strength.

## Making Contact

If you must be at your office during the business day, then you have additional problems to deal with. How can you work interviews into the business day? And if you work in an open office, how can you even call to set up interviews? Obviously, you should keep up the effort and the appearances on your present job. So maximize your use of the lunch hour, early mornings, and late afternoons for calling. If you keep trying, you'll be surprised how often you will be able to reach the executive you are trying to contact during your out-of-office hours. You can catch people as early as 8 a.m. and as late as 6 p.m. on frequent occasions.

## Scheduling Interviews

Your inability to interview at any time other than lunch just might work to your advantage. If you can, try to set up as many interviews as possible for your lunch hour. This will go a long way to creating a relaxed atmosphere. But be sure the interviews don't stray too far from the agenda on hand.

Lunchtime interviews are much easier to obtain if you have substantial career experience. People with less experience will often find no alternative to taking time off for interviews. If you have to take time off, you have to take time off. But try to do this as little as possible. Try to take the whole day off in order to avoid being blatantly obvious about your job search, and try to schedule two to three interviews for the same day. (It is very difficult to maintain an optimum level of energy at more than three interviews in one day.) Explain to the interviewer why you might have to juggle your interview schedule; he/she should honor the respect you're showing your current employer by minimizing your days off and will probably appreciate the fact that another prospective employer is interested in you.

> **Try calling as early as 8 a.m. and as late as 6 p.m. You'll be surprised how often you will be able to reach the executive you want during these times of the day.**

## References

What do you tell an interviewer who asks for references from your current employer? Just say that while you are happy to have your former employers contacted, you are trying to keep your job search confidential and would rather that your current employer not be contacted until you have been given a firm offer.

# IF YOU'RE FIRED OR LAID OFF:
## Picking Yourself Up and Dusting Yourself Off

If you've been fired or laid off, you are not the first and will not be the last to go through this traumatic experience. In today's changing economy, thousands of professionals lose their jobs every year. Even if you were terminated with just cause, do not lose heart. Remember, being fired is not a reflection on you as a person. It is usually a reflection of your company's staffing needs and its perception of your recent job performance and attitude. And if you were not performing up to par or enjoying your work, then you will probably be better off at another company anyway.

> **Be prepared for the question "Why were you fired?" during job interviews.**

A thorough job search could take months, so be sure to negotiate a reasonable severance package, if possible, and determine to what benefits, such as health insurance, you are still legally entitled. Also, register for unemployment compensation immediately. Don't be surprised to find other professionals collecting unemployment compensation – it is for everyone who has lost their job.

Don't start your job search with a flurry of unplanned activity. Start by choosing a strategy and working out a plan. Now is not the time for major changes in your life. If possible, remain in the same career and in the same geographical location, at least until you have been working again for a while. On the other hand, if the only industry for which you are trained is leaving, or is severely depressed in your area, then you should give prompt consideration to moving or switching careers.

Avoid mentioning you were fired when arranging interviews, but be prepared for the question "Why were you fired?" during an interview. If you were laid off as a result of downsizing, briefly explain, being sure to reinforce that your job loss was not due to performance. If you were in fact fired, be honest, but try to detail the reason as favorably as possible and portray what you have learned from your mistakes. If you are confident one of your past managers will give you a good reference, tell the interviewer to contact that person. Do not to speak negatively of your past employer and try not to sound particularly worried about your status of being temporarily unemployed.

Finally, don't spend too much time reflecting on why you were let go or how you might have avoided it. Think positively, look to the future, and be sure to follow a careful plan during your job search.

## THE COLLEGE STUDENT:
### Conducting Your First Job Search

While you will be able to apply many of the basics covered earlier in this chapter to your job search, there are some situations unique to the college student's job search.

---

### THE GPA QUESTION

You are interviewing for the job of your dreams. Everything is going well: You've established a good rapport, the interviewer seems impressed with your qualifications, and you're almost positive the job is yours. Then you're asked about your GPA, which is pitifully low. Do you tell the truth and watch your dream job fly out the window?

*Never* lie about your GPA (they may request your transcript, and no company will hire a liar). You can, however, explain if there is a reason you don't feel your grades reflect your abilities, and mention any other impressive statistics. For example, if you have a high GPA in your major, or in the last few semesters (as opposed to your cumulative college career), you can use that fact to your advantage.

---

Perhaps the biggest problem college students face is lack of experience. Many schools have internship programs designed to give students exposure to the field of their choice, as well as the opportunity to make valuable contacts. Check out your school's career services department to see what internships are available. If your school does not have a formal internship program, or if there are no available internships that appeal to you, try contacting local businesses and offering your services. Often, businesses will be more than willing to have an extra pair of hands (especially if those hands are unpaid!) for a day or two each week. Or try contacting school alumni to see if you can "shadow" them for a few days, and see what their daily duties are like.

## Informational Interviews

Although many jobseekers do not do this, it can be extremely helpful to arrange an informational interview with a college alumnus or someone else who works in your desired industry. You interview them about their job, their company, and their industry with questions you have prepared in advance. This can be done over the phone but is usually done in person. This will provide you with a contact in the industry who may give you more valuable information – or perhaps even a job opportunity – in the future. Always follow up with a thank you letter that includes your contact information.

*The goal is to try to begin building experience and establishing contacts as early as possible in your college career.*

What do you do if, for whatever reason, you weren't able to get experience directly related to your desired career? First, look at your previous jobs and see if there's anything you can highlight. Did you supervise or train other employees? Did you reorganize the accounting system, or boost productivity in some way? Accomplishments like these demonstrate leadership, responsibility, and innovation -- qualities that most companies look for in employees. And don't forget volunteer activities and school clubs, which can also showcase these traits.

## On-Campus Recruiting

Companies will often send recruiters to interview on-site at various colleges. This gives students a chance to interview with companies that may not have interviewed them otherwise. This is particularly true if a company schedules "open" interviews, in which the only screening process is who is first in line at the sign-ups. Of course, since many more applicants gain interviews in this format, this also means that many more people are rejected. The on-campus interview is generally a screening interview, to see if it is worth the company's time to invite you in for a second interview. So do everything possible to make yourself stand out from the crowd.

The first step, of course, is to check out any and all information your school's career center has on the company. If the information seems out of date, check out the company on the Internet or call the company's headquarters and ask for any printed information.

Many companies will host an informational meeting for interviewees, often the evening before interviews are scheduled to take place. DO NOT MISS THIS MEETING. The recruiter will almost certainly ask if you attended. Make an effort to stay after the meeting and talk with the company's representatives. Not only does this give you an opportunity to find out more information about both the company and the position, it also makes you stand out in the recruiter's mind. If there's a particular company that you had your heart set on, but you weren't able to get an interview with them, attend the information session anyway. You may be able to persuade the recruiter to squeeze you into the schedule. (Or you may discover that the company really isn't the right fit for you after all.)

Try to check out the interview site beforehand. Some colleges may conduct "mock" interviews that take place in one of the standard interview rooms. Or you may be able to convince a career counselor (or even a custodian) to let you sneak a peek during off-hours. Either way, having an idea of the room's setup will help you to mentally prepare.

Arrive at least 15 minutes early to the interview. The recruiter may be ahead of schedule, and might meet you early. But don't be surprised if previous interviews have run over, resulting in your 30-minute slot being reduced to 20 minutes (or less). Don't complain or appear anxious; just use the time you do have as efficiently as possible to showcase the reasons *you* are the ideal candidate. Staying calm and composed in these situations will work to your advantage.

## LAST WORDS

A parting word of advice. Again and again during your job search you will face rejection. You will be rejected when you apply for interviews. You will be rejected after interviews. For every job offer you finally receive, you probably will have been rejected many times. Don't let rejections slow you down. Keep reminding yourself that the sooner you go out, start your job search, and get those rejections flowing in, the closer you will be to obtaining the job you want.

## RESUMES AND COVER LETTERS

When filling a position, an employer will often have 100-plus applicants, but time to interview only a handful of the most promising ones. As a result, he or she will reject most applicants after only briefly skimming their resumes.

Unless you have phoned and talked to the employer – which you should do whenever you can – you will be chosen or rejected for an interview entirely on the basis of your resume and cover letter. *Your cover letter must catch the employer's attention, and your resume must hold it.* (But remember – a resume is no substitute for a job search campaign. You must seek a job. Your resume is only one tool, albeit a critical one.)

# RESUME FORMAT:
## Mechanics of a First Impression

### The Basics

Employers dislike long resumes, so unless you have an unusually strong background with many years of experience and a diversity of outstanding achievements, keep your resume length to one page. If you must squeeze in more information than would otherwise fit, try using a smaller typeface or changing the margins. Watch also for "widows" at the end of paragraphs. You can often free up some space if you can shorten the information enough to get rid of those single words taking up an entire line. Another tactic that works with some word processing programs is to decrease the font size of your paragraph returns and changing the spacing between lines.

Print your resume on standard 8 1/2" x 11" paper. Since recruiters often get resumes in batches of hundreds, a smaller-sized resume may be lost in the pile. Oversized resumes are likely to get crumpled at the edges, and won't fit easily in their files.

*First impressions matter, so make sure the recruiter's first impression of your resume is a good one.* Never hand-write your resume (or cover letter)! Print your resume on quality paper that has weight and texture, in a conservative color such as white, ivory, or pale gray. Good resume paper is easy to find at many stores that sell stationery or office products. It is even available at some drug stores. Use *matching* paper and envelopes for both your resume and cover letter. One hiring manager at a major magazine throws out all resumes that arrive on paper that differs in color from the envelope!

Do not buy paper with images of clouds and rainbows in the background or anything that looks like casual stationery that you would send to your favorite aunt. Do not spray perfume or cologne on your resume. Do not include your picture with your resume unless you have a specific and appropriate reason to do so.

Another tip: Do a test print of your resume (and cover letter), to make sure the watermark is on the same side as the text so that you can read it. Also make sure it is right-side up. As trivial as this may sound, some recruiters check for this! One recruiter at a law firm in New Hampshire sheepishly admitted this is the first thing he checks. *"I open each envelope and check the watermarks on the resume and cover letter. Those candidates that have it wrong go into a different pile."*

## Getting it on Paper

Modern photocomposition typesetting gives you the clearest, sharpest image, a wide variety of type styles, and effects such as italics, bold-facing, and book-like justified margins. It is also too expensive for many jobseekers. The quality of today's laser printers means that a computer-generated resume can look just as impressive as one that has been professionally typeset.

A computer with a word processing or desktop publishing program is the most common way to generate your resume. This allows you the flexibility to make changes almost instantly and to store different drafts on disk. Word processing and desktop publishing programs also offer many different fonts to choose from, each taking up different amounts of space. (It is generally best to stay between 9-point and 12-point font size.) Many other options are also available, such as bold-facing or italicizing for emphasis and the ability to change and manipulate spacing. It is generally recommended to leave the right-hand margin unjustified as this keeps the spacing between the text even and therefore easier to read. It is not wrong to justify both margins of text, but if possible try it both ways before you decide.

For a resume on paper, the end result will be largely determined by the quality of the printer you use. Laser printers will generally provide the best quality. Do not use a dot matrix printer.

Many companies now use scanning equipment to screen the resumes they receive, and certain paper, fonts, and other features are more compatible with this technology. White paper is preferable, as well as a standard font such as Courier or Helvetica. You should use at least a 10-point font, and avoid bolding, italics, underlining, borders, boxes, or graphics.

Household typewriters and office typewriters with nylon or other cloth ribbons are *not* good enough for typing your resume. If you don't have access to a quality word processing program, hire a professional with the resources to prepare your resume for you. Keep in mind that businesses such as Kinko's (open 24 hours) provide access to computers with quality printers.

*Don't* make your copies on an office photocopier. Only the human resources office may see the resume you mail. Everyone else may see only a copy of it, and copies of copies quickly become unreadable. Furthermore, sending photocopies of your resume or cover letter is completely unprofessional. Either print out each copy individually, or take your resume to a professional copy shop, which will generally offer professionally-maintained, extra-high-quality photocopiers and charge fairly reasonable prices. You want your resume to represent you with the look of polished quality.

## Proof with Care

Whether you typed it or paid to have it produced professionally, mistakes on resumes are not only embarrassing, but will usually remove you from consideration (particularly if something obvious such as your name is misspelled). No matter how much you paid someone else to type, write, or typeset your resume, *you* lose if there is a mistake. So proofread it as carefully as possible. Get a friend to help you. Read your draft aloud as your friend checks the proof copy. Then have your friend read aloud while you check. Next, read it letter by letter to check spelling and punctuation.

If you are having it typed or typeset by a resume service or a printer, and you don't have time to proof it, pay for it and take it home. Proof it there and bring it back later to get it corrected and printed.

If you wrote your resume with a word processing program, use the built-in spell checker to double-check for spelling errors. Keep in mind that a spell checker will not find errors such as "to" for "two" or "wok" for "work." Many spell check programs do not recognize missing or misused punctuation, nor are they set to check the spelling of capitalized words. It's important that you still proofread your resume to check for grammatical mistakes and other problems, even _after_ it has been spellchecked. If you find mistakes, do not make edits in pen or pencil or use white-out to fix them on the final copy!

## Electronic Resumes

As companies rely increasingly on emerging technologies to find qualified candidates for job openings, you may opt to create an electronic resume in order to remain competitive in today's job market. Why is this important? Companies today sometimes request that resumes be submitted by e-mail, and many hiring managers regularly check online resume databases for candidates to fill unadvertised job openings. Other companies enlist the services of electronic employment database services, which charge jobseekers a nominal fee to have their resumes posted to the database to be viewed by potential employers. Still other companies use their own automated applicant tracking systems, in which case your resume is fed through a scanner that sends the image to a computer that "reads" your resume, looking for keywords, and files it accordingly in its database.

Whether you're posting your resume online, e-mailing it directly to an employer, sending it to an electronic employment database, or sending it to a company you suspect uses an automated applicant tracking system, you must create some form of electronic resume to take advantage of the technology. Don't panic! An electronic resume is simply a modified version of your conventional resume. An electronic resume is one that is sparsely formatted, but filled with keywords and important facts.

In order to post your resume to the Internet – either to an online resume database or through direct e-mail to an employer – you will need to change the way your resume is formatted. Instead of a Word, WordPerfect, or other word processing document, save your resume as a plain text, DOS, or ASCII file. These three terms are basically interchangeable, and describe text at its simplest, most basic level, without the formatting such as boldface or italics that most jobseekers use to make their resumes look more interesting. If you use e-mail, you'll notice that all of your messages are written and received in this format. First, you should remove all formatting from your resume including boldface, italics, underlining, bullets, differing font sizes, and graphics. Then, convert and save your resume as a plain text file. Most word processing programs have a "save as" feature that allows you to save files in different formats. Here, you should choose "text only" or "plain text."

Another option is to create a resume in HTML (hypertext markup language), the text formatting language used to publish information on the World Wide Web. However, the real usefulness of HTML resumes is still being explored. Most of the major online databases do not accept HTML resumes, and the vast majority of companies only accept plain text resumes through their e-mail.

Finally, if you simply wish to send your resume to an electronic employment database or a company that uses an automated applicant tracking system, there is no need to convert your resume to a plain text file. The only change you need to make is to organize the information in your resume by keywords. Employers are likely to do keyword searches for information, such as degree held or knowledge of particular types of software. Therefore, using the right keywords or key phrases in your resume is critical to its ultimate success. Keywords are usually nouns or short phrases that the computer searches for which refer to experience, training, skills, and abilities. For example, let's say an employer searches an employment database for a sales representative with the following criteria:

BS/BA
exceeded quota
cold calls
high energy
willing to travel

Even if you have the right qualifications, neglecting to use these keywords would result in the computer passing over your resume. Although there is no way to know for sure which keywords employers are most likely to search for, you can make educated guesses by checking the help-wanted ads or online job postings for your type of job. You should also arrange keywords in a keyword summary, a paragraph listing your qualifications that immediately follows your name and address (see sample letter in this chapter). In addition, choose a nondecorative font with clear, distinct characters, such as Helvetica or Times. It is more difficult for a scanner to accurately pick up the more unusual fonts. Boldface and all capital letters are best used only for major section headings, such as "Experience" and "Education." It is also best to avoid using italics or underlining, since this can cause the letters to bleed into one another.

For more specific information on creating and sending electronic resumes, see *The Adams Internet Job Search Almanac.*

## Types of Resumes

The most common resume formats are the functional resume, the chronological resume, and the combination resume. (Examples can be found at the end of this chapter.) A functional resume focuses on skills and de-emphasizes job titles, employers, etc. A functional resume is best if you have been out of the work force for a long time or are changing careers. It is also good if you want to highlight specific skills and strengths, especially if all of your work experience has been at one company. This format can also be a good choice if you are just out of school or have no experience in your desired field.

Choose a chronological format if you are currently working or were working recently, and if your most recent experiences relate to your desired field. Use reverse chronological order and include dates. To a recruiter your last job and your latest schooling are the most important, so put the last first and list the rest going back in time.

A combination resume is perhaps the most common. This resume simply combines elements of the functional and chronological resume formats. This is used by many jobseekers with a solid track record who find elements of both types useful.

## Organization

Your name, phone number, e-mail address (if you have one), and a complete mailing address should be at the top of your resume. Try to make your name stand out by using a slightly larger font size or all capital letters. Be sure to spell out everything. Never abbreviate St. for Street or Rd. for Road. If you are a college student, you should also put your home address and phone number at the top.

Change your message on your answering machine if necessary – RUSH blaring in the background or your sorority sisters screaming may not come across well to all recruiters. If you think you may be moving within six months then include a second address and phone number of a trusted friend or relative who can reach you no matter where you are.

*Remember that employers will keep your resume on file and may contact you months later if a position opens that fits your qualifications. All too often, candidates are unreachable because they have moved and had not previously provided enough contact options on their resume.*

Next, list your experience, then your education. If you are a recent graduate, list your education first, unless your experience is more important than your education. (For example, if you have just graduated from a teaching school, have some business experience, and are applying for a job in business, you would list your business experience first.)

Keep everything easy to find. Put the dates of your employment and education on the left of the page. Put the names of the companies you worked for and the schools you attended a few spaces to the right of the dates. Put the city and state, or the city and country, where you studied or worked to the right of the page.

The important thing is simply to break up the text in some logical way that makes your resume visually attractive and easy to scan, so experiment to see which layout works best for your resume. However you set it up, *stay consistent*. Inconsistencies in fonts, spacing, or tenses will make your resume look sloppy. Also, be sure to use tabs to keep your information vertically lined up, rather than the less precise space bar.

## RESUME CONTENT:
### Say it with Style
### Sell Yourself

You are selling your skills and accomplishments in your resume, so it is important to inventory yourself and know yourself. If you have achieved something, say so. Put it in the best possible light, but avoid subjective statements, such as "I am a hard worker" or "I get along well with my coworkers." Just stick to the facts.

While you shouldn't hold back or be modest, don't exaggerate your achievements to the point of misrepresentation. Be honest. Many companies will immediately drop an applicant from consideration (or fire a current employee) upon discovering inaccurate or untrue information on a resume or other application material.

Write down the important (and pertinent) things you have done, but do it in as few words as possible. Your resume will be scanned, not read, and short, concise phrases are much more effective than long-winded sentences. Avoid the use of "I" when emphasizing your accomplishments. Instead, use brief phrases beginning with action verbs.

While some technical terms will be unavoidable, you should try to avoid excessive "technicalese." Keep in mind that the first person to see your resume may be a human resources person who won't necessarily know all the jargon – and how can they be impressed by something they don't understand?

## Keep it Brief

Also, try to hold your paragraphs to six lines or less. If you have more than six lines of information about one job or school, put it in two or more paragraphs. A short resume will be examined more carefully. Remember: Your resume usually has between eight and 45 seconds to catch an employer's eye. So make every second count.

## Job Objective

A functional resume may require a job objective to give it focus. One or two sentences describing the job you are seeking can clarify in what capacity your skills will be best put to use. Be sure that your stated objective is in line with the position you're applying for.

*Examples:*

An entry-level editorial assistant position in the publishing industry.
A senior management position with a telecommunications firm.

Don't include a job objective on a chronological resume unless your previous work experiences are <u>completely</u> unrelated to the position for which you're applying. The presence of an overly specific job objective might eliminate you from consideration for other positions that a recruiter feels are a better match for your qualifications. But even if you don't put an objective on paper, having a career goal in mind as you write can help give your resume a solid sense of direction.

---

### USE ACTION VERBS

*How* you write your resume is just as important as *what* you write. In describing previous work experiences, the strongest resumes use short phrases beginning with action verbs. Below are a few you may want to use. (This list is not all-inclusive.)

| | | | |
|---|---|---|---|
| achieved | developed | integrated | purchased |
| administered | devised | interpreted | reduced |
| advised | directed | interviewed | regulated |
| arranged | distributed | launched | represented |
| assisted | established | managed | resolved |
| attained | evaluated | marketed | restored |
| budgeted | examined | mediated | restructured |
| built | executed | monitored | revised |
| calculated | expanded | negotiated | scheduled |
| collaborated | expedited | obtained | selected |
| collected | facilitated | operated | served |
| compiled | formulated | ordered | sold |
| completed | founded | organized | solved |
| computed | generated | participated | streamlined |
| conducted | headed | performed | studied |
| consolidated | identified | planned | supervised |
| constructed | implemented | prepared | supplied |
| consulted | improved | presented | supported |
| controlled | increased | processed | tested |
| coordinated | initiated | produced | trained |
| created | installed | proposed | updated |
| determined | instructed | published | wrote |

Some jobseekers may choose to include both "Relevant Experience" and "Additional Experience" sections. This can be useful, as it allows the jobseeker to place more emphasis on certain experiences and to de-emphasize others.

Emphasize continued experience in a particular job area or continued interest in a particular industry. De-emphasize irrelevant positions. It is okay to include one opening line providing a general description of each company you've worked at. Delete positions that you held for less than four months (unless you are a very recent college grad or still in school). Stress your <u>results</u> and your achievements, elaborating on how you contributed in your previous jobs. Did you increase sales, reduce costs, improve a product, implement a new program? Were you promoted? Use specific numbers (i.e., quantities, percentages, dollar amounts) whenever possible.

## Education

Keep it brief if you have more than two years of career experience. Elaborate more if you have less experience. If you are a recent college graduate, you may choose to include any high school activities that are directly relevant to your career. If you've been out of school for a while you don't need to list your education prior to college.

Mention degrees received and any honors or special awards. Note individual courses or projects you participated in that might be relevant for employers. For example, if you are an English major applying for a position as a business writer, be sure to mention any business or economics courses. Previous experience such as Editor-in-Chief of the school newspaper would be relevant as well.

If you are uploading your resume to an online job hunting site such as CareerCity.com, action verbs are still important, but the key words or key nouns that a computer would search for become more important. For example, if you're seeking an accounting position, key nouns that a computer would search for such as "Lotus 1-2-3" or "CPA" or "payroll" become very important.

## Highlight Impressive Skills

Be sure to mention any computer skills you may have. You may wish to include a section entitled "Additional Skills" or "Computer Skills," in which you list any software programs you know. An additional skills section is also an ideal place to mention fluency in a foreign language.

## Personal Data

This section is optional, but if you choose to include it, keep it brief. A one-word mention of hobbies such as fishing, chess, baseball, cooking, etc., can give the person who will interview you a good way to open up the conversation.

Team sports experience is looked at favorably. It doesn't hurt to include activities that are somewhat unusual (fencing, Akido, '70s music) or that somehow relate to the position or the company to which you're applying. For instance, it would be worth noting if you are a member of a professional organization in your industry of interest. Never include information about your age, alias, date of birth, health, physical characteristics, marital status, religious affiliation, or political/moral beliefs.

## References

The most that is needed is the sentence "References available upon request" at the bottom of your resume. If you choose to leave it out, that's fine. This line is not really necessary. It is understood that references will most likely be asked for and provided by you later on in the interviewing process. Do not actually send references with your resume and cover letter unless specifically requested.

# HIRING A RESUME WRITER:
## Is it the Right Choice for You?

If you write reasonably well, it is to your advantage to write your own resume. Writing your resume forces you to review your experiences and figure out how to explain your accomplishments in clear, brief phrases. This will help you when you explain your work to interviewers. It is also easier to tailor your resume to each position you're applying for when you have put it together yourself.

If you write your resume, everything will be in your own words; it will sound like you. It will say what you want it to say. If you are a good writer, know yourself well, and have a good idea of which parts of your background employers are looking for, you should be able to write your own resume better than someone else. If you decide to write your resume yourself, have as many people as possible review and proofread it. Welcome objective opinions and other perspectives.

## When to Get Help

If you have difficulty writing in "resume style" (which is quite unlike normal written language), if you are unsure which parts of your background to emphasize, or if you think your resume would make your case better if it did not follow one of the standard forms outlined either here or in a book on resumes, then you should consider having it professionally written.

Even some professional resume writers we know have had their resumes written with the help of fellow professionals. They sought the help of someone who could be objective about their background, as well as provide an experienced sounding board to help focus their thoughts.

## If You Hire a Pro

The best way to choose a writer is by reputation: the recommendation of a friend, a personnel director, your school placement officer, or someone else knowledgeable in the field.

*Important questions:*
- "How long have you been writing resumes?"
- "If I'm not satisfied with what you write, will you go over it with me and change it?"
- "Do you charge by the hour or a flat rate?"

There is no sure relation between price and quality, except that you are unlikely to get a good writer for less than $50 for an uncomplicated resume and you shouldn't have to pay more than $300 unless your experience is very extensive or complicated. There will be additional charges for printing. Assume nothing no matter how much you pay. It is your career at stake if there are mistakes on your resume!

Few resume services will give you a firm price over the phone, simply because some resumes are too complicated and take too long to do for a predetermined price. Some services will quote you a price that applies to almost all of their customers. Once you decide to use a specific writer, you should insist on a firm price quote *before* engaging their services. Also, find out how expensive minor changes will be.

# COVER LETTERS:
## Quick, Clear, and Concise

*Always* mail a cover letter with your resume. In a cover letter you can show an interest in the company that you can't show in a resume. You can also point out one or two of your skills or accomplishments the company can put to good use.

## Make it Personal

The more personal you can get, the better, so long as you keep it professional. If someone known to the person you are writing has recommended that you contact the company, get permission to include his/her name in the letter. If you can get the name of a person to send the letter to, address it directly to that person (after first calling the company to verify the spelling of the person's name, correct title, and mailing address). Be sure to put the person's name and title on both the letter and the envelope. This will ensure that your letter will get through to the proper person, even if a new person now occupies this position. It will not always be possible to get the name of a person. Always strive to get at least a title.

Be sure to mention something about why you have an interest in the company - - *so many candidates apply for jobs with no apparent knowledge of what the company does!* This conveys the message that they just want any job.

Type cover letters in full. Don't try the cheap and easy ways, like using a computer mail merge program or photocopying the body of your letter and typing in the inside address and salutation. You will give the impression that you are mailing to a host of companies and have no particular interest in any one.

Print your cover letter on the same color and same high-quality paper as your resume.

### Cover letter basic format

Paragraph 1: State what the position is that you are seeking. It is not always necessary to state how you found out about the position – often you will apply without knowing that a position is open.

Paragraph 2: Include what you know about the company and why you are interested in working there. Mention any prior contact with the company or someone known to the hiring person if relevant. Briefly state your qualifications and what you can offer. (Do not talk about what you cannot do).

Paragraph 3: Close with your phone number and where/when you can be reached. Make a request for an interview. State when you will follow up by phone (or mail or e-mail if the ad requests no phone calls). Do not wait long – generally five working days. If you say you're going to follow up, then actually do it! This phone call can get your resume noticed when it might otherwise sit in a stack of 225 other resumes.

## Cover letter do's and don'ts

- *Do* keep your cover letter brief and to the point.
- *Do* be sure it is error-free.
- *Do* accentuate what you can offer the company, not what you hope to gain.
- *Do* be sure your phone number and address is on your cover letter just in case it gets separated from your resume (this happens!).
- *Do* check the watermark by holding the paper up to a light – be sure it is facing forward so it is readable – on the same side as the text, and right-side up.
- *Do* sign your cover letter (or type your name if you are sending it electronically). Blue or black ink are both fine. Do not use red ink.
- *Don't* just repeat information verbatim from your resume.
- *Don't* overuse the personal pronoun "I."
- *Don't* send a generic cover letter – show your personal knowledge of and interest in that particular company.

# THANK YOU LETTERS:
## Another Way to Stand Out

As mentioned earlier, *always* send a thank you letter after an interview (see the sample later in this section). So few candidates do this and it is yet another way for you to stand out. Be sure to mention something specific from the interview and restate your interest in the company and the position.

It is generally acceptable to handwrite your thank you letter on a generic thank you card (but *never* a postcard). Make sure handwritten notes are neat and legible. However, if you are in doubt, typing your letter is always the safe bet. If you met with several people it is fine to send them each an individual thank you letter. Call the company if you need to check on the correct spelling of their names.

**Remember to:**
- Keep it short.
- Proofread it carefully.
- Send it *promptly.*

# FUNCTIONAL RESUME

## C.J. RAVENCLAW
129 Pennsylvania Avenue
Washington DC 20500
202/555-6652
e-mail: ravenclaw@dcpress.net

### Objective
A position as a graphic designer commensurate with my acquired skills and expertise.

### Summary
Extensive experience in plate making, separations, color matching, background definition, printing, mechanicals, color corrections, and personnel supervision. A highly motivated manager and effective communicator. Proven ability to:

- **Create Commercial Graphics**
- **Produce Embossed Drawings**
- **Color Separate**
- **Control Quality**
- **Resolve Printing Problems**
- **Analyze Customer Satisfaction**

### Qualifications
**Printing:**
Knowledgeable in black and white as well as color printing. Excellent judgment in determining acceptability of color reproduction through comparison with original. Proficient at producing four- or five-color corrections on all media, as well as restyling previously reproduced four-color artwork.

**Customer Relations:**
Routinely work closely with customers to ensure specifications are met. Capable of striking a balance between technical printing capabilities and need for customer satisfaction through entire production process.

**Specialties:**
Practiced at creating silk screen overlays for a multitude of processes including velo bind, GBC bind, and perfect bind. Creative design and timely preparation of posters, flyers, and personalized stationery.

**Personnel Supervision:**
Skillful at fostering atmosphere that encourages highly talented artists to balance high-level creativity with maximum production. Consistently beat production deadlines. Instruct new employees, apprentices, and students in both artistry and technical operations.

### Experience
Graphic Arts Professor, Ohio State University, Columbus OH (1992-1996).
Manager, Design Graphics, Washington DC (1997-present).

### Education
Massachusetts Conservatory of Art, Ph.D. 1990
University of Massachusetts, B.A. 1988

# CHRONOLOGICAL RESUME

**HARRY SEABORN**
**557 Shoreline Drive**
**Seattle, WA 98404**
**(206) 555-6584**
**e-mail: hseaborn@centco.com**

## EXPERIENCE

THE CENTER COMPANY                                    Seattle, WA
*Systems Programmer*                                  1996-present
  • Develop and maintain customer accounting and order tracking
  database using a Visual Basic front end and SQL server.
  • Plan and implement migration of company wide transition from
  mainframe-based dumb terminals to a true client server environment
  using Windows NT Workstation and Server.
  • Oversee general local and wide area network administration
  including the development of a variety of intranet modules to
  improve internal company communication and planning across
  divisions.

INFO TECH, INC.                                       Seattle, WA
*Technical Manager*                                   1994-1996
  • Designed and managed the implementation of a network providing
  the legal community with a direct line to Supreme Court cases
  across the Internet using SQL Server and a variety of Internet tools.
  • Developed a system to make the entire library catalog available on
  line using PERL scripts and SQL.
  • Used Visual Basic and Microsoft Access to create a registration
  system for university registrar.

## EDUCATION

SALEM STATE UNIVERSITY                                Salem, OR
        M.S. in Computer Science.                     1993
        B.S. in Computer Science.                     1991

## COMPUTER SKILLS

  • Programming Languages: Visual Basic, Java, C++, SQL, PERL
  • Software: SQL Server, Internet Information Server, Oracle
  • Operating Systems: Windows NT, UNIX, Linux

# FUNCTIONAL RESUME

**Donna Hermione Moss**
703 Wizard's Way
Chicago, IL 60601
(312) 555-8841
e-mail: donna@cowfire.com

**OBJECTIVE:**
To contribute over five years of experience in promotion, communications, and administration to an entry-level position in advertising.

**SUMMARY OF QUALIFICATIONS:**
- Performed advertising duties for small business.
- Experience in business writing and communications skills.
- General knowledge of office management.
- Demonstrated ability to work well with others, in both supervisory and support staff roles.
- Type 75 words per minute.

**SELECTED ACHIEVEMENTS AND RESULTS:**
Promotion:
Composing, editing, and proofreading correspondence and public relations materials for own catering service. Large-scale mailings.

Communication:
Instruction; curriculum and lesson planning; student evaluation; parent-teacher conferences; development of educational materials. Training and supervising clerks.

Computer Skills:
Proficient in MS Word, Lotus 1-2-3, Excel, and Filemaker Pro.

Administration:
Record-keeping and file maintenance. Data processing and computer operations, accounts receivable, accounts payable, inventory control, and customer relations. Scheduling, office management, and telephone reception.

**PROFESSIONAL HISTORY:**
Teacher; Self-Employed (owner of catering service); Floor Manager; Administrative Assistant; Accounting Clerk.

**EDUCATION:**
Beloit College, Beloit, WI, BA in Education, 1991

# CHRONOLOGICAL RESUME

**PERCY ZIEGLER**
16 Josiah Court
Marlborough CT 06447
203/555-9641 (h)
203/555-8176, x14 (w)

**EDUCATION**  Keene State College, Keene NH
Bachelor of Arts in Elementary Education, 1998
• Graduated *magna cum laude*
• English minor
• Kappa Delta Pi member, inducted 1996

**EXPERIENCE**  Elmer T. Thienes Elementary School, Marlborough CT
September 1998-  *Part-time Kindergarten Teacher*
Present  • Instruct kindergartners in reading, spelling, language arts, and music.
• Participate in the selection of textbooks and learning aids.
• Organize and supervise class field trips and coordinate in-class presentations.

Summers  Keene YMCA, Youth Division, Keene NH
1995-1997  *Child-care Counselor*
• Oversaw summer program for low-income youth.
• Budgeted and coordinated special events and field trips, working with Program Director to initiate variations in the program.
• Served as Youth Advocate in cooperation with social worker to address the social needs and problems of participants.

Spring 1997  Wheelock Elementary School, Keene NH
*Student Teacher*
• Taught third-grade class in all elementary subjects.
• Designed and implemented a two-week unit on Native Americans.
• Assisted in revision of third-grade curriculum.

Fall 1996  Child Development Center, Keene NH
*Daycare Worker*
• Supervised preschool children on the playground and during art activities.
• Created a "Wishbone Corner," where children could quietly look at books or take a voluntary "time-out."

**ADDITIONAL INTERESTS**
Martial arts, Pokemon, politics, reading, skiing, writing.

# ELECTRONIC RESUME

## GRIFFIN DORE
69 Dursley Drive
Cambridge, MA 02138
(617) 555-5555

### KEYWORD SUMMARY

Senior financial manager with over ten years experience in Accounting and Systems Management, Budgeting, Forecasting, Cost Containment, Financial Reporting, and International Accounting. MBA in Management. Proficient in Lotus, Excel, Solomon, and Windows.

### EXPERIENCE

COLWELL CORPORATION, Wellesley, MA
Director of Accounting and Budgets, 1990 to present
    Direct staff of twenty in General Ledger, Accounts Payable, Accounts Receivable, and International Accounting.
    Facilitate month-end closing process with parent company and auditors.
    Implemented team-oriented cross-training program within accounting group, resulting in timely month-end closings and increased productivity of key accounting staff.
    Developed and implemented a strategy for Sales and Use Tax Compliance in all fifty states.
    Prepare monthly financial statements and analyses.

FRANKLIN AND DELANEY COMPANY, Melrose, MA
Senior Accountant, 1987-1990
    Managed Accounts Payable, General Ledger, transaction processing, and financial reporting. Supervised staff of five.

Staff Accountant, 1985-1987
    Managed Accounts Payable, including vouchering, cash disbursements, and bank reconciliation.
    Wrote and issued policies.
    Maintained supporting schedules used during year-end audits.
    Trained new employees.

### EDUCATION

MBA in Management, Northeastern University, Boston, MA, 1989
BS in Accounting, Boston College, Boston, MA, 1985

### ASSOCIATIONS

National Association of Accountants

# GENERAL MODEL
# FOR A COVER LETTER

Your mailing address
Date

Contact's name
Contact's title
Company
Company's mailing address

Dear Mr./Ms. _____:

Immediately explain why your background makes you the best candidate for the position that you are applying for. Describe what prompted you to write (want ad, article you read about the company, networking contact, etc.). Keep the first paragraph short and hard-hitting.

Detail what you could contribute to this company. Show how your qualifications will benefit this firm. Describe your interest in the corporation. Subtly emphasizing your knowledge about this firm and your familiarity with the industry will set you apart from other candidates. Remember to keep this letter short; few recruiters will read a cover letter longer than half a page.

If possible, your closing paragraph should request specific action on the part of the reader. Include your phone number and the hours when you can be reached. Mention that if you do not hear from the reader by a specific date, you will follow up with a phone call. Lastly, thank the reader for their time, consideration, etc.

Sincerely,

(signature)

Your full name (typed)

Enclosure (use this if there are other materials, such as your resume, that are included in the same envelope)

# SAMPLE COVER LETTER

16 Josiah Court
Marlborough CT 06447
January 16, 2000

Ms. Leona Malfoy
Assistant Principal
Laningham Elementary School
43 Mayflower Drive
Keene NH 03431

Dear Ms. Malfoy:

Toby Potter recently informed me of a possible opening for a third grade teacher at Laningham Elementary School. With my experience instructing third-graders, both in schools and in summer programs, I feel I would be an ideal candidate for the position. Please accept this letter and the enclosed resume as my application.

Laningham's educational philosophy that every child can learn and succeed interests me, since it mirrors my own. My current position at Elmer T. Thienes Elementary has reinforced this philosophy, heightening my awareness of the different styles and paces of learning and increasing my sensitivity toward special needs children. Furthermore, as a direct result of my student teaching experience at Wheelock Elementary School, I am comfortable, confident, and knowledgeable working with third-graders.

I look forward to discussing the position and my qualifications for it in more detail. I can be reached at 203/555-9641 evenings or 203/555-8176, x14 weekdays. If I do not hear from you before Tuesday of next week, I will call to see if we can schedule a time to meet. Thank you for your time and consideration.

Sincerely,

*Percy Ziegler*

Percy Ziegler

Enclosure

# GENERAL MODEL FOR A
# THANK YOU/FOLLOW-UP LETTER

Your mailing address
Date

Contact's name
Contact's title
Company
Company's mailing address

Dear Mr./Ms._____:

Remind the interviewer of the reason (i.e., a specific opening, an informational interview, etc.) you were interviewed, as well as the date. Thank him/her for the interview, and try to personalize your thanks by mentioning some specific aspect of the interview.

Confirm your interest in the organization (and in the opening, if you were interviewing for a particular position). Use specifics to re-emphasize that you have researched the firm in detail and have considered how you would fit into the company and the position. This is a good time to say anything you wish you had said in the initial meeting. Be sure to keep this letter brief; a half page is plenty.

If appropriate, close with a suggestion for further action, such as a desire to have an additional interview, if possible. Mention your phone number and the hours you can be reached. Alternatively, you may prefer to mention that you will follow up with a phone call in several days. Once again, thank the person for meeting with you, and state that you would be happy to provide any additional information about your qualifications.

Sincerely,

(signature)

Your full name (typed)

# PRIMARY EMPLOYERS

## ACCOUNTING AND MANAGEMENT CONSULTING

**You can expect to find the following types of companies in this chapter:**
*Consulting and Research Firms • Industrial Accounting Firms •
Management Services • Public Accounting Firms •
Tax Preparation Companies*

**AON CONSULTING**
2540 North First Street, Suite 400, San Jose CA 95131. 408/321-2500. **Contact:** Human Resources. **World Wide Web address:** http://www.aon.com. **Description:** An international human resources consulting and benefits brokerage firm providing integrated advisory and support services in retirement planning, health care management, organizational effectiveness, compensation, human resources-related communications, and information technologies. The company's organizational effectiveness services include advisory and support services in compensation, strategy development, organizational design, business process redesign, human resources development, management training and development, organizational communications, and information technology applications. Strategic health care services include advisory and support services in traditional group health and welfare programs, strategic health planning, strategic health care management, quality assurance, flexible benefits and compensation, financial and data management, vendor oversight, and communications. Strategic retirement planning and educational services include consulting and support services in core actuarial applications, retirement health and welfare benefits, funding and investment strategy, record keeping and administration, employee sensing and communications, personalized retirement modeling, holistic lifestyle and family planning, and database information and proprietary studies. Information technologies services include human resources information systems development (information management strategies, systems, databases, software, and technology advisement) and human resources systems applications (human resources planning, record keeping, communication, and education). **Positions advertised include:** Manager Trainee. **Corporate headquarters location:** Chicago IL. **Other area locations:** Fresno CA; Irvine CA; Sacramento CA; San Francisco CA; Woodland Hills CA. **Listed on:** New York Stock Exchange. **Stock exchange symbol:** AOC.

## BAIN & COMPANY
3 Embarcadero Center, Suite 3600, San Francisco CA 94111. 415/627-1000. **Contact:** Recruiting Manager. **World Wide Web address:** http://www.bain.com. **Description:** An international management consulting firm that helps major companies achieve higher levels of competitiveness and profitability. Founded in 1973. **Special programs:** Internships. **Corporate headquarters location:** Boston MA.

## BENSON & NEFF
One Post Street, Suite 2150, San Francisco CA 94104-5225. 415/705-5615. **Fax:** 415/705-5633. **Contact:** Director of Personnel. **E-mail address:** bn@bensonneff.com. **World Wide Web address:** http://www.bensonneff.com. **Description:** A certified public accounting firm offering accounting, auditing, tax, computer, and other consulting services. **Corporate headquarters location:** This location. **Operations at this facility include:** Service.

## CRAWFORD PIMENTEL & COMPANY, INC.
2150 Trade Zone Boulevard, Suite 200, San Jose CA 95131. 408/942-6888. **Contact:** Human Resources. **E-mail address:** recruiting@cpconet.com. **World Wide Web address:** http://www. 1040tax.com. **Description:** A public accounting firm that also offers management advisory, technology consulting, and business consulting services. **Special programs:** Training. **Corporate headquarters location:** This location. **Operations at this facility include:** Service. **Listed on:** Privately held. **Annual sales/revenues:** Less than $5 million. **Number of employees at this location:** 25.

## DELOITTE & TOUCHE
50 Fremont Street, San Francisco CA 94105. 415/247-4000. **Contact:** Human Resources. **World Wide Web address:** http://www. us.deloitte.com. **Description:** An international firm of certified public accountants providing professional accounting, auditing, tax, and management consulting services to widely diversified clients. The company has a specialized program consisting of national industry groups and functional groups that cross industry lines. Groups are involved in various disciplines including accounting, auditing, taxation management advisory services, small and growing businesses, mergers and acquisitions, and computer applications. **Positions advertised include:** A&A Technology Director; Marketing Manager; PC Specialist; Consultant; Dispute Manager, Health Care; Dispute Senior Associate, Loss Prevention Services.

**ERNST & YOUNG LLP**
555 California Street, Suite 1700, San Francisco CA 94104. 415/951-3000. **Contact:** Director of Human Resources. **World Wide Web address:** http://www.ey.com. **Description:** A certified public accounting firm that also provides management consulting services. Services include data processing, financial modeling, financial feasibility studies, production planning and inventory management, management sciences, health care planning, human resources, cost accounting, and budgeting systems. **Positions advertised include:** Tax Consulting Client Serving Associate; Tax Consulting Manager; Senior Designer; Audit Senior; Assurance Manager. **Corporate headquarters location:** New York NY.

**ERNST & YOUNG LLP**
303 Almaden Boulevard, San Jose CA 95110. 408/947-5500. **Contact:** Director of Human Resources. **World Wide Web address:** http://www.ey.com. **Description:** A certified public accounting firm that also provides management consulting services. Services include data processing, financial modeling, financial feasibility studies, production planning and inventory management, management sciences, health care planning, human resources, cost accounting, and budgeting systems. **Positions advertised include:** Technology and Security Risk Services Staff Member; Tax Consulting Manager; Senior Recruiter; Assurance Staff Member; Assurance Manager. **Corporate headquarters location:** New York NY.

**GRANT THORTON**
One California Street, Suite 1100, San Francisco CA 94111. 415/986-3900. **Contact:** Human Resources. **E-mail address:** californiaauditcareers@gt.com. **World Wide Web address:** http://www.grantthorton.com. **Description:** An accounting, tax, and business advisory firm. **Positions advertised include:** Manager of Assurance; Senior Tax Manager.

**H&R BLOCK**
266 West Portal Avenue, San Francisco CA 94127. 415/665-4540. **Recorded jobline:** 888/244-6860. **Contact:** Personnel. **E-mail address:** taxprepcareers@hrblock.com. **World Wide Web address:** http://www.hrblock.com. **Description:** Engaged in consumer tax preparation. H&R Block operates more than 9,500 offices nationwide and prepares more than 10 million tax returns each year. The company has offices in over 750 Sears, Roebuck & Co. stores in both the United States and Canada. The company is also engaged in

a number of other tax-related activities including group tax programs, executive tax service, tax training schools, and real estate awareness seminars. **Other U.S. locations:** Nationwide. **Listed on:** New York Stock Exchange. **Stock exchange symbol:** HRB.

## KPMG CONSULTING
3 Embarcadero Center, Suite 2000, San Francisco CA 94111. 415/951-0100. **Contact:** Human Resources. **World Wide Web address:** http://www.kpmgconsulting.com. **Description:** Delivers a wide range of value-added assurance, tax, and consulting services. **NOTE:** Jobseekers should send resumes to: KPMG HR Service Center, 8200 Brookriver Drive, Suite 200, Dallas TX 75247. Jobseekers should include a cover letter and the location in which they are interested. **Positions advertised include:** VS Consultant. **Special programs:** Internships. **Corporate headquarters location:** McLean VA. **Operations at this facility include:** Regional Headquarters. **Number of employees at this location:** 1,200. **Listed on:** NASDAQ. **Stock exchange symbol:** KCIN.

## ARTHUR D. LITTLE, INC.
505 Hamilton Avenue, Suite 201, Palo Alto CA 94301-2008. 650/752-2600. **Contact:** Human Resources. **World Wide Web address:** http://www.arthurdlittle.com. **Description:** A management consulting firm that serves corporations and institutions worldwide. The company offers services in three areas: management consulting; technology and product development; and environmental, health, and safety consulting. Founded in 1886. **Number of employees nationwide:** 2,500.

## PRICEWATERHOUSECOOPERS
333 Market Street, 21st Floor, San Francisco CA 94105. 415/498-5000. **Contact:** Human Resources. **E-mail address:** westpwcjobs@us.pwcglobal.com. **World Wide Web address:** http://www.pwcglobal.com. **Description:** One of the largest certified public accounting firms in the world. PricewaterhouseCoopers provides public accounting, business advisory, management consulting, and taxation services. **Positions advertised include:** SAP Senior Associate; Executive Assistant; Manager; Senior Associate; Assurance Manager; Manager Internal Audit. **Corporate headquarters location:** New York NY. **Other U.S. locations:** Nationwide.

## PRICEWATERHOUSECOOPERS

199 Fremont Street, San Francisco CA 94105. 415/498-5000. **Contact:** Human Resources. **E-mail address:** westpwcjobs@ us.pwcglobal.com. **World Wide Web address:** http://www. pwcglobal.com. **Description:** One of the largest certified public accounting firms in the world. PricewaterhouseCoopers provides public accounting, business advisory, management consulting, and taxation services. **Positions advertised include:** SAP Senior Associate; Executive Assistant; Manager; Senior Associate; Assurance Manager; Manager Internal Audit. **Special programs:** Internships. **Corporate headquarters location:** New York NY. **Other U.S. locations:** Nationwide.

## ADVERTISING, MARKETING, AND PUBLIC RELATIONS

**You can expect to find the following types of companies in this chapter:**
*Advertising Agencies • Direct Mail Marketers •*
*Market Research Firms • Public Relations Firms*

### A&R PARTNERS
201 Baldwin Avenue, San Mateo CA 94401-3914. 650/762-2800. **Fax:** 650/762-2801. **Contact:** Human Resources. **E-mail address:** hr@arpartners.com. **World Wide Web address:** http://www. arpartners.com. **Description:** A public relations firm. **NOTE:** Entry-level positions are offered. **Special programs:** Internships; Apprenticeships; Training. **Corporate headquarters location:** This location. **President:** Robert Angus. **Annual sales/revenues:** $5 - $10 million.

### ACCESS COMMUNICATIONS
101 Howard Street, 2nd Floor, San Francisco CA 94105-1629. 415/904-7070. **Fax:** 415/904-7055. **Contact:** Human Resources. **E-mail address:** info@accesspr.com. **World Wide Web address:** http:// www.accesspr.com. **Description:** A public relations firm whose clients include software and other high-tech corporations. **Corporate headquarters location:** This location. **Other U.S. locations:** New York NY.

### AVISO INC.
1336-C Park Street, Alameda CA 94501. 510/865-5100. **Fax:** 510/865-5165. **Contact:** Human Resources. **E-mail address:** personnel@avisoinc.com. **World Wide Web address:** http://www. avisoinc.com. **Description:** A marketing and communications firm that primarily serves the real estate and development industries. **Corporate headquarters location:** This location.

### BBDO WEST
637 Commercial Street, 3rd Floor, San Francisco CA 94111. 415/274-6200. **Contact:** Human Resources. **World Wide Web address:** http://www.bbdo.com. **Description:** One location of the worldwide network of advertising agencies with related businesses in public relations, direct marketing, sales promotion, graphic arts, and printing. **Corporate headquarters location:** New York NY. **Other area locations:** Los Angeles CA. **Other U.S. locations:** Miami FL; Atlanta GA; Chicago IL; Wellesley MA; Southfield MI. **Parent**

**company:** BBDO Worldwide operates 156 offices in 42 countries and 96 cities. The company operates 83 subsidiaries, affiliates, and associates engaged in advertising and related operations.

### BLANC & OTUS
303 Second Street, Suite 800 South, San Francisco CA 94102. 415/856-5100. **Contact:** Human Resources. **E-mail address:** jobs@blancandotus.com. **World Wide Web address:** http://www. bando.com. **Description:** A public relations firm that primarily serves the high-tech industry. **Positions advertised include:** Conference Strategist. **Corporate headquarters location:** This location. **Other U.S. locations:** Washington DC; Boston MA. **Parent company:** Hill and Knowlton.

### BURSON-MARSTELLER
100 Pine Street, Suite 2300, San Francisco CA 94111. 415/591-4000. **Contact:** Human Resources. **World Wide Web address:** http:// www.bm.com. **Description:** A public relations firm. **NOTE:** Please mail resumes to: 1800 Century Park East, Suite 200, Los Angeles CA 90067. **Special programs:** Internships. **Corporate headquarters location:** New York NY. **Other area locations:** Los Angeles CA; Sacramento CA; San Diego CA; San Francisco CA. **Other U.S. locations:** Miami FL; Chicago IL; Pittsburgh PA; Austin TX; Dallas TX. **International locations:** Worldwide. **Parent company:** Young and Rubicam, Inc.

### CITIGATE CUNNINGHAM
1510 Page Mill Road, Palo Alto CA 94304. 650/858-3700. **Contact:** Human Resources. **E-mail address:** careers@cunningham.com. **World Wide Web address:** http://www.cunningham.com. **Description:** A public relations agency specializing in the high-tech industry. **Corporate headquarters location:** This location. **Other U.S. locations:** Cambridge MA; Austin TX. **Parent company:** Incepta Group plc. **Operations at this facility include:** Administration; Service. **Listed on:** Privately held. **Number of employees at this location:** 55. **Number of employees nationwide:** 80.

### EDELMAN PUBLIC RELATIONS WORLDWIDE
350 California Street, Suite 1600, San Francisco CA 94104. 415/433-5381. **Contact:** Human Resources. **World Wide Web address:** http:// www.edelman.com. **Description:** A public relations firm. **Positions advertised include:** Senior Account Executive. **Corporate headquarters location:** Chicago IL. **Special programs:** Internships.

## THE FINANCIAL RELATIONS BOARD INC.

180 Montgomery Street, Suite 710, San Francisco CA 94104. 415/986-1591. **Contact:** Human Resources. **World Wide Web address:** http://www.frbinc.com. **Description:** A public relations firm that primarily serves the financial industry. **NOTE:** Please send resumes to: The Financial Relations Board Inc., Attn: Susan Walia, Human Resources Manager, 1888 Century Park East, Suite 920, Los Angeles CA 90067. **Corporate headquarters location:** Chicago IL. **Parent company:** Weber Shandwick Financial Communications.

## FOOTE, CONE & BELDING

600 Battery Street, San Francisco CA 94111. 415/820-8000. **Fax:** 415/820-8087. **Contact:** Eileen McCarthy, Human Resources Manager. **E-mail address:** careerssc@fcb.com. **World Wide Web address:** http://www.fcb.com. **Description:** One of the five largest advertising agencies in the world. Foote, Cone & Belding develops integrated marketing campaigns for a broad range of clients. The firm offers additional services such as merchandising, product research, package design, e-business marketing, direct marketing, sports marketing, and events marketing. **NOTE:** Entry-level positions are offered. **Special programs:** Internships; Training. **Corporate headquarters location:** Chicago IL. **Other U.S. locations:** Nationwide. **Parent company:** True North Communications. **Chairman and CEO:** Geoff Thompson. **Number of employees at this location:** 400.

## GCI GROUP

188 The Embarcadero, Suite 500, San Francisco CA 94105. 415/974-6200. **Fax:** 415/974-6226. **Contact:** Suzanne Fayfette, Human Resources. **E-mail address:** working@gcigroup.com **World Wide Web address:** http://www.gcigroup.com. **Description:** A high-tech public relations firm. **Corporate headquarters location:** New York NY.

## GARTNER GROUP

251 River Oaks Parkway, San Jose CA 95134. 408/468-8000. **Contact:** Human Resources. **World Wide Web address:** http://www. gartner.com. **Description:** A market research company. **Positions advertised include:** Relationship Manager; Vice President, Private Sector; Vice President, State and Local Government; Senior Account Executive; Client Director. **Corporate headquarters location:** Stamford CT. **Listed on:** New York Stock Exchange. **Stock exchange symbol:** IT.

## GOLIN HARRIS INTERNATIONAL

90 New Montgomery Street, 15th Floor, San Francisco CA 94105. 415/808-9800. **Fax:** 415/808-9890. **Contact:** Human Resources. **E-mail address:** careers@golinharris.com. **World Wide Web address:** http://www.golinharris.com. **Description:** A public relations firm that primarily serves high-tech industries. **Corporate headquarters location:** Chicago IL. **Other U.S. locations:** Bellevue WA.

## HILL AND KNOWLTON INC.

303 Second Street, Suite 900 South, San Francisco 94107. 415/281-7120. **Contact:** Donna Renella, Human Resources. **E-mail address:** anicosia@hillandknowlton.com. **World Wide Web address:** http://www.hillandknowlton.com. **Description:** One of the world's largest public relations/public affairs counseling firms, serving more than 1,000 clients worldwide, Hill and Knowlton Inc. serves clients through more than 60 company offices and through associate arrangements with 50 leading regional firms worldwide. **Corporate headquarters location:** New York NY. **Other U.S. locations:** Washington DC.

## THE HORN GROUP INC.

612 Howard Street, Suite 100, San Francisco CA 94105. 415/905-4000. **Fax:** 415/905-4001. **Contact:** Director of Training. **World Wide Web address:** http://www.horngroup.com. **Description:** A public relations firm that primarily serves high-tech industries. Founded in 1991. **NOTE:** Entry-level positions are offered. **Company slogan:** Pride, passion, results. **Special programs:** Internships; Summer Jobs. **Office hours:** Monday - Friday, 8:30 a.m. - 5:30 p.m. **Corporate headquarters location:** This location. **Other U.S. locations:** Braintree MA. **Listed on:** Privately held. **Annual sales/revenues:** $5 - $10 million. **Number of employees at this location:** 40. **Number of employees nationwide:** 50.

## MACKENZIE COMMUNICATIONS, INC.

601 California Street, Suite 1501, San Francisco CA 94108. 415/433-8200. **Contact:** Human Resources. **E-mail address:** info@mackenziesf.com. **World Wide Web address:** http://www.mackenziesf.com. **Description:** A public relations firm that serves a wide range of industries including banking, law, and public service. **Corporate headquarters location:** This location.

## PORTER NOVELLI CONVERGENCE GROUP

100 First Street, San Francisco CA 94107. 415/284-5200. **Fax:** 415/975-2201. **Contact:** Patricia Tey, Personnel. **E-mail address:** patricia.tey@porternovelli.com. **World Wide Web address:** http://www.poternovelli.com. **Description:** A public relations firm primarily serving the high-tech and consumer electronics industries. **Corporate headquarters location:** New York NY. **Other U.S. locations:** Boston MA.

## SOLEM & ASSOCIATES

550 Kearny Street, Suite 1010, San Francisco CA 94108. 415/788-7788. **Fax:** 415/788-7858. **Contact:** Personnel. **World Wide Web address:** http://www.solem.com. **Description:** A public relations firm that primarily serves the health care, transportation, and government advocacy industries. **Corporate headquarters location:** This location.

## STERLING COMMUNICATIONS, INC.

750 University Avenue, Suite 250, Los Gatos CA 95032. 408/395-5500. **Contact:** Human Resources. **E-mail address:** jobs@sterlingpr.com. **World Wide Web address:** http://www.sterlingpr.com. **Description:** A public relations firm that provides services to technology-based companies. **Corporate headquarters location:** This location.

## TBWA/CHIAT/DAY

55 Union Street, San Francisco CA 94111. 415/315-4100. **Recorded jobline:** 415/315-4264. **Contact:** Human Resources. **E-mail address:** hr-sf@tbwachiat.com. **World Wide Web address:** http://www.tbwachiat.com. **Description:** An advertising agency.

## TMP WORLDWIDE

799 Market Street, 8th Floor, San Francisco CA 94103. 415/820-7800. **Fax:** 415/820-0540. **Contact:** Human Resources. **World Wide Web address:** http://www.tmpw.com. **Description:** An advertising agency specializing in human resources and employee communications. TMP is a member of the American Association of Advertising Agencies. **NOTE:** Jobseekers should send resumes to: TMP Worldwide Human Resources, 622 Third Avenue, 36th Floor, New York NY 10017. **Office hours:** 9:00 a.m. - 5:00 p.m. **Corporate headquarters location:** New York NY. **Other area locations:** Santa Monica CA. **Other U.S. locations:** Boston MA. **Listed on:** NASDAQ. **Stock exchange symbol:** TMPW.

## J. WALTER THOMPSON COMPANY

945 Front Street, San Francisco CA 94111. 415/733-0700. **Contact:** Roman Lesnau, Human Resources. **E-mail address:** roman.lesnau@ jwt.com. **World Wide Web address:** http://www.jwtworld.com. **Description:** A full-service advertising agency. **NOTE:** Entry-level positions are offered. **Corporate headquarters location:** New York NY. **International locations:** Worldwide. **Parent company:** WPP Group. **Listed on:** NASDAQ. **Stock exchange symbol:** WPPGY. **Number of employees at this location:** 175.

## UPSTART COMMUNICATIONS

6425 Christie Avenue, Suite 300, Emeryville CA 94608. 510/457- 3000. **Fax:** 510/457-3010. **Contact:** Human Resources Department. **E-mail address:** careers@upstart.com. **World Wide Web address:** http://www.upstart.com. **Description:** A public relations firm that primarily serves high-tech industries. **Corporate headquarters location:** This location.

## WILSON McHENRY COMPANY

393 Vintage Park Drive, Suite 140, Foster City CA 94404. 650/356- 5200. **Fax:** 650/356-5252. **Contact:** Human Resources. **E-mail address:** hr@wmc.com. **World Wide Web address:** http://www. wmc.com. **Description:** A public relations and marketing firm that primarily serves high-tech industries. Founded in 1990. **NOTE:** If sending a resume via e-mail, please make sure the document is in MS Word or ASCII text format. **Positions advertised include:** Warehouse Officer; Project Engineer; Maintenance Engineer; Geotechnical Engineer; Business Improvement Engineer; HR Analyst; Refinery Process Technician; Radiation Safety Officer.

## YOUNG & RUBICAM WEST

100 First Street, Suite 1800, San Francisco CA 94105. 415/882- 0600. **Fax:** 415/882-0797. **Contact:** Ms. Whitney Ball, Human Resources Manager. **World Wide Web address:** http://www.yr.com. **Description:** An international advertising agency. The company operates through three divisions: Young & Rubicam International; Marsteller Inc., a worldwide leader in business-to-business and consumer advertising; and Young & Rubicam USA, with 14 consumer advertising agencies operating through four regional groups (except Young & Rubicam Detroit), and five specialized advertising and marketing agencies. **Corporate headquarters location:** New York NY.

# AEROSPACE

**You can expect to find the following types of companies in this chapter:**
*Aerospace Products and Services • Aircraft Equipment and Parts*

## AEROJET

P.O. Box 13222, Sacramento CA 95813-6000. 916/355-4000. **Contact:** Human Resources. **E-mail address:** careers.sac@ aerojet.com. **World Wide Web address:** http://www.aerojet.com. **Description:** Engaged in the research, development, testing, and production of liquid propellant rocket engines, solid rocket motors, sounding rockets, defense and aerospace systems, and waterjet propulsion systems. **Positions advertised include:** Accountant; Associate Program Planner; Chemist; Chemistry Specialist; Engineering Specialist; Environmental Specialist; Financial Specialist; Inspector; Janitor; Program Manager. **Corporate headquarters location:** This location. **Other area locations:** Rancho Cordova CA. **Other U.S. locations:** Huntsville AL; Washington DC; Arlington NJ; Socono NM; Jonesboro TN. **Parent company:** GenCorp, through its subsidiaries, manufactures products for the aerospace, pharmaceutical, fine chemical, and automotive industries. **Listed on:** New York Stock Exchange. **Stock Exchange Symbol:** GY.

## INVISION TECHNOLOGIES

7151 Gateway Boulevard, Newark CA 94560. 510/739-2400. **Fax:** 510/608-0764. **Contact:** Human Resources. **E-mail address:** hr@invision.iip.com. **World Wide Web address:** http://www. invision-tech.com. **Description:** Provider of explosives detection systems for the aviation security industry. **Positions advertised include:** Systems Design Engineer; Technical Support Engineer; Senior Engineering Program Manager. **Corporate headquarters location:** This location. **Listed on:** NASDAQ. **Stock exchange symbol:** INVN.

## KAISER ELECTRONICS

2701 Orchard Parkway, Mail Stop 10, San Jose CA 95134. 408/432-3000. **Contact:** Jerry De La Piedra, Human Resources. **E-mail address:** delapiedraj@kaisere.com. **World Wide Web address:** http://www.kaiserelectronics.com. **Description:** Designs, develops, and manufactures avionic display systems. **Corporate headquarters location:** This location. **Parent company:** Rockwell Collins. **Operations at this facility include:** Administration; Manufacturing; Research and Development; Service. **Listed on:** New York Stock

Exchange. **Stock exchange symbol:** COL. **Number of employees at this location:** 800.

**LOCKHEED MARTIN SPACE SYSTEMS**
P.O. Box 3504, RRC Building 150, Sunnyvale CA 94088-3504. 408/742-7151. **Fax:** 877/244-0989. **Contact:** Personnel. **E-mail address:** jobs.lmms@lmco.com. **World Wide Web address:** http://lmms.external.lmco.com. **Description:** Develops missile systems and high-tech space-related products. **Special programs:** Internships. **Corporate headquarters location:** Bethesda MD. **Parent company:** Lockheed Martin Corporation operates in five major areas: Space Systems (develops space technology systems such as rocket systems, Space Shuttle support technology, and other products); Missile Systems (produces fleet ballistic missiles for military applications); Advanced Systems (operates as the research and development organization exploring military, commercial, and scientific needs); Information Processing (develops comprehensive database systems to process the specific needs of other company divisions); and the Austin Division (responsible for designing and producing military tactical support systems). **Operations at this facility include:** Administration; Research and Development. **Listed on:** New York Stock Exchange. **Stock exchange symbol:** LMT. **Number of employees at this location:** 12,000. **Number of employees nationwide:** 14,000.

**PACIFIC SCIENTIFIC QUANTIC**
1010 Commercial Street, San Carlos CA 94070. 650/595-1100. **Contact:** Personnel. **Description:** Produces sophisticated aerospace equipment such as satellite guidance systems and aerospace ordnance devices. **World Wide Web address:** http://www.psemc.com. **Office hours:** Monday - Friday, 8:00 a.m. - 5:00 p.m. **Corporate headquarters location:** Chandler AZ.

**ROLLS ROYCE ENGINE SERVICES**
7200 Earhart Road, Oakland CA 94621. 510/613-1000. **Fax:** 510/635-6911. **Recorded jobline:** 510/613-1011. **Contact:** Peter Caldwell, Human Resources Manager. **E-mail address:** rolls-roycecareers@rolls-royce.com. **World Wide Web address:** http://www.rolls-royce.com. **Description:** Engaged in the maintenance, repair, and overhaul of aviation and industrial gas turbine engines. Founded in 1960. **NOTE:** Entry-level positions and part-time jobs are offered. **Company slogan:** Engines fueled by people. **Positions advertised include:** IT General Manager; QA Auditor; Supervisor;

Project Engineer. **Special programs:** Internships; Apprenticeships; Training; Co-ops. **Corporate headquarters location:** This location. **Parent company:** First Aviation Services, Inc. **President/CEO:** Raj Sharma. **Purchasing Manager:** Barry Lynch. **Sales Manager:** Joe Ghantous. **Annual sales/revenues:** More than $100 million. **Number of employees at this location:** 340. **Number of employees nationwide:** 360. **Listed on:** NASDAQ. **Stock exchange symbol:** FAVS.

### SANMINA-SCI CORPORATION
2000 Ringwood Avenue, San Jose CA 95131. 408/943-6100. **Contact:** Human Resources. **World Wide Web address:** http://www.sci.com. **Description:** Sanmina-SCI designs, develops, manufactures, markets, distributes, and services electronic products for the computer, aerospace, defense, telecommunications, medical, and banking industries, as well as for the United States government. Sanmina-SCI is one of the world's largest contract electronics manufacturers and operates one of the largest surface mount technology production capacities in the merchant market. Operations are conducted through a Commercial Division and a Government Division. The Commercial Division operates in five geographically organized business units: Eastern, Central, and Western North America; Europe; and Asia. Each unit operates multiple plants that manufacture components, subassemblies, and finished products primarily for original equipment manufacturers. Design, engineering, purchasing, manufacturing, distribution, and support services are also offered. The Governmental Division provides data management, instrumentation, communication, and computer subsystems to the U.S. government and several foreign governments. **Positions advertised include:** Business Analyst; Tax Accountant; External Reporting Manager; Financial Analyst; Process Engineer; Regional Quality Manager; Senior Tax Accountant. **International locations:** Canada; France; Ireland; Mexico; Scotland; Singapore; Thailand. **Operations at this facility include:** This location is engaged in printed circuit board assembly. **Listed on:** NASDAQ. **Stock exchange symbol:** SANM. **Annual sales/revenues:** More than $100 million. **Number of employees at this location:** 350. **Number of employees nationwide:** 8,000. **Number of employees worldwide:** 10,000.

### SANMINA-SCI CORPORATION
2700 North First Street, San Jose CA 95131. 408/964-3500. **Fax:** 408/964-3799. **Contact:** Human Resources. **World Wide Web**

**address:** http://www.sanmina.com. **Description:** Manufactures custom-designed backplane assemblies and subassemblies; multilayer, high-density printed circuit boards; testing equipment; and surface mount technology assemblies used in sophisticated electronics equipment with primary customers in the telecommunications, data communications, industrial/medical, computer systems, and contract assembly business sectors. **Listed on:** NASDAQ. **Stock exchange symbol:** SANM. **Annual sales/revenues:** More than $100 million. **Number of employees at this location:** 100. **Number of employees nationwide:** 750.

## UNIVERSAL PROPULSION COMPANY

P.O. Box KK, Fairfield CA 94533. 707/422-1880. **Fax:** 707/422-3242. **Contact:** Human Resources. **World Wide Web address:** http://www.upco.goodrich.com. **Description:** Manufactures explosive devices and systems for the aerospace industry. **Corporate headquarters location:** Charlotte NC. **Parent company:** Goodrich Corporation. **Listed on:** New York Stock Exchange. **Stock exchange symbol:** GR.

## WYMAN-GORDON COMPANY

414 Hester Street, San Leandro CA 94577. 510/568-6400. **Fax:** 510/635-1922. **Contact:** Lana Gossett, Human Resources Manager. **E-mail address:** lgossett@wyman.com. **World Wide Web address:** http://www.wyman-gordon.com. **Description:** An aerospace investment casting foundry that manufactures high-technology ferrous and nonferrous castings. **NOTE:** Entry-level positions and second and third shifts are offered. **Special programs:** Internships; Training. **Internship information:** The company offers product and process engineering internships as well as management trainee internships. **Corporate headquarters location:** North Grafton MA. **Other U.S. locations:** Nationwide. **Operations at this facility include:** Administration; Manufacturing; Sales; Service. **Listed on:** NASDAQ. **Annual sales/revenues:** $21 - $50 million. **Number of employees at this location:** 250.

## APPAREL, FASHION, AND TEXTILES

**You can expect to find the following types of companies in this chapter:**
*Broadwoven Fabric Mills • Knitting Mills • Curtains and Draperies •*
*Footwear • Nonwoven Fabrics • Textile Goods and Finishing •*
*Yarn and Thread Mills*

## BYER CALIFORNIA
66 Potrero Avenue, San Francisco CA 94103. 415/626-7844. **Fax:**
415/626-7865. **Contact:** Personnel Department. **E-mail address:**
clee@byer.com. **World Wide Web address:** http://www.byer.com.
**Description:** Manufactures women's apparel. **Corporate
headquarters location:** This location.

## KORET OF CALIFORNIA, INC.
505 14th Street, Oakland CA 94612. 510/622-7037. **Contact:**
Human Resources Department. **E-mail address:** resumes@
koretsf.com. **World Wide Web address:** http://www.koretsf.com.
**Description:** Manufactures and markets women's apparel. **Special
programs:** Internships. **Corporate headquarters location:** This
location. **Other area locations:** Chico CA; Los Angeles CA; Napa
CA. **Other U.S. locations:** Miami FL; New York NY; Price UT.
**Subsidiaries include:** Koret Canada; Mr. Jax. **Parent company:**
Kellwood Company. **Operations at this facility include:**
Administration; Sales; Service. **Listed on:** New York Stock Exchange.
**Stock exchange symbol:** KWD. **Number of employees nationwide:**
1,200.

## LEVI STRAUSS & COMPANY
1155 Battery Street, San Francisco CA 94111. 415/501-6000.
**Contact:** Human Resources. **World Wide Web address:** http://www.
levistrauss.com. **Description:** Designs, manufactures, and markets a
diversified line of apparel, primarily jeans and jeans-related products
under the Levi's and Brittania brand names. The company also
manufactures the Dockers line of clothing for U.S. markets. **Positions
advertised include:** Administrator; Senior Manager of
Communications; Assistant Designer; Design Division Coordinator;
Designer; Business Analyst; Cost Accounting Specialist; Customer
Fulfillment Performance Analyst; Performance Consultant; Tax
Specialist. **Corporate headquarters location:** This location.

## THE TOM JAMES COMPANY
220 Montgomery Street, San Francisco CA 94104. 415/837-53803. **Fax:** 208/977-3655. **Contact:** Shelbi Lavender, Human Resources. **E-mail address:** tjmrecruiting@tomjamesco.com. **World Wide Web address:** http://www.tomjamesco.com. **Description:** A clothing company. **Positions advertised include:** Salesperson; Manager.

## UNIFIRST CORPORATION
2602 Bearrington Court, Hayward CA 94545. 510/293-1380. **Fax:** 510/293-1385. **Contact:** Chris Phelps, Human Resources. **E-mail address:** chris_phelps@unifirst.com. **World Wide Web address:** http://www.unifirst.com. **Description:** A supplier of work clothing for many different types of businesses. Founded in 1936. **Positions advertised include:** Telemarketer; Sales Associate. **Corporate headquarters location:** Wilmington MA. **Other U.S. locations:** Nationwide. **Listed on:** New York Stock Exchange. **Stock exchange symbol:** UNF.

## ARCHITECTURE, CONSTRUCTION, AND ENGINEERING

**You can expect to find the following types of companies in this chapter:**
*Architectural and Engineering Services • Civil and Mechanical Engineering Firms • Construction Products, Manufacturers, and Wholesalers • General Contractors/ Specialized Trade Contractors*

### BECHTEL CORPORATION
P.O. Box 193965, San Francisco CA 94119-3965. 415/768-1234. **Physical address:** 50 Beale Street, San Francisco CA 94105-1895. **Contact:** Human Resources. **E-mail address:** staffpx@bechtel.com. **World Wide Web address:** http://www.bechtel.com. **Description:** Operations focus on engineering, construction, financing operations and maintenance, electricity, nuclear fuel, metals, minerals, procurement management, transportation, and pollution control. **NOTE:** Resumes should be sent to Bechtel Staffing Support Center-SF, P.O. Box 36359, Phoenix AZ 85067-6359. All resumes should be in a scannable format. **Positions advertised include:** Senior Science Specialist; Principal Automation Support Analyst; Principal Engineer; Administrative Assistant; Administrative Support Analyst; Senior Engineer. **Corporate headquarters location:** This location. **Other area locations:** Martinez CA; Los Angeles CA; San Diego CA. **Other U.S. locations:** AZ; CO; KY; MD; NY; TN; TX; WA.

### BURKE MERCER
2250 South 10th Street, San Jose CA 95112. 408/297-3500. **Fax:** 408/291-8401. **Contact:** Karen Lerma, Personnel Director. **World Wide Web address:** http://www.burkemercer.com. **Description:** Manufactures a wide variety of flooring products including carpet base, tile, transition strip accessories, stair tread, and floor adhesives. **Corporate headquarters location:** This location.

### CH2M HILL CALIFORNIA INC.
P.O. Box 12681, Oakland CA 94604. 510/251-2426. **Physical address:** 155 Grand Avenue, Suite 1000, Oakland CA 94612. **Fax:** 510/893-8205. **Contact:** Human Resources Department. **World Wide Web address:** http://www.ch2m.com. **Description:** A group of employee-owned companies operating under the names CH2M Hill, Inc., Industrial Design Corporation, Operations Management International, CH2M Hill International, and CH2M Hill Engineering. The company provides planning, engineering design, and operation and construction management services to help clients apply

technology, safeguard the environment, and develop infrastructure. The professional staff includes specialists in environmental engineering and waste management, water management, transportation, industrial facilities, and a broad spectrum of infrastructure systems. Founded in 1946. **Positions advertised include:** Stormwater Engineer; Water Resource Senior Product Manager; General Superintendent; Senior Schedule Engineer; Contracts Administrator; Environmental Data Manager; Associate Air Quality Engineer. **Corporate headquarters location:** Greenwood Village CO. **International locations:** Worldwide. **Operations at this facility include:** Regional Headquarters.

## CAL-AIR CONDITIONING
1555 South Seventh Street, Building K, San Jose CA 95112. 408/947-0155. **Fax:** 562/698-4396. **Contact:** Administration Manager. **World Wide Web address:** http://www.calair.com. **Description:** A mechanical contractor. Cal-Air Conditioning installs and services air conditioning and heating systems, and is also engaged in energy management and sheet metal fabrication. **Positions advertised include:** Energy Service Sales Representative; Service Technician. **Corporate headquarters location:** Whittier CA. **Other U.S. locations:** Glendale CA; Sacramento CA. **Parent company:** Cal-Air, Inc. **Operations at this facility include:** Administration; Divisional Headquarters; Sales; Service. **Number of employees at this location:** 150. **Number of employees nationwide:** 400.

## THE CLARK CONSTRUCTION GROUP, INC.
7677 Oakport Street, Suite 1040, Oakland CA 94621. 510/430-1700. **Fax:** 510/430-1705. **Contact:** Human Resources. **E-mail address:** hr@clarkconstruction.com. **World Wide Web address:** http://www.clarkus.com. **Description:** One of the nation's leading general contractors. Construction and renovation projects include sports facilities, civic centers, hotels, educational facilities, laboratories, and office buildings. **NOTE:** All resumes should be sent to Human Resources, The Clark Construction Group, Inc., P.O. Box 5937, Bethesda MD 20814. **Corporate headquarters location:** Bethesda MD. **Other U.S. locations:** Nationwide. **Other area locations:** Irvine CA.

## EXPONENT, INC.
149 Commonwealth Drive, Menlo Park CA 94025. 650/326-9400. **Fax:** 650/328-3049. **Contact:** Human Resources Department. **E-mail address:** hr@exponent.com. **World Wide Web address:** http://

www.exponent.com. **Description:** A technical consulting firm dedicated to the investigation, analysis, and prevention of accidents and failures of an engineering or scientific nature. The company provides a multidisciplinary approach to analyze how failures occur. The company specializes in accident reconstruction, biomechanics, construction/structural engineering, aviation and marine investigations, environmental assessment, materials and product testing, warning and labeling issues, accident statistical data analysis, and risk prevention/mitigation. Founded in 1967. **NOTE:** You must hold a master's or doctorate degree in a suitable background to be considered for employment. **Positions advertised include:** Data/Risk Analyst; Environmental Engineer; Senior Hydorgeologist; Engineer; Contract Recruiter; Contracts/Business Manager; Administrative Assistant; Executive Assistant; Receptionist; Controller; Scientist; Senior Geological Engineer; Respiratory Toxicologist. **Special programs:** Internships. **Office hours:** Monday - Friday, 8:00 a.m. - 5:00 p.m. **Corporate headquarters location:** This location. **Other U.S. locations:** Nationwide. **Subsidiaries include:** Exponent Environmental Group; Exponent Failure Analysis; Exponent Health Group. **Listed on:** NASDAQ. **Stock exchange symbol:** EXPO. **CEO:** Michael Gaulke. **Annual sales/revenues:** $51 - $100 million. **Number of employees at this location:** 600.

### GENSLER
600 California Street, Suite 1000, San Francisco CA 94108-2740. 415/433-3700. **Contact:** Human Resources. **E-mail address:** info@ gensler.com. **World Wide Web address:** http://www.gensler.com. **Description:** Provides architectural space planning, graphics, and interior design services nationwide. **NOTE:** Resumes may be sent to the above e-mail address. **Special programs:** Internships. **Corporate headquarters location:** This location. **Other area locations:** Irvine CA; Los Angeles CA. **Other U.S. locations:** Denver CO; Washington DC; Atlanta GA; Boston MA; Detroit MI; New York NY; Houston TX. **Listed on:** Privately held. **Number of employees at this location:** 175. **Number of employees nationwide:** 800.

### HATHAWAY DINWIDDIE CONSTRUCTION COMPANY
275 Battery Street, Suite 300, San Francisco CA 94111. 415/986-2718. **Fax:** 415/956-5669. **Contact:** Human Resources. **E-mail address:** hr@hdcco.com. **World Wide Web address:** http://www. hdcco.com. **Description:** A full-service general contractor. **Corporate headquarters location:** This location. **Other area locations:** Los Angeles CA; Santa Clara CA.

## LATHROP CONSTRUCTION COMPANY

P.O. Box 2005, Benicia CA 94510. 707/746-8000. **Physical address:** 4001 Park Road, Benicia CA 94510. **Contact:** Human Resources. **E-mail address:** info@lathropconstruction.com. **World Wide Web address:** http://www.lathropconstruction.com. **NOTE:** Resumes may be sent to the above e-mail address. **Description:** A general contractor that offers a variety of services including construction management, budget development, document review, and cost estimation. **Positions advertised include:** Project Manager; Superintendent; Project Engineer. **Corporate headquarters location:** This location.

## LOCUS TECHNOLOGIES

299 Fairchild Drive, Mountain View CA 94043. 650/960-1640. **Fax:** 650/960-0739. **Contact:** Human Resources. **E-mail address:** humanresources@locustec.com. **World Wide Web address:** http:// www.locustec.com. **Description:** A leading environmental consulting, engineering, and remediation services provider. **NOTE:** Candidates should send a resume with salary requirements and references. **Corporate headquarters location:** Walnut Creek CA. **Other area locations:** El Segundo CA; Newark CA. **Listed on:** Privately held.

## PARSONS BRINCKERHOFF INC.

303 Second Street, Suite 700 North, San Francisco CA 94107. 415/243-4600. **Contact:** Betsy Hume, Human Resources Department. **World Wide Web address:** http://www.pbworld.com. **Description:** Provides total engineering and construction management services from project conception through completion. Services include the development of major bridges, tunnels, highways, marine facilities, buildings, industrial complexes, and railroads. **Positions advertised include:** Systems Analyst. **Special programs:** Internships. **Corporate headquarters location:** New York NY. **Other U.S. locations:** Nationwide. **Subsidiaries include:** Parsons Brinckerhoff Construction Services; Parsons Brinckerhoff International. **Number of employees worldwide:** 1,400.

## SWINERTON AND WALBERG BUILDERS

580 California Street, 12th Floor, San Francisco CA 94104. 415/421-2980. **Fax:** 415/984-1262. **Contact:** Marina Aviles, Director of Employment and Staffing. **World Wide Web address:** http://www. swinerton.com. **Description:** A general contracting firm that specializes in consulting, value management, and conceptual

design. The company's expertise lies with the assisted living, healthcare, public facilities, renovation and restoration, tenant improvement, and transportation markets. **Positions advertised include:** Receptionist/Administrative Assistant; Senior Estimator; Senior Administrative Assistant; Senior Project Engineer; Superintendent; Project Manager. **Special programs:** Internships. **Corporate headquarters location:** This location. **Other area locations:** Los Angeles CA. **Other U.S. locations:** Tucson AZ; Denver CO; Portland OR. **Operations at this facility include:** Administration. **Listed on:** Privately held. **Number of employees at this location:** 100. **Number of employees nationwide:** 500.

## THOMAS OUTDOOR LIGHTING
P.O. Box 2013, San Leandro CA 94577. 510/357-6900. **Physical address:** 2661 Alvarado Street, San Leandro CA 94577. **Contact:** Human Resources. **World Wide Web address:** http://www. sitelighting.com. **Description:** Thomas Industries provides lighting and compressor/vacuum pump products. **Special programs:** Internships. **Corporate headquarters location:** Louisville KY. **Other U.S. locations:** Nationwide. **Operations at this facility include:** This location produces and installs outdoor area lighting and flood lighting for parking lots, pathways, gardens, and garages. **Listed on:** New York Stock Exchange. **Stock exchange symbol:** TII. **Number of employees at this location:** 200. **Number of employees nationwide:** 3,000.

## URS CORPORATION
100 California Street, Suite 500, San Francisco CA 94111. 415/774-2700. **Contact:** Personnel Department. **World Wide Web address:** http://www.urscorp.com. **Description:** An international professional services organization with substantial engineering, training, architectural planning, environmental, and construction management capabilities. **Positions advertised include:** Civil-Geotechnical Engineer; Graduate Civil Engineer; Project Biologist; Project Manager; Structural Technician; Field Technician; Program Manager. **Corporate headquarters location:** This location. **Listed on:** New York Stock Exchange. **Stock exchange symbol:** URS.

## WENTZ GROUP
P.O. Box 610, San Carlos CA 94070. 650/592-3950. **Physical address:** 1599 Industrial Road, San Carlos CA 94070. **World Wide Web address:** http://www.wentzgroup.com. **Description:** Provides general construction services. **Corporate headquarters location:** This

location. **Other U.S. locations:** Los Angeles CA. **Listed on:** Privately held. **Number of employees at this location:** 30.

# ARTS, ENTERTAINMENT, SPORTS, AND RECREATION

**You can expect to find the following types of companies in this chapter:**
*Botanical and Zoological Gardens • Entertainment Groups • Motion Picture and Video Tape Production and Distribution • Museums and Art Galleries • Physical Fitness Facilities • Professional Sports Clubs • Public Golf Courses • Racing and Track Operations • Sporting and Recreational Camps • Theatrical Producers*

## ALLIED VAUGHN
480 Valley Drive, Brisbane CA 94005. 415/656-2200. **Toll-free phone:** 888/691-3381. **Contact:** Human Resources. **World Wide Web address:** http://www.allied-digital.com. **Description:** One of the nation's leading independent multimedia manufacturing companies, offering CD-audio and CD-ROM mastering and replication; videocassette and audiocassette duplication; laser video disc recording; off-line and online video editing; motion picture film processing; film-to-tape and tape-to-film transfers; and complete finishing, packaging, warehousing, and fulfillment services. **Other U.S. locations:** Nationwide.

## LUCAS DIGITAL LTD. LLC
P.O. Box 2459, San Rafael CA 94912. 415/258-2200. **Recorded jobline:** 415/448-2100. **Contact:** Recruitment Department. **E-mail address:** hrdept@lucasdigital.com. **World Wide Web address:** http://www.ilm.com. **Description:** A digital effects company engaged in motion picture film production. The company is comprised of Industrial Light & Magic (ILM), a visual effects company; and Skywalker Sound, a state-of-the-art audio facility. **Positions advertised include:** Technical Editor; Digital Matte Artist; Visual Effects Art Director; Storyboard/Concept Artist; Visual Effects Art Director. **Corporate headquarters location:** This location.

## LUCASFILM LTD.
P.O. Box 2009, San Rafael CA 94912-2009. 415/662-1700. **Fax:** 415/662-5697. **Contact:** Human Resources. **World Wide Web address:** http://www.lucasfilm.com. **Description:** A leading film production company specializing in visual and sound effects. **Positions advertised include:** Payroll Coordinator; Network Systems Administrator; Oracle Programmer Analyst; Director of Toys; Documentary Manager; Security Officer. **Special programs:** Internships. **Corporate headquarters location:** This location.

## THE OAKLAND ATHLETICS (A'S)
7000 Coliseum Way, Oakland CA 94621. 510/638-4900. **Recorded jobline:** 510/638-4900x2817. **Contact:** Human Resources. **E-mail address:** hr@oaklandathletics.com. **World Wide Web address:** http://oakland.athletics.mlb.com. **Description:** Business offices for the Major League Baseball team. **NOTE:** Entry-level positions and part-time jobs are offered. **Special programs:** Internships. **Office hours:** Monday - Friday, 8:00 a.m. - 5:00 p.m. **Corporate headquarters location:** This location. **Listed on:** Privately held.

## PIXAR ANIMATION STUDIOS
1200 Park Avenue, Emeryville CA 94608. 510/752-3000. **Contact:** Recruiting. **E-mail address:** hr@pixar.com. **World Wide Web address:** http://www.pixar.com. **Description:** A computer animation studio. Pixar Animation Studios produces various computer animated entertainment products in the form of feature films and computer software. **Positions advertised include:** Mac/PC Systems Administrator; MacOS X Systems Administrator; QA Engineer; Project Coordinator; Film-On-Line Tools Engineer; Software Project Manager; QA/Automated Test Engineer. **Corporate headquarters location:** This location. **Listed on:** NASDAQ. **Stock exchange symbol:** PIXR. **Number of employees at this location:** 430.

## SAN FRANCISCO OPERA
301 Van Ness Avenue, San Francisco CA 94102. 415/861-4008. **Fax:** 415/551-6297. **Recorded jobline:** 415/565-6464. **Contact:** Human Resources. **E-mail address:** employment@sfopera.com. **World Wide Web address:** http://www.sfopera.com. **Description:** An opera house. Founded in 1923. **Positions advertised include:** Audience Development Manager; Leadership Gifts Officer; Development Services Manager; Administrative Assistant; Annual and Planned Giving Assistant; Subscription Associate.

## SAN JOSE SHARKS
525 West Santa Clara Street, San Jose CA 95113. 408/287-7070. **Contact:** Human Resources. **World Wide Web address:** http://www.sj-sharks.com. **Description:** A professional hockey team. **Corporate headquarters location:** This location.

# AUTOMOTIVE

**You can expect to find the following types of companies in this chapter:**
*Automotive Repair Shops • Automotive Stampings • Industrial Vehicles and Moving Equipment • Motor Vehicles and Equipment • Travel Trailers and Campers*

## CONEXANT SYSTEMS INC.
3600 Pruneridge Avenue, Suite 100, Santa Clara CA 95051. 408/551-0270. **Contact:** Personnel. **World Wide Web address:** http://www.conexant.com. **Description:** Provides products for the printing, military, automotive, and aerospace industries through its electronics, automotive, and graphics divisions. Products include military and commercial communications equipment, guidance systems, electronics, components for automobiles, and printing presses. **Corporate headquarters location:** This location. **Other U.S. locations:** Austin TX. **Listed on:** NASDAQ. **Stock exchange symbol:** CNXT.

## CUMMINS WEST INC.
14775 Wicks Boulevard, San Leandro CA 94577-6779. 510/351-6101. **Contact:** Michael Doherty, Vice President of Finance. **World Wide Web address:** http://www.cummins.com. **Description:** Cummins West Inc. manufactures in-line and V-type diesel engines from 145 to 1600 horsepower, and replacement parts for these engines. The company also manufactures and markets a broad range of heavy-duty filters and reconditioned diesel engines and parts. **Positions advertised include:** Applications Developer; Database Administrator; Network Administrator; Systems Analyst; Web Developer. **Corporate headquarters location:** Columbus IN. **Operations at this facility include:** This facility is primarily a wholesale dealership. **Listed on:** New York Stock Exchange.

## CUSTOM CHROME, INC.
16100 Jacqueline Court, Morgan Hill CA 95037. 408/778-0500. **Fax:** 408/778-0530. **Contact:** Personnel. **E-mail address:** mary_profeta@customchrome.com. **World Wide Web address:** http://www.customchrome.com. **Description:** A leading independent supplier of aftermarket parts and accessories for Harley-Davidson motorcycles. Custom Chrome distributes its own products under brand names including Rev Tech, Premium, Dyno Power, and C.C. Rider. The company also supplies products by manufacturers such as Dunlop, Champion, Hastings, and Accel. Founded in 1970. **Parent

company: Global Motorsport Group Inc. **Listed on:** NASDAQ. **Stock exchange symbol:** CSTM.

## FIRESTONE TIRE & SERVICE CENTER
4637 Watt Avenue, North Highlands CA 95660. 916/486-9807. **Contact:** Human Resources. **World Wide Web address:** http://www.bridgestone-firestone.com. **Description:** One location in a chain of tire and automotive service centers. **Positions advertised include:** Store Manager; Manager of Tire Sales; Service Manager; Master Technician; Senior Technician; Maintenance Technician. **Parent company:** Bridgestone/Firestone, Inc. (Nashville TN).

## HONEYWELL
1430 Tully Road, Suite 415, San Jose CA 95122. 650/965-2414. **Contact:** Human Resources. **World Wide Web address:** http://www.honeywell.com. **Description:** Honeywell is engaged in the research, development, manufacture, and sale of advanced technology products and services in the fields of chemicals, electronics, automation, and controls. The company's major businesses are home and building automation and control, performance polymers and chemicals, industrial automation and control, space and aviation systems, and defense and marine systems. **Corporate headquarters location:** Plymouth MN. **Operations at this facility include:** This location manufactures industrial chemicals. **Listed on:** New York Stock Exchange. **Stock exchange symbol:** HON.

## NEW UNITED MOTOR MANUFACTURING INC.
45500 Fremont Boulevard, Fremont CA 94538. 510/498-5500. **Fax:** 510/770-4116. **Contact:** Human Resources Department. **E-mail address:** careers@nummi.com. **World Wide Web address:** http://www.nummi.com. **Description:** Through a joint venture between General Motors Corporation and Toyota Motor Corporation, New United Motor Manufacturing manufactures Chevrolet Prizms for the Chevrolet Motor Division of General Motors and Toyota Corolla sedans and Tacoma pickup trucks for Toyota. Founded in 1984. **NOTE:** Entry-level positions are offered. **Positions advertised include:** Financial Analyst; Industrial Electrician. **Special programs:** Co-ops. **Internship information:** The company offers a six-month cooperative education program. **Corporate headquarters location:** This location. **Listed on:** Privately held. **Number of employees at this location:** 4,800.

# BANKING/SAVINGS AND LOANS

**You can expect to find the following types of companies in this chapter:**
*Banks • Bank Holding Companies and Associations •*
*Lending Firms/Financial Services Institutions*

## BANK OF AMERICA
1275 Fell Street, San Francisco CA 94117. 650/615-4700. **Contact:** Human Resources Department. **World Wide Web address:** http://www.bankofamerica.com. **Description:** Bank of America is a full-service banking and financial institution. The company operates through four business segments: Global Corporate and Investment Banking, Principal Investing and Asset Management, Commercial Banking, and Consumer Banking. **Positions advertised include:** Teller; Trust Officer; Manager of Information Research; Group Banking Account Specialist. **Corporate headquarters location:** Charlotte NC. **Other U.S. locations:** Nationwide. **International locations:** Worldwide. **Annual sales/revenues:** More than $100 million. **Listed on:** New York Stock Exchange. **Stock exchange symbol:** BAC.

## BAY BANK OF COMMERCE
1495 East 14th Street, San Leandro CA 94577. 510/357-2265. **Contact:** Personnel. **World Wide Web address:** http://www.baybankofcommerce.com. **Description:** A full-service bank. The bank's Construction Lending Division provides residential construction financing to individuals and builders throughout the East Bay area. **Corporate headquarters location:** This location. **Parent company:** Greater Bay Bankcorp. **Number of employees at this location:** 60. **Listed on:** NASDAQ. **Stock exchange symbol:** GBBK.

## BAY VIEW BANK
136 Second Avenue, San Mateo CA 94403. 650/312-7200. **Contact:** Human Resources. **E-mail address:** humanresources@ bayviewcapitalcapital.com. **World Wide Web address:** http://www.bayviewbank.com. **Description:** A commercial bank. Founded in 1911. **NOTE:** Please send resumes to Human Resources, Bay View Capital Corporation, 1840 Gateway Drive, San Mateo CA 94404. **Corporate headquarters location:** This location. **Other U.S. locations:** IL; TX. **Parent company:** Bay View Capital Corporation is a diversified, financial institution. **Listed on:** New York Stock Exchange. **Stock exchange symbol:** BVC.

## BAY VIEW BANK
1098 Shell Boulevard, Foster City CA 94404. 650/574-4034. **Contact:** Human Resources. **World Wide Web address:** http://www. bayviewbank.com. **Description:** A commercial bank. Founded in 1911. **NOTE:** Please send resumes to Human Resources, Bay View Capital Corporation, 1840 Gateway Drive, San Mateo CA 94404. **Corporate headquarters location:** San Mateo CA. **Other U.S. locations:** IL; TX. **Parent company:** Bay View Capital Corporation is a diversified, financial institution. **Listed on:** New York Stock Exchange. **Stock exchange symbol:** BVC.

## CITY NATIONAL BANK
2101 Webster Street, 14th Floor, Oakland CA 94612. 510/836-6500. **Contact:** Human Resources. **E-mail address:** careers@cnb. com. **World Wide Web address:** http://www.cnb.com. **Description:** A commercial bank with 50 offices in Northern and Southern California. **Corporate headquarters location:** Beverly Hills CA. **Other area locations:** Statewide. **Listed on:** New York Stock Exchange. **Stock exchange symbol:** CYN. **Number of employees at this location:** 115.

## COMERICA BANK CALIFORNIA
55 Almaden Boulevard, 2nd Floor, Mail Code 4113, San Jose CA 95113. 408/556-5000. **Toll-free phone:** 800/522-2265. **Contact:** Human Resources. **World Wide Web address:** http://www. comerica.com. **Description:** A bank with more than 30 offices across the state. **Positions advertised include:** Computer Operator; Operations Specialist, Legal and Compliance. **Corporate headquarters location:** Detroit MI. **Other area locations:** Alameda CA; Los Angeles CA; Monterey CA; San Francisco CA; San Mateo CA; Santa Clara CA; Santa Cruz CA. **Other U.S. locations:** FL; IL; MI; TX. **Parent company:** Comerica, Inc. (Detroit MI) is a bank holding company. The company offers a wide range of financial products and services for businesses and individuals through more than 400 offices nationwide. The five core business markets Comerica covers are corporate banking, consumer banking, private banking, institutional trust and investment management, and international finance and trade services. Including its subsidiaries, Comerica has operations in 16 states and two Canadian provinces. **Listed on:** New York Stock Exchange. **Stock exchange symbol:** CMA. **Number of employees at this location:** 1,000. **Number of employees nationwide:** 14,000.

## CUPERTINO NATIONAL BANK & TRUST

20230 Stevens Creek Boulevard, Cupertino CA 95014. 408/996-1144. **Toll-free phone:** 800/226-5262. **Fax:** 650/843-1287. **Contact:** Human Resources. **World Wide Web address:** http://www.gbbk.com. **Description:** A bank offering a variety of services including corporate and personal relationship banking, residential lending, SBA lending, and personal and corporate trust services. **Corporate headquarters location:** This location. **Other area locations:** Palo Alto CA; San Jose CA. **Parent company:** Greater Bay Bankcorp. **Listed on:** NASDAQ. **Stock exchange symbol:** GBBK.

## FEDERAL HOME LOAN BANK OF SAN FRANCISCO

P.O. Box 7948, San Francisco CA 94120. 415/616-1000. **Physical address:** 600 California Street, Suite 300, San Francisco CA 94018. **Fax:** 415/616/-2864. **Contact:** Human Resources Department. **E-mail address:** web_hr@fhlbnsf.com. **World Wide Web address:** http://www.fhlbsf.com. **Description:** The central bank and regulating agency to more than 200 savings and loan associations in California, Arizona, and Nevada. **Positions advertised include:** Facilities Coordinator; Collateral Operations Specialist; Applications Consultant; Mortgage Finance Director; Financial Analyst; Derivatives Accountant; Treasury Assistant; Senior Trader.

## FIRST BANK AND TRUST

550 Montgomery Street, San Francisco CA 94111. 415/781-7810. **World Wide Web address:** http://www.firstbank.com. **Description:** A bank holding company. **Corporate headquarters location:** This location. **Operations at this facility include:** Administration. **Listed on:** Privately held. **Number of employees at this location:** 40.

## FIRST REPUBLIC BANCORP INC.

111 Pine Street, 5th floor, San Francisco CA 94111-5602. 415/392-1400. **Toll-free phone:** 800/392-1400. **Contact:** Human Resources. **World Wide Web address:** http://www.firstrepublic.com. **Description:** A leading banking and mortgage institution with growing operations in San Francisco, Los Angeles, San Diego, and Las Vegas. **Corporate headquarters location:** This location.

## GOLDEN STATE BANCORP
## CALIFORNIA FEDERAL BANK

135 Main Street, San Francisco CA 94105. 415/904-1100. **Contact:** Human Resources. **World Wide Web address:** http://www.calfed.com. **Description:** A bank holding company. **Corporate**

**headquarters location:** This location. **Subsidiaries include:** California Federal Bank (also at this location) offers mortgage services, consumer and business banking products, and automobile financing. **Listed on:** New York Stock Exchange. **Stock exchange symbol:** GSB. **Annual sales/revenues:** More than $100 million.

### GREATER BAY BANCORP
900 Veterens Boulevard, Redwood City CA 94063. 650/813-8200. **Fax:** 650/843-1287. **Contact:** Human Resources. **E-mail address:** careersearch@gbbk.com. **World Wide Web address:** http://www. gbbk.com. **Description:** A bank holding company. **NOTE:** To request an application, applicants should call 650/813-8267. **Corporate headquarters location:** This location. **Listed on:** NASDAQ. **Stock exchange symbol:** GBBK. **Annual sales/revenues:** More than $100 million.

### PATELCO CREDIT UNION
156 Second Street, San Francisco CA 94105. 415/442-6200. **Fax:** 415/442-6248. **Contact:** Human Resources. **E-mail address:** jobs@ patelco.org. **World Wide Web address:** http://www.patelco.org. **Description:** A full service credit union. Founded in 1936. **Positions advertised include:** Internal Auditor; HR Recruiter; Manager of Financial Analysis and Reporting; Member Service Representative; Credit Union Representative; Credit Union Direct Lending Representative.

### U.S. BANK
1440 Ethan Way, Suite 101, Sacramento CA 95825. 916/920-4111. **Contact:** Employment Services. **World Wide Web address:** http:// www.usbank.com. **Description:** A bank. **NOTE:** Resumes should either be accompanied by an application (available at local offices) or a specific job number. **Positions advertised include:** Account Service Representative; In Store Banker; Mortgage Loan Officer; Personal Broker; Sales and Service Manager; Teller. **Corporate headquarters location:** Minneapolis MN.

### U.S. BANK
1440 Ethan Way, Suite 101, Sacramento CA 95825. 916/920-4111. **Contact:** Employment Services. **World Wide Web address:** http:// www.usbank.com. **Description:** A bank. **NOTE:** Resumes should either be accompanied by an application (available at local offices) or a specific job number. **Positions advertised include:** Account Service Representative; In Store Banker; Mortgage Loan Officer;

Personal Broker; Sales and Service Manager; Teller. **Corporate headquarters location:** Minneapolis MN.

## U.S. FEDERAL RESERVE BANK OF SAN FRANCISCO

101 Market Street, San Francisco CA 94105. 415/974-2000. **Contact:** Human Resources Department. **World Wide Web address:** http://www.frbsf.org. **Description:** One of 12 regional Federal Reserve banks that, along with the Federal Reserve Board of Governors in Washington DC and the Federal Open Market Committee (FOMC), comprise the Federal Reserve System, the nation's central bank. As the nation's central bank, Federal Reserve is charged with three major responsibilities: setting monetary policy, banking supervision and regulation, and payment processing. **NOTE:** Entry-level positions and second and third shifts are offered. **Positions advertised include:** Chief Stationary Engineer; Contract Administrator; Credit Analyst; Executive Staff Assistant; Project Applications Consultant. **Corporate headquarters location:** This location. **Number of employees at this location:** 1,400.

## UNION BANK OF CALIFORNIA

400 California Street, 10th Floor, San Francisco CA 94104. 415/765-3434. **Fax:** 415/765-2202. **Contact:** Corporate Staffing. **E-mail address:** careers05@uboc.com. **World Wide Web address:** http://www.uboc.com. **Description:** A full-service commercial bank providing a broad mix of financial services including retail and small business banking, middle market banking, personal and business trust services, real estate finance, corporate banking, trade finance (with a focus on the Pacific Rim), and financial management services through 246 branch offices. **NOTE:** Union Bank offers management training programs in several areas: community (retail) banking, commercial lending, and business relationships. **Positions advertised include:** Private Bank Relationship Manager; Management Trainee; Branch Manager; Audit Relationship Manager; Fixed Income Funds Manager. **Subsidiaries include:** U.S. Investment Services, Inc. **Corporate headquarters location:** This location. **Parent company:** UnionBanCal Corporation. **Listed on:** New York Stock Exchange. **Stock exchange symbol:** UB. **Number of employees at this location:** 3,500. **Number of employees nationwide:** 10,000.

## WELLS FARGO & COMPANY

490 Brannan Street, San Francisco CA 94107. 415/396-6181. **Contact:** Recruitment Services. **World Wide Web address:** http://www.wellsfargo.com. **Description:** A diversified financial institution.

Wells Fargo serves over 17 million customers through 5,300 independent locations worldwide. The company also maintains several stand-alone ATMs and branches within retail outlets. Services include community banking, credit and debit cards, home equity and mortgage loans, online banking, student loans, and insurance. Wells Fargo also offers a complete line of commercial and institutional financial services. Founded in 1852. **Special programs:** Internships; Training; Summer Jobs. **Internship information:** The company offers summer internships only. **Corporate headquarters location:** This location. **Other U.S. locations:** Nationwide. **International locations:** Worldwide. **Parent company:** Wells Fargo & Company is one of the largest bank holding companies in the United States with 5,000 branch locations. **Listed on:** New York Stock Exchange. **Stock exchange symbol:** WFC. **President/CEO:** Dick Kovacevich. **Annual sales/revenues:** More than $100 million. **Number of employees worldwide:** 104,000.

## WESTAMERICA BANK
424 Grass Valley Highway, Auburn CA 95603. 530/888-3747. **Recorded jobline:** 707/863-6400. **Contact:** Human Resources. **E-mail address:** recruiting@westamerica.com. **World Wide Web address:** http://www.westamerica.com. **Description:** Offers a wide range of general commercial banking services including money market accounts, NOW accounts, checking accounts, savings accounts, and certificates of deposit. **Positions advertised include:** Teller; Assistant Customer Service Manager. **Corporate headquarters location:** San Rafael CA. **Listed on:** NASDAQ. **Stock exchange symbol:** WBKC.

## WORLD SAVINGS & LOAN ASSOCIATION
1901 Harrison Street, Oakland CA 94612. 510/446-6000. **Contact:** Human Resources. **World Wide Web address:** http://www.worldsavings.com. **Description:** One of the largest savings and loan associations in the United States, with more than 50 locations nationwide. **Positions advertised include:** Benefits Manager. **Corporate headquarters location:** This location. **Other area locations:** Sacramento CA; San Francisco CA; Walnut Creek CA. **Other U.S. locations:** Nationwide. **Parent company:** Golden West Financial (also at this location). **Operations at this facility include:** Administration; Service. **Listed on:** New York Stock Exchange. **Stock exchange symbol:** GDW.

# BIOTECHNOLOGY, PHARMACEUTICALS, AND SCIENTIFIC R&D

**You can expect to find the following types of companies in this chapter:**
*Clinical Labs • Lab Equipment Manufacturers*
*Pharmaceutical Manufacturers and Distributors*

## A.P. PHARMA
123 Saginaw Drive, Redwood City CA 94063. 650/366–2626. **Fax:** 650/365-6490. **Contact:** Sandra Squires, Human Resources. **E-mail address:** jobs@appharma.com. **World Wide Web address:** http://www.appharma.com. **Description:** A developer and marketer of polymer-based delivery systems and related technologies for use in pharmaceuticals, over-the-counter drugs, toiletries, and specialty applications. **Corporate headquarters location:** This location. **Listed on:** NASDAQ. **Stock exchange symbol:** APPA

## ABAXIS, INC.
3240 Whipple Road, Union City CA 94587. 510/675-6500. **Fax:** 510/441-6151. **Contact:** Human Resources. **World Wide Web address:** http://www.abaxis.com. **Description:** A research and development firm. Abaxis, Inc. is focused on the commercialization of the Piccolo System, which consists of a small, whole-blood analyzer and blood chemistry reagent rotors. The company developed Primary Health Profile, a nine-test reagent rotor marketed to veterinarians. Founded in 1989. **Corporate headquarters location:** This location.

## ALZA CORPORATION
P.O. Box 7210, Mountain View CA 94039-7210. 650/564-5000. **Physical address:** 1900 Charlestown Road, Mountain View CA 94043. **Fax:** 650/564-5656. **Recorded jobline:** 650/494-5319. **Contact:** Darlene Markovitch, Human Resources Director. **E-mail address:** jobs@alza.com. **World Wide Web address:** http://www.alza.com. **Description:** Develops, manufactures, and markets therapeutic systems for both humans and animals. Products include drug delivery technologies that focus on the areas of urology and oncology and are used in the treatment of angina, hypertension, respiratory allergies, motion sickness, and nicotine withdrawal. Founded in 1968. **Positions advertised include:** Associate Director of Product Development; Director of Macroflux Product Development; Process Engineer; Director of New Product Planning; Senior Financial Analyst; Facilities Planning Manager; Production

Supervisor; Mechanic; Clinical Data Coordinator; Research Scientist. **Special programs:** Internships. **Corporate headquarters location:** This location. **Other U.S. locations:** Vacaville CA; Minneapolis MN. **International locations:** Canada. **Parent company:** Johnson & Johnson. **Operations at this facility include:** Administration; Manufacturing; Research and Development. **Listed on:** New York Stock Exchange. **Stock exchange symbol:** JNJ. **Number of employees at this location:** 1,000. **Number of employees nationwide:** 1,370.

### APPLIED BIOSYSTEMS
850 Lincoln Centre Drive, Foster City CA 94404. 650/638-5800. **Contact:** Employment. **World Wide Web address:** http://www. appliedbiosystems.com. **Description:** Manufactures life science systems and analytical tools for use in such markets as biotechnology, pharmaceuticals, environmental testing, and chemical manufacturing. **Positions advertised include:** Senior Systems Integration Engineer; Staff Administrator; Design Specialist; Client Engineering Manager; Process Development Scientist; Senior Coordinator, Helpdesk; Brand Programs Manager; Network Services Engineer; Science Facilitator; Design Specialist. **Corporate headquarters location:** This location. **Operations at this facility include:** Administration; Manufacturing; Research and Development; Sales; Service. **Listed on:** New York Stock Exchange. **Stock exchange symbol:** ABI. **Number of employees nationwide:** 900.

### ARADIGM
3929 Point Eden Way, Hayward CA 94545. 510/265-9000. **Contact:** Human Resources. **Description:** A drug delivery company. **Positions advertised include:** Engineering Technician; Cleanroom Packaging Operator; Nozzle Manufacturing Operator; Compounding Operator Specialist; QA Compliance Manager; Senior Quality/Validation and Testing Engineer; Quality Systems Developer; Microbiologist; Materials and Process Science Director.

### BD BIOSCIENCES
2350 Qume Drive, San Jose CA 95131. 408/432-9475. **Toll-free phone:** 800/223-8226. **Contact:** Personnel. **World Wide Web address:** http://www.bdbiosciences.com. **Description:** BD Biosciences serves laboratories worldwide with research and clinical applications in immunology, hematology, and cell biology. The company also provides products and instruments for infectious disease diagnosis, which screen for microbial presence; grow and identify organisms; and test for antibiotic susceptibility. Products for

the industrial microbiology market are used for food testing, environmental monitoring, and biopharmaceutical fermentation media. Tissue culture products help advance the understanding of diseases and potential therapies. **Positions advertised include:** Commodity Team Leader; Director of Finance; Director of Regulatory Affairs; Dispatch Coordinator; Intellectual Property Counsel; Manager of Customer Service; Manufacturing Group Leader; Planner/Scheduler; Senior Change Order Drafter; Senior Applications Analyst. **Corporate headquarters location:** Franklin Lakes NJ. **Other U.S. locations:** Palo Alto CA; San Diego CA; Bedford MA. **International locations:** Worldwide. **Listed on:** New York Stock Exchange. **Stock exchange symbol:** BOX. **Number of employees at this location:** 500. **Number of employees nationwide:** 600.

### BAYER CORPORATION
P.O. Box 1986, Berkeley CA 94701. 510/705-5000. **Contact:** Personnel. **World Wide Web address:** http://www.bayerus.com. **Description:** Bayer is engaged in the development, manufacture, and distribution of health care products including pharmaceuticals and a wide range of hospital equipment. **NOTE:** Electronic submissions are preferred and will receive more immediate consideration. Please send to appropriate contact person for each job listing on the job page. **Corporate headquarters location:** Pittsburgh PA. **Other U.S. locations:** Nationwide. **International locations:** Worldwide. **Operations at this facility include:** This location conducts pharmaceutical research and development. **Listed on:** New York Stock Exchange. **Stock exchange symbol:** BAY. **Number of employees nationwide:** 23,000. **Number of employees worldwide:** 120,000.

### BIO-RAD LABORATORIES
2000 Alfred Nobel Drive, Hercules CA 94547. 510/724-7000. **Contact:** Human Resources. **World Wide Web address:** http://www. bio-rad.com. **Description:** Develops, manufactures, and markets diagnostic test kits, specialty chemicals, and related equipment used for separating complex mixtures. The company also produces analytical instruments used to detect and measure chemical components in minute quantities, as well as products for electron microscopy. **NOTE:** Resumes can be sent to their resume processing center at Bio-Rad Laboratories, P.O. Box 445, Burlington MA 01803. **Positions advertised include:** Account Executive; Chemist; Division Manager; Attorney; Group Leader; Information Systems and Services

Manager. **Corporate headquarters location:** This location. **Other U.S. locations:** Randolph MA; Philadelphia PA. **International locations:** Worldwide. **Operations at this facility include:** Administration; Manufacturing; Research and Development; Service. **Listed on:** American Stock Exchange. **Stock exchange symbol:** BIO.

### BIOTIME, INC.

935 Pardee Street, Berkeley CA 94710. 510/845-9535. **Fax:** 510/845-7914. **Contact:** contacts@biotimemail.com. **World Wide Web address:** http://www.biotimeinc.com. **Description:** Engaged in the research and development of aqueous-based synthetic solutions. Products are used as plasma expanders, organ preservation solutions, or solutions to replace blood volume. Founded in 1990. **Listed on:** American Stock Exchange. **Stock exchange symbol:** BTX.

### CALGENE, INC.

1920 Fifth Street, Davis CA 95616. 530/753-6313. **Fax:** 530/792-2453. **Contact:** Human Resources. **World Wide Web address:** http://www.monsanto.com. **Description:** Develops genetically-engineered plants and plant products for the food and seed industries. The company's research and business efforts are focused in three main crop areas: fresh market tomato, edible and industrial plant oils, and cotton. **Corporate headquarters location:** St. Louis MO.

### CELERA

180 Kimball Way, South San Francisco CA 94080. 650/829-1000. **Toll-free phone:** 877/CELERA1. **Contact:** Human Resources. **World Wide Web address:** http://www.celera.com. **Description:** Engaged in the discovery and development of innovative drugs, with a focus in oncology. **Positions advertised include:** Research Associate; Senior Scientist; Research Assistant; Process and Scale Up Chemist; EHS Manager. **Corporate headquarters location:** This location. **Listed on:** New York Stock Exchange. **Stock exchange symbol:** CRA.

### CELL GENESYS, INC.

500 Forbes Boulevard, South San Francisco CA 94080. 650/266-3000. **Contact:** Human Resources. **E-mail address:** hr@cellgenesys.com. **World Wide Web address:** http://www.cellgenesys.com. **Description:** Develops and commercializes gene therapies to treat major life-threatening diseases including cancer and cardiovascular disease. The company is conducting two multicenter Phase II human clinical trials for its GVAX cancer vaccine in prostate cancer and

plans to initiate a multicenter Phase I/II trial of GVAX vaccine in lung cancer. Preclinical stage programs include gene therapy for cancer, cardiovascular disorders, hemophilia, and Parkinson's disease. **Positions advertised include:** Supervisor, Payroll and Stock Administration; Director of Finance; Director of Regulatory Affairs; Vice President of Regulatory Affairs and Quality Assurance; Animal Technician; Senior Clinical Research Associate. **Corporate headquarters location:** This location. **Other area locations:** San Diego CA. **Other U.S. locations:** Memphis TN. **Listed on:** NASDAQ. **Stock exchange symbol:** CEGE.

## CHIRON CORPORATION
4560 Horton Street, Emeryville CA 94608-2916. 510/655-8730. **Fax:** 510/623-2514. **Contact:** Human Resources. **E-mail address:** jobs@chiron.com. **World Wide Web address:** http://www.chiron. com. **Description:** A biotechnology company that operates within three global health care sectors including biopharmaceuticals, blood testing, and vaccines. The company specializes in products designed to prevent and treat cancer, cardiovascular disease, and infectious diseases. **Positions advertised include:** Administrative Assistant; Clinical Studies Assistant; Drug Safety Specialist; Process Engineer; Master Mechanic; Senior Mechanical Engineer. **Corporate headquarters location:** This location. **Other area locations:** Vacaville CA. **Other U.S. locations:** Annandale NJ; Seattle WA. **International locations:** Canada; France; Germany; Italy; Netherlands; United Kingdom. **Subsidiaries include:** IOLAB. **Listed on:** NASDAQ. **Stock exchange symbol:** CHIR. **Number of employees nationwide:** 1,900.

## CHOLESTECH CORPORATION
3347 Investment Boulevard, Hayward CA 94545. 510/732-7200. **Fax:** 510/732-7227. **Contact:** Human Resources. **E-mail address:** ctec_hr@cholestech.com. **World Wide Web address:** http://www. cholestech.com. **Description:** Develops and markets diagnostics systems that measure cholesterol. **Corporate headquarters location:** This location. **Listed on:** NASDAQ. **Stock exchange symbol:** CTEC.

## CYGNUS, INC.
400 Penobscot Drive, Redwood City CA 94063. 650/369-4300. **Fax:** 650/599-3938. **Contact:** Human Resources. **E-mail address:** recruiting@cygn.com. **World Wide Web address:** http://www.cygn. com. **Description:** Develops and manufactures diagnostic medical devices. Founded in 1985. **Positions advertised include:** Engineer.

**Corporate headquarters location:** This location. **Listed on:** NASDAQ. **Stock exchange symbol:** CYGN.

## DNA PLANT TECHNOLOGY CORPORATION
6701 San Pablo Avenue, Oakland CA 94608. 510/547-2395. **Contact:** Human Resources. **World Wide Web address:** http://www.dnap.com. **Description:** A leading agricultural biotechnology company focused on developing and marketing premium, fresh, and processed fruits and vegetables, using advanced breeding, genetic engineering, and other biotechniques. **Corporate headquarters location:** This location. **Subsidiaries include:** FreshWorld Farms markets a line of premium vegetables under the FreshWorld Farms brand name including tomatoes, carrot bites, sweet red mini-peppers, and carrot sticks.

## DADE BEHRING, INC.
20400 Mariani Avenue, Cupertino CA 95014. 408/239-2000. **Contact:** Professional Employment. **World Wide Web address:** http://www.dadebehring.com. **Description:** Manufactures and distributes diagnostic instrument systems and other labware that serve clinical and research laboratories worldwide. Dade Behring also offers its customers support services. **Corporate headquarters location:** Deerfield IL. **International locations:** Worldwide. **Number of employees worldwide:** 7,500.

## ELAN PHARMACEUTICALS, INC.
800 Gateway Boulevard, South San Francisco CA 94080. 650/877-0900. **Fax:** 650/553-7138. **Contact:** Recruiter. **E-mail address:** careers@elanpharma.com. **World Wide Web address:** http://www.elan.com. **Description:** A research-based pharmaceutical company with a focus on drug delivery systems and specializing in neurology, cancer, pain management, and infectious diseases. **Positions advertised include:** Associate Director of PK; RA, Molecular Biology; Associate Project Manager, Clinical Trials Materials; Manager; LIMS Administrator; Research Associate; Research Assistant; Associate Scientist. **Corporate headquarters location:** Dublin, Ireland. **Parent company:** Elan Corporation. **Listed on:** New York Stock Exchange. **Stock exchange symbol:** ELN. **Annual sales/revenues:** More than $100 million. **Number of employees at this location:** 1,000.

## GENELABS TECHNOLOGIES, INC.
505 Penobscot Drive, Redwood City CA 94063. 650/369-9500. **Contact:** Human Resources. **E-mail address:** hr@genelabs.com.

**World Wide Web address:** http://www.genelabs.com. **Description:** Develops, manufactures, and provides products for the treatment, prevention, and diagnosis of viral and severely debilitating or life-threatening diseases. The company operates through its biopharmaceutical and diagnostic divisions to clinical laboratories and physicians' offices worldwide. **Corporate headquarters location:** This location. **Listed on:** NASDAQ. **Stock exchange symbol:** GNLB.

## GENENTECH, INC.

One DNA Way, South San Francisco CA 94080. 650/225-1000. **Contact:** Human Resources. **E-mail address:** genentechjobpost@webhirepc.com. **World Wide Web address:** http://www.gene.com. **Description:** A biotechnology company that develops, manufactures, and markets pharmaceuticals using human genetic information. Genentech specializes in products designed to treat growth deficiencies, breast cancer, and AMI. **NOTE:** If sending a hard copy of your resume, please make sure that it is in a scannable format and mail to Genentech, Inc., Human Resources, P.O. Box 1950, South San Francisco CA 94083-1950. **Positions advertised include:** Associate Accountant; Global Procurement Director. **Corporate headquarters location:** This location. **Listed on:** New York Stock Exchange. **Stock exchange symbol:** DNA.

## GILEAD SCIENCES

333 Lakeside Drive, Foster City CA 94404. 650/574-3000. **Toll-free phone:** 800/GILEAD5. **Fax:** 650/578-9264. **Contact:** Human Resources. **E-mail address:** gilead@rpc.webhire.com. **World Wide Web address:** http://www.gilead.com. **Description:** A biopharmaceutical company dedicated to the discovery, development, and commercialization of treatments for human diseases. The company's business is focused on making new therapies available to patients, physicians, and health care systems. The company has also developed treatments for diseases caused by HIV, the Hepatitis B virus, the Herpes simplex virus, human papilloma virus, and the influenza virus. **NOTE:** Entry-level positions are offered. **Positions advertised include:** Tax Manager; Human Resources Manager; Environmental Health and Safety Specialist; Project Manager; Director of Internal Audit; Senior Research Associate; Network Specialist. **Corporate headquarters location:** This location. **Listed on:** NASDAQ. **Stock exchange symbol:** GILD. **Annual sales/revenues:** $11 - $20 million. **Number of employees at this location:** 270.

## INSITE VISION INCORPORATED

965 Atlantic Avenue, Alameda CA 94501. 510/865-8800. **Fax:** 510/865-5700. **Contact:** Human Resources. **World Wide Web address:** http://www.insitevision.com. **Description:** Manufactures ophthalmic pharmaceuticals. InSite Vision is responsible for the development of the DuraSite eyedrop-based drug delivery system, which provides a steady drug flow to the eye over an elapsed period of time. **Corporate headquarters location:** This location. **Listed on:** American Stock Exchange. **Stock exchange symbol:** ISV.

## NORTHVIEW PACIFIC LABORATORIES

552 Linus Pauling Drive, Hercules CA 94547. 510/964-9000. **Fax:** 510/964-3551. **Contact:** Human Resources. **E-mail address:** hr@ northviewlabs.com. **World Wide Web address:** http://www. northviewlabs.com. **Description:** A laboratory with testing capabilities in microbiology; sterility assurance; analytical chemistry, biocompatibility, and toxicology. **Positions advertised include:** Research Assistant; Quality Assurance Auditor; Client Services Coordinator; Animal Care Technician; Animal Care Supervisor; Research Associate.

## ONCOLOGY THERAPEUTICS NETWORK

395 Oyster Point Boulevard, Suite 405, South San Francisco CA 94080. 650/952-8400. **Toll-free phone:** 800/482-6700. **Contact:** Human Resources. **World Wide Web address:** http://www.otnnet. com. **Description:** Distributes pharmaceuticals and related products for the treatment of cancer to oncology physicians. **Corporate headquarters location:** New York NY. **Parent company:** Bristol-Myers Squibb. **Listed on:** New York Stock Exchange. **Stock exchange symbol:** BMY.

## ONYX PHARMACEUTICALS, INC.

3031 Research Drive, Building A, Richmond CA 94806. 510/222-9700. **Contact:** Human Resources. **E-mail address:** resumes@onyx-pharm.com. **World Wide Web address:** http://www.onyx-pharm. com. **Description:** Engaged in the discovery and development of innovative therapeutics based on the genetics of human disease. The company's main focus is on the discovery of cancer treatments. **Corporate headquarters location:** This location. **Listed on:** NASDAQ. **Stock exchange symbol:** ONXX.

## PROTEIN DESIGN LABS, INC.

34801 Campus Drive, Fremont CA 94555. 510/574-1400. **Contact:** Human Resources. **E-mail address:** careers@pdl.com. **World Wide Web address:** http://www.pdl.com. **Description:** A research and development company focused on the development of humanized and human monoclonal antibodies for the treatment and prevention of various diseases. **Positions advertised include:** Associate Director, Clinical Operations; Maintenance Technician; Development Assistant; QA Associate; Scientist; Meetings Events Planner; Electronic Document Management Specialist. **Corporate headquarters location:** This location. **Listed on:** NASDAQ. **Stock exchange symbol:** PDH.

## SRI INTERNATIONAL

333 Ravenswood Avenue, Menlo Park CA 94025-3493. 650/326-6200. **Contact:** Personnel. **E-mail address:** careers@sri.com. **World Wide Web address:** http://www.sri.com. **Description:** A multidisciplinary research, development, and consulting organization engaged in government and private industry research. SRI International provides solutions in a variety of areas including pharmaceutical discovery; biopharmaceutical development; education, health, and state policy; engineering sciences; and systems development. **Positions advertised include:** Biologist; Computer Scientist; Electrical Engineer; Medicinal Chemist; Laboratory Director. **Corporate headquarters location:** This location. **Listed on:** NASDAQ. **Stock exchange symbol:** STRC.

## SANGSTAT MEDICAL CORPORATION

6300 Dumbarton Circle, Fremont CA 94555. 510/789-4300. **Contact:** Human Resources. **E-mail address:** hr@sangstat.com. **World Wide Web address:** http://www.sangstat.com. **Description:** Produces diagnostic and therapeutic pharmaceutical products for use in organ transplantation. **Positions advertised include:** Medical Science Liaison; Regulatory Affairs Director; Regulatory Affairs Manager; Quality Assurance Specialist; Scientist; Research Associate. **Corporate headquarters location:** This location. **Listed on:** NASDAQ. **Stock exchange symbol:** SANG.

## SCIOS INC.

820 West Maude Avenue, Sunnyvale CA 94085. 408/616-8200. **Contact:** Human Resources. **E-mail address:** jobs@sciosinc.com. **World Wide Web address:** http://www.sciosinc.com. **Description:** Researches, develops, and manufactures pharmaceuticals for the

treatment of cardiovascular and neurological disorders. Founded in 1981. **Positions advertised include:** Clinical Research Associate; Application Administrator; Publications Coordinator; Market Research Analyst. **Office hours:** Monday - Friday, 8:00 a.m. - 5:00 p.m. **Corporate headquarters location:** This location. **Listed on:** NASDAQ. **Stock exchange symbol:** SCIO. **Number of employees at this location:** 240. **Number of employees nationwide:** 340.

### THERMO FINNIGAN
355 River Oaks Parkway, San Jose CA 95134. 408/965-6000. **Contact:** Human Resources. **E-mail address:** jobs@thermofinnigan. com. **World Wide Web address:** http://www.thermofinnigan.com. **Description:** Manufactures laboratory instruments and supplies for the health care industry. **Corporate headquarters location:** This location. **Parent company:** Thermo Electron. **Listed on:** New York Stock Exchange. **Stock exchange symbol:** TMO. **Number of employees at this location:** 300.

### UNILAB CORPORATION
3714 North Gate Boulevard, Sacramento CA 95834. 916/444-3500. **Fax:** 916/927-4124. **Contact:** Human Resources. **E-mail address:** hrsacramento@unilab.com. **World Wide Web address:** http://www. unilab.com. **Description:** A clinical laboratory that analyzes a wide variety of medical tests. Unilab also performs drug testing. **NOTE:** At time of publication, Quest Diagnostics announced plans to acquire Unilab Corporation. Please see Web site for more details. **Positions advertised include:** Client Billing Representative; Patient Billing Clerk; Insurance Billing Clerk; File Clerk; Warehouse Worker; Computer Operator; Clinical Data Processor. **Corporate headquarters location:** Tarzana CA. **Listed on:** NASDAQ. **Stock exchange symbol:** ULAB.

### XENOGEN CORPORATION
860 Atlantic Avenue, Alameda CA 94501. 510/291-6100. **Contact:** Human Resources. **E-mail address:** employment@xenogen.com. **World Wide Web address:** http://www.xenogen.com. **Description:** Offers real-time in vivo imaging services. Xenogen's in vivo biophotonic imaging system assists pharmaceutical companies in drug discovery and development. **Positions advertised include:** Research Associate. **Corporate headquarters location:** This location.

## BUSINESS SERVICES AND NON-SCIENTIFIC RESEARCH

**You can expect to find the following types of companies in this chapter:**
*Adjustment and Collection Services • Cleaning, Maintenance, and Pest Control Services • Credit Reporting • Detective, Guard, and Armored Car Services • Miscellaneous Equipment Rental and Leasing • Secretarial and Court Reporting Services*

### ABM INDUSTRIES INCORPORATED
160 Pacific Avenue, Suite 222, San Francisco CA 94111. 415/733-4000. **Fax:** 415/733-5122. **Contact:** Human Resources. **World Wide Web address:** http://www.abm.com. **Description:** A national contract maintenance firm providing janitorial, maintenance, and building management products and services in more than 60 metropolitan areas throughout the United States and Canada. **Corporate headquarters location:** This location. **Listed on:** New York Stock Exchange. **Stock exchange symbol:** ABM.

### AUTOMATIC DATA PROCESSING (ADP)
3300 Olcott Street, Santa Clara CA 95054. 408/970-7671. **Toll-free phone:** 800/225-5237. **Contact:** Human Resources. **World Wide Web address:** http://www.adp.com. **Description:** Automatic Data Processing is engaged in payroll processing services including unemployment claims management, and local, state, and federal tax filing. **Corporate headquarters location:** Roseland NJ. **Operations at this facility include:** This location is part of the major accounts division. **Listed on:** New York Stock Exchange. **Stock exchange symbol:** ADP. **Number of employees at this location:** 500. **Number of employees nationwide:** 20,000.

### BUCK CONSULTANTS
100 California Street, San Francisco CA 94111. 415/392-0616. **Contact:** Irene Gutierrez, Human Resources. **E-mail address:** careers@buckconsultants.com. **World Wide Web address:** http://www.buckconsultants.com. **Description:** A human resources consulting company. **Positions advertised include:** Client Services Specialist.

### CJ LASER BUSINESS SERVICES
654 14th Street, Oakland CA 94612. 510/832-2828. **Contact:** Human Resources. **World Wide Web address:** http://www.cjlaser.

com. **Description:** Provides laser printer repair services and reconditions toner cartridges.

## COMPUTER HORIZONS CORPORATION
350 Sansome Street, Suite 810, San Francisco CA 94104. 415/434-2424. **Toll-free phone:** 800/475-7779. **Fax:** 415/434-2650. **Contact:** Human Resources. **World Wide Web address:** http://www. computerhorizons.com. **Description:** A full-service technology solutions company offering contract staffing, outsourcing, re-engineering, migration, downsizing support, and network management. The company has a worldwide network of 43 offices. Founded in 1969. **Corporate headquarters location:** Mountain Lakes NJ. **Other U.S. locations:** Nationwide. **International locations:** Canada; England. **Listed on:** NASDAQ. **Stock exchange symbol:** CHRZ.

## COPART, INC.
5500 East Second Street, 2nd Floor, Benicia CA 94510. 707/748-5027. **Contact:** Personnel. **E-mail address:** jobs@copart.com. **World Wide Web address:** http://www.copart.com. **Description:** Copart auctions salvage vehicles as a service to vehicle suppliers, principally major insurance companies. Copart services numerous vehicle suppliers including many of the largest insurance, financial, and rental car companies in the country. **Corporate headquarters location:** This location.

## FAIR, ISAAC AND CO., INC.
111 Smith Ranch Road, San Rafael CA 94903. 415/472-2211. **Toll-free phone:** 800/999-2955. **Fax:** 415/491-5100. **Contact:** Human Resources. **World Wide Web address:** http://www.fairisaac.com. **Description:** Develops and provides data management software and services for the consumer credit, personal lines insurance, and direct marketing industries. Founded in 1956. **Positions advertised include:** Director of Financial Planning and Analysis; Programming Manager. **Corporate headquarters location:** This location. **Other U.S. locations:** New Castle DE; Wilmington DE; Atlanta GA; Chicago IL. **Subsidiaries include:** Dynamark (Minneapolis MN); European Analytic Products Group (Birmingham, England). **Listed on:** New York Stock Exchange. **Stock exchange symbol:** FIC. **Number of employees at this location:** 800. **Number of employees nationwide:** 1,400.

## JETRO SAN FRANCISCO
235 Pine Street, Suite 1700, San Francisco CA 94104. 415/392-1333. **Contact:** Human Resources Department. **World Wide Web address:** http://www.jetro.org/sanfrancisco. **Description:** A nonprofit organization that provides assistance to area businesses regarding trade and investment opportunities in Japan. This location also has a Japanese information center that is open to the public. **Corporate headquarters location:** This location.

## QUEST DISCOVERY SERVICES, INC.
2025 Gateway Plaza, San Jose CA 95110. 408/441-7000. **Fax:** 408/441-7070. **Contact:** Director of Human Resources. **E-mail address:** jbetonio@questds.com. **World Wide Web address:** http://www.questds.com. **Description:** Provides litigation support services such as deposition reporting, process serving, and large volume copy work. **Corporate headquarters location:** This location.

## UNDERWRITERS LABORATORIES INC.
1655 Scott Boulevard, Santa Clara CA 95050. 408/985-2400. **Contact:** Human Resources Department. **E-mail address:** scjobs@ul.com. **World Wide Web address:** http://www.ul.com. **Description:** An independent, nonprofit corporation established to help reduce or prevent bodily injury, loss of life, and property damage. Underwriters Laboratories accomplishes its objectives by scientific investigation of various materials, devices, equipment, constructions, methods, and systems; and by the publication of standards, classifications, specifications, and other information. Engineering functions are divided between six departments: Electrical; Burglary Protection and Signaling; Casualty and Chemical Hazards; Fire Protection; Heating, Air-Conditioning, and Refrigeration; and Marine. The company also performs factory inspections. **Corporate headquarters location:** Northbrook IL.

## CHARITIES AND SOCIAL SERVICES

**You can expect to find the following types of organizations in this chapter:**
*Social and Human Service Agencies • Job Training and Vocational Rehabilitation Services • Nonprofit Organizations*

### AMERICAN CANCER SOCIETY
1700 Webster Street, Oakland CA 94612. 510/832-7012. **Toll-free phone:** 800/ACS-2345. **Fax:** 510/893-0951. **Contact:** Malene Yip, Human Resources Assistant. **World Wide Web address:** http://www. cancer.org. **Description:** A nationwide, community-based, nonprofit, voluntary health organization dedicated to eliminating cancer as a major health problem by funding cancer research and public education. The society helps patients directly by offering services including transportation to treatment and rehabilitation services. **Positions advertised include:** Staff Assistant. **Special programs:** Training. **Corporate headquarters location:** Atlanta GA. **Other U.S. locations:** Nationwide. **CEO:** Patricia M. Felts. **Information Systems Manager:** Steve Levinson.

### BOY SCOUTS OF AMERICA
970 West Julian Street, San Jose CA 95126. 408/280-5088. **Contact:** Human Resources. **E-mail address:** leadership@sccc-scouting.org. **World Wide Web address:** http://www.sccc-scouting.org. **Description:** Western regional office of the national scouting organization for young adults. The Boy Scouts of America has 340 local councils nationwide. **Corporate headquarters location:** Irving TX.

### CATHOLIC CHARITIES
P.O. Box 4900, Santa Rosa CA 95402. 707/528-8712. **Contact:** Personnel. **E-mail address:** ccharity@sonic.net. **World Wide Web address:** http://www.srcharities.org. **Description:** Provides social service programs for the needy in several counties of California. **Positions advertised include:** Director of Development and Communications.

### FILIPINOS FOR AFFIRMATIVE ACTION
310 Eighth Street, Suite 306, Oakland CA 94607. 510/465-9876. **Fax:** 510/465-7548. **Contact:** Ms. Lillian Galedo, Executive Director of Human Resources Department. **E-mail address:** lgaledo@ filipinos4action.org. **World Wide Web address:** http://www.

filipinos4action.org. **Description:** A private, nonprofit, advocacy organization that provides employment and immigration assistance, information, and other services to the Filipino community. **Corporate headquarters location:** This location.

## INTEGRATED COMMUNITY SERVICES
3020 Kerner Boulevard, Suite A, San Rafael CA 94901. 415/455-8481. **Fax:** 415/455-8483. **Contact:** Donna Lemmon, Executive Director. **E-mail address:** connectics@aol.com. **World Wide Web address:** http://www.connectics.org. **Description:** Provides job placement services and independent living skills training for individuals with disabilities. **Positions advertised include:** Job Coach; Independent Living Skills Trainer.

## THE SALVATION ARMY
832 Folsom Street, San Francisco CA 94107. 415/553-3500. **Fax:** 415/553-3537. **Contact:** Personnel. **World Wide Web address:** http://www.salvationarmy.org. **Description:** A nonprofit organization providing several service programs including day-care centers, programs for people with disabilities, substance abuse programs and tutoring for at-risk students. The Salvation Army targets its programs to assist alcoholics, battered women, drug addicts, the elderly, the homeless, people with AIDS, prison inmates, teenagers, and the unemployed. **Corporate headquarters location:** Alexandria VA.

## SAN JOSE JOB CORPS CENTER
3485 East Hills Drive, San Jose CA 95127. 408/254-5627. **Fax:** 408/254-5663. **Contact:** Human Resources Department. **E-mail address:** coronav@jcdc.jobcorps.org. **World Wide Web address:** http://www.sanjosejobcorps.org. **Description:** Offers vocational and educational training for youths. **Corporate headquarters location:** Rochester NY. **Number of employees at this location:** 200. **Parent company:** Career Systems Development Corporation.

## SIERRA CLUB
85 Second Street, 2nd Floor, San Francisco CA 94105. 415/977-5500. **Recorded jobline:** 415/977-5744. **Contact:** Personnel. **E-mail address:** resumes@sierraclub.org. **World Wide Web address:** http://www.sierraclub.org. **Description:** A national, volunteer-based, nonprofit company chiefly concerned with the maintenance and preservation of national natural resources, wildlife, and wilderness areas. **NOTE:** Please call the jobline for a listing of available positions before sending a resume. **Positions advertised include:**

Member Services Representative. **Corporate headquarters location:** This location.

**YMCA OF THE EAST BAY**
2350 Broadway, Oakland CA 94612. 510/451-9622. **Fax:** 510/987-7449. **Contact:** Human Resources Director. **World Wide Web address:** http://www.ymca.com. **Description:** The YMCA provides health and fitness; social and personal development; sports and recreation; education and career development; and camps and conferences to children, youths, adults, the elderly, families, the disabled, refugees and foreign nationals, YMCA residents, and community residents, through a broad range of specific programs. Founded in 1879. **NOTE:** Entry-level positions are offered. **Special programs:** Internships; Training. **Corporate headquarters location:** Chicago IL. **Other U.S. locations:** Nationwide. **Number of employees at this location:** 650. **Number of employees nationwide:** 20,000.

## CHEMICALS/RUBBER AND PLASTICS

**You can expect to find the following types of companies in this chapter:**
*Adhesives, Detergents, Inks, Paints, Soaps, Varnishes • Agricultural Chemicals and Fertilizers • Carbon and Graphite Products • Chemical Engineering Firms• Industrial Gases*

### BOC GASES
2389 Lincoln Avenue, Hayward CA 94545. 510/786-2611. **Contact:** Joe Clark, Regional Sales Manager. **World Wide Web address:** http://www.boc.com. **Description:** BOC Gases manufactures industrial, electronic, and medical gases; and cryogenic equipment. **Corporate headquarters location:** Murray Hill NJ. **International locations:** Hong Kong; Indonesia; Japan; Korea; Malaysia; Singapore. **Parent company:** The BOC Group, Inc. **Operations at this facility include:** This location manufactures industrial specialty gases.

### CARGILL SALT COMPANY
7220 Central Avenue, Newark CA 94560. 510/797-1820. **Contact:** Ilene Fox, Human Resources Manager. **E-mail address:** employment@cargill.com (for inquiries only). **World Wide Web address:** http://www.cargill.com. **Description:** Processes and distributes table and industrial salts. **NOTE:** Entry-level positions are offered. **Corporate headquarters location:** Minneapolis MN. **Parent company:** Cargill Inc. and its subsidiaries and affiliates are involved in nearly 50 individual lines of business. The company has over 130 years of service and international expertise in commodity trading, handling, transporting, processing, and risk management. Cargill is a major trader of grains and oilseeds, as well as a marketer of many other agricultural and nonagricultural commodities. Cargill is a leader in developing high-quality, competitively priced farm products and in supplying them to growers. The company's agricultural products include a wide variety of feed, seed, fertilizers, and other goods and services needed by producers worldwide. Cargill is also a leader in producing and marketing seed varieties and hybrids. Cargill's Financial Markets Division (FMD) supports Cargill and its subsidiaries with financial products and services that address the full spectrum of market conditions. Cargill's worldwide food processing businesses supply products ranging from basic ingredients used in food production to recognized brand names. Cargill also operates a number of industrial businesses including the steel production, industrial-grade starches, ethanol, and salt

products. **Other U.S. locations:** Nationwide. **Listed on:** Privately held. **Number of employees worldwide:** 70,000.

## FLINT INK
750 Gilman Street, Berkeley CA 94710. 510/525-1188. **Contact:** Human Resources. **World Wide Web address:** http://www.flintink. com. **Description:** A leading manufacturer of printing inks, inkjet inks, and toners for various printing applications. **NOTE:** Please send resumes to: Flint Ink, 4600 Arrow Head Drive, Ann Arbor MI 48105. **Corporate headquarters location:** Ann Arbor MI. **Other U.S. locations:** Nationwide. **International locations:** Worldwide.

## KELLY-MOORE PAINT COMPANY, INC.
1075 Commercial Avenue, San Carlos CA 94070. 650/595-1654. **Contact:** Human Resources. **World Wide Web address:** http://www. kellymoore.com. **Description:** Manufactures and sells paint through four manufacturing facilities and more than 150 retail locations in 10 states. **Corporate headquarters location:** This location.

## THE SHERWIN-WILLIAMS COMPANY INC.
696 Broadway, Redwood City CA 94063-3103. 650/366-5786. **Contact:** Human Resources. **World Wide Web address:** http:// www.sherwin.com. **Description:** Sherwin-Williams manufactures, sells, and distributes coatings and related products. Coatings are produced for original equipment manufacturers in various industries, as well as for the automotive aftermarket, the industrial maintenance market, and the traffic paint market. Sherwin-Williams labeled architectural and industrial coatings are sold through company-owned specialty paint and wall covering stores. The Sherwin-Williams Company also manufactures paint under the Acme, Dutch Boy, Kem-Tone, Lucas, Martin-Senour, Minwax, Pratt & Lambert, Rogers, and Thompson brand names, as well as private labels, and markets its products to independent dealers, mass merchandisers, and home improvement centers. **Corporate headquarters location:** Cleveland OH. **Other U.S. locations:** Nationwide. **Operations at this facility include:** This location is a retail paint and wall covering store. **Listed on:** New York Stock Exchange. **Stock exchange symbol:** SHW.

## THE SHERWIN-WILLIAMS COMPANY INC.
1450 Sherwin Avenue, Emeryville CA 94608. 510/420-7232. **Contact:** Human Resources Manager. **World Wide Web address:** http://www.sherwin.com. **Description:** Sherwin-Williams Company

manufactures, sells, and distributes coatings and related products. Coatings are produced for original equipment manufacturers in various industries, as well as for the automotive aftermarket, the industrial maintenance market, and the traffic paint market. Sherwin-Williams labeled architectural and industrial coatings are sold through company-owned specialty paint and wall covering stores. The Sherwin-Williams Company also manufactures paint under the Acme, Dutch Boy, Kem-Tone, Lucas, Martin-Senour, Minwax, Pratt & Lambert, Rogers, and Thompson brand names, as well as private labels, and markets its products to independent dealers, mass merchandisers, and home improvement centers. **Special programs:** Internships. **Office hours:** Monday - Friday, 6:30 a.m. - 3:00 p.m. **Corporate headquarters location:** Cleveland OH. **Other U.S. locations:** Nationwide. **Operations at this facility include:** This location is a support office for area stores and a facility for manufacturing emulsion paints. **Listed on:** New York Stock Exchange. **Stock exchange symbol:** SHW.

## COMMUNICATIONS: TELECOMMUNICATIONS AND BROADCASTING

You can expect to find the following types of companies in this chapter:
*Cable/Pay Television Services • Communications Equipment•
Radio and Television Broadcasting Systems • Telephone, Telegraph, and
other Message Communications*

### ABC7/KGO-TV
900 Front Street, San Francisco CA 94111. 415/954-7777. **Recorded jobline:** 415/954-7958. **Contact:** Human Resources. **World Wide Web address:** http://www.abc7news.com. **Description:** An ABC-affiliated television station. **Positions advertised include:** Director of Engineering; General Assignment Reporter; Engineering Management Supervisor; Promotions Manager; News Topical Promotions Producer. **Special programs:** Internships. **Internship information:** Internships are offered to college juniors, seniors, and graduate students. Interns are paid minimum wage and receive college credit for their work. Approximately 16 interns are selected each semester. **Corporate headquarters location:** New York NY. **Other U.S. locations:** New York NY; Seattle WA. **Parent company:** Disney Corporation.

### AT&T MEDIA SERVICES
737 Southpoint Boulevard, Suite H, Petaluma CA 94954. 707/781-1840. **Contact:** Human Resources. **World Wide Web address:** http://www.cableistv.com. **Description:** Provides cable television services. **Other U.S. locations:** Nationwide. **Listed on:** New York Stock Exchange. **Stock exchange symbol:** T.

### ACCOM, INC.
1490 O'Brien Drive, Menlo Park CA 94025. 650/328-3818. **Fax:** 650/327-2511. **Contact:** Human Resources. **E-mail address:** personnel@accom.com. **World Wide Web address:** http://www.accom.com. **Description:** Designs, manufactures, and sells digital video production, recording, and editing equipment for the television, broadcasting, computer, and video industries. **Corporate headquarters location:** This location. **CEO:** Junaid Sheikh.

### ALLIED TELESYN, INC.
960 Stewart Drive, Suite B, Sunnyvale CA 94085. 408/730-0950. **Contact:** Human Resources. **E-mail address:** jobs-na@alliedtelesyn.com. **World Wide Web address:** http://www.

alliedtelesyn.com. **Description:** Manufactures a variety of hardware for the communications industry. **Positions advertised include:** Hardware Engineer; Marketing Manager; Public Relations Manager; Software Engineer.

## APPLIED SIGNAL TECHNOLOGY
400 West California Avenue, Sunnyvale CA 94086. 408/749-1888. **Fax:** 408/523-2800. **Contact:** Human Resources Department. **E-mail address:** resume@appsig.com. **World Wide Web address:** http://www.appsig.com. **Description:** Designs, develops, manufactures, and markets signal reconnaissance equipment to collect and process telecommunications signals. The equipment is purchased by the U.S. government for foreign signal reconnaissance. Founded in 1984. **Positions advertised include:** Systems Engineer; Software Engineer; Junior Design Engineer; Program Scheduler; Security Specialist. **Corporate headquarters location:** This location. **Other U.S. locations:** MD; OR; UT; VA.

## ASPECT TELECOMMUNICATIONS
1310 Ridder Park Drive, San Jose CA 95131. 408/325-2200. **Fax:** 408/325-2260. **Contact:** Staffing Department. **E-mail address:** staffing@aspect.com. **World Wide Web address:** http://www.aspect.com. **Description:** Provides comprehensive business solutions for mission-critical call centers worldwide. Products include automatic call distributors, computer-telephony integration solutions, call center management and reporting software, automation solutions, and planning and forecasting packages. Founded in 1985. **NOTE:** Entry-level positions are offered. **Positions advertised include:** Employee Communications Director; Senior Services Manager; Senior Global Applications Director; Regional Partner Manager; Inside Sales Representative; Director of Financial Reporting; Vice President of General Counsel. **Special programs:** Internships. **Corporate headquarters location:** This location. **Other U.S. locations:** Nationwide. **International locations:** Worldwide. **Listed on:** NASDAQ. **Stock exchange symbol:** ASPT. **CEO:** Jim Carreker. **Annual sales/revenues:** More than $100 million. **Number of employees at this location:** 850. **Number of employees nationwide:** 1,600. **Number of employees worldwide:** 2,000.

## CNET NETWORKS, INC.
235 Second Street, San Francisco CA 94105. 415/344-2000. **Contact:** Human Resources. **E-mail address:** careers@cnet.com. **World Wide Web address:** http://www.cnet.com. **Description:** A

new media company that provides services and information related to computers and technology. Products and services include technology-related Internet sites, television shows, radio shows, and comparison shopping. **Positions advertised include:** Account Manager; Copy Editor; Online Commerce Designer; Knowledge Base Editor; Payroll Assistant; Producer; Downloads Production Manager; Project Leader, Knowledge Base Development; Research Analyst, Media & Market Intelligence; Staff Writer, News.com; Technical Producer, Outbound Marketing Solutions. **Corporate headquarters location:** This location. **Listed on:** NASDAQ. **Stock exchange symbol:** CNET.

## COPPERCOM
2860 De La Cruz Boulevard, Santa Clara CA 95050. 408/987-8500. **Toll-free phone:** 866/COPPER1. **Contact:** Human Resources. **E-mail address:** hr1@coppercom.com; jobs@coppercom.com. **World Wide Web address:** http://www.coppercom.com. **Description:** Designs, develops, and markets DSL products that allow telephone companies to deliver high-speed data. **Corporate headquarters location:** Boca Raton FL. **Other U.S. locations:** Raleigh NC. **Listed on:** Privately held.

## CYLINK CORPORATION
3131 Jay Street, Santa Clara CA 95054. 408/855-6000. **Fax:** 408/855-6126. **Contact:** Human Resources. **E-mail address:** jobs@cylink.com. **World Wide Web address:** http://www.cylink.com. **Description:** Develops and markets secure e-business solutions that protect information. The company's products protect information on the Internet as well as in local and wide area networks. Founded in 1983. **Corporate headquarters location:** This location. **Other U.S. locations:** DC; IL; NJ. **International locations:** China; Singapore; United Kingdom. **Listed on:** NASDAQ. **Stock exchange symbol:** CYLK. **Annual sales/revenues:** $21 - $50 million. **Number of employees worldwide:** 350.

## CXR TELCOM
47971 Fremont Boulevard, Fremont CA 94538-6502. 510/657-8810. **Contact:** Human Resources. **World Wide Web address:** http://www.cxr.com. **Description:** Designs, manufactures, and markets electronic telecommunications test equipment and data communications equipment. The company's customers include interconnect carriers, independent telephone operating companies, private communications networks, banks, brokerage firms, and

government agencies. **Corporate headquarters location:** Ontario CA.

## EARTHLINK
220 Cochrane Circle, Morgan Hill CA 95037. 408/779-1162. **Fax:** 408/779-3106. **Contact:** Human Resources. **World Wide Web address:** http://www.earthlink.com. **Description:** Designs, develops, and markets telephone and Internet equipment such as Caller ID, voicemail, and e-mail. **Corporate headquarters location:** Atlanta GA. **Other area locations:** Pasadena CA; Pleasanton CA; Roseville CA; Sacramento CA; San Jose CA. **Other U.S. locations:** Phoenix AZ; Kansas City KS; Jackson MN; Harrisburg PA; Knoxville TN; Dallas TX. **Listed on:** NASDAQ. **Stock exchange symbol:** ELNK.

## GRASS VALLEY GROUP
P.O. Box 599000, Nevada City CA 95959. 530/478-3000. **Physical address:** 400 Providence Mine Road, Nevada City CA 95959. **Contact:** Carole E. Johnson, Human Resources Consultant. **E-mail address:** carolj@grassvalleygroup.com. **World Wide Web address:** http://www.grassvalleygroup.com. **Description:** Manufactures television broadcasting line equipment, terminal equipment, and video switching systems and related products. **Corporate headquarters location:** Beaverton OR.

## JDS UNIPHASE CORPORATION
163 Baypointe Parkway, San Jose CA 95134. 408/434-1800. **Contact:** Human Resources. **World Wide Web address:** http://www.jdsunph.com. **Description:** Develops, manufactures, and distributes fiber-optic products including cable assemblies, fusion splicers, couplers, and lasers. Products are primarily sold to companies in the cable television and telecommunications fields. **Listed on:** NASDAQ. **Stock exchange symbol:** JDSU.

## KCRA-TV
3 Television Circle, Sacramento CA 95814. 916/446-3333. **Contact:** Human Resources. **World Wide Web address:** http://www.thekcrachannel.com. **Description:** Operates one of the nation's largest television stations. In May 1999, KCRA-TV launched KCRA-DT, Northern California's first digital television station. Founded in 1955. **Company slogan:** Where the news comes first. **Parent company:** Hearst-Argyle Television, Inc. **Listed on:** New York Stock Exchange. **Stock exchange symbol:** HTV.

## L3 COMMUNICATIONS, INC.
107 Woodmere Road, Folson CA 95630. 916/351-4500. **Fax:** 916/351-4568. **Contact:** Personnel. **E-mail address:** cooljobs@l-3com.com. **World Wide Web address:** http://www.l-3com.com. **Description:** Manufactures filters/multiplexers, isolators, circulators, gain equalizers, oscillators (cavity and DRO), and integrated assemblies. **Corporate headquarters location:** New York NY. **Listed on:** New York Stock Exchange. **Stock exchange symbol:** LLL.

## LUCENT TECHNOLOGIES INTERNETWORKING SYSTEMS
1701 Harbor Bay Parkway, Alameda CA 94502. 510/769-6001. **Contact:** Human Resources. **World Wide Web address:** http://www.lucent.com. **Description:** Develops, manufactures, markets, and supports a family of high-performance, multiservice wide area network (WAN) switches that enable public carrier providers and private network managers to provide cost-effective, high-speed, enhanced data communications services. These products direct and manage data communications across wide area networks that utilize different network architectures and services, and are designed to support, on a single platform, the major high-speed packet data communications services. These services include frame relay, switched multimegabit data service, and asynchronous transfer mode. The company markets its products to public network providers, including interexchange carriers, local exchange carriers, competitive access providers, other public network providers, and private network managers. **Corporate headquarters location:** Murray Hill NJ. **Listed on:** New York Stock Exchange. **Stock exchange symbol:** LU. **Number of employees at this location:** 80.

## METRO TEL CORPORATION
374 South Milpitas Boulevard, Milpitas CA 95035. 408/946-4600. **Toll-free phone:** 888/998-8300. **Fax:** 408/946-4069. **Contact:** Human Resources. **World Wide Web address:** http://www.metrotelcorp.com. **Description:** Manufactures and sells telephone test, station, and customer premise equipment and related accessories. Metro Tel's products are marketed to independently operating telephone companies, long-distance resellers, telephone interconnect companies, and large corporations with their own telecommunications systems. **Corporate headquarters location:** This location.

## NEXTIRAONE
975 Island Drive, Redwood City CA 94065. 650/802-3600. **Contact:** Human Resources. **World Wide Web address:** http://www. nextiraone.com. **Description:** Designs, manufactures, and supports voice-processing and health care communications systems including call center management, telephone systems, locator systems, videoconferencing, health care communications, and network and data services. **Positions advertised include:** Senior Manager; Network Consultant. **Number of employees nationwide:** 2,400.

## RFI ENTERPRISES
360 Turtle Creek Court, San Jose CA 95125. 408/298-5400. **Fax:** 408/882-4305. **Contact:** Human Resources. **E-mail address:** jobs@ rfi.com. **World Wide Web address:** http://www.rfi-ent.com. **Description:** A multisystem integrator for low-voltage systems including alarm systems, public announcement systems, and closed circuit television. Founded in 1979. **NOTE:** Entry-level positions are offered. **Positions advertised include:** Dispatcher; Fire Alarm Test Technician; Installation Service Technician; Senior Fire Technician; Sound Technician. **Special programs:** Internships; Apprenticeships. **Corporate headquarters location:** This location. **Other U.S. locations:** Reno NV; Beaverton OR; Kent WA. **Listed on:** Privately held. **Number of employees at this location:** 250. **Number of employees nationwide:** 320.

## SS8 NETWORKS
91 East Tasman Drive, San Jose CA 95134. 408/944-0250. **Fax:** 408/428-3732. **Contact:** Human Resources. **E-mail address:** jobs@ ss8.com. **World Wide Web address:** http://www.ss8.com. **Description:** Designs, manufactures, and markets communications systems that enable users to access and interact with a broad range of information in a variety of formats including voice, text, data, e-mail, and facsimile from a touch-tone telephone. The company's applications, such as voice messaging, facsimile store-and-forward, and interactive voice response, are integrated on the company's Adaptive Information Processing platform, a communication server that is based on industry-standard hardware and software. **Corporate headquarters location:** This location. **Operations at this facility include:** Administration; Divisional Headquarters; Manufacturing; Research and Development; Sales.

## SIEMENS ICN

4900 Old Ironsides Drive, Santa Clara CA 95054. 408/492-2000. **Contact:** Human Resources. **World Wide Web address:** http://www.siemens.icn.com. **Description:** A leading provider of communications and communications integration technology such as OfficePoint ISDN systems, a high-speed integration product enabling transmission and reception of voice, data, image, and video over a single phone line. **Positions advertised include:** Business Development/Strategic Account Manager. **Corporate headquarters location:** Boca Raton FL. **Parent company:** Siemens A.G. (Germany). **Listed on:** New York Stock Exchange. **Stock exchange symbol:** SI.

## STRATEX NETWORKS

170 Rose Orchard Way, San Jose CA 95134. 408/943-0777. **Fax:** 408/944-1701. **Contact:** Human Resources. **E-mail address:** careers@stratexnet.com. **World Wide Web address:** http://www. stratexnet.com. **Description:** Designs, manufactures, and markets wireless products for communications networks. **Positions advertised include:** Order Process Manager; Solutions Marketing Manager; Commodities Manager. **Corporate headquarters location:** This location. **International locations:** Asia; Europe; Latin America; Singapore; United Kingdom. **Listed on:** NASDAQ. **Stock exchange symbol:** STXN.

## TCI (TECHNOLOGY FOR COMMUNICATIONS INTERNATIONAL)

47300 Kato Road, Fremont CA 94538. 510/687-6100. **Contact:** Personnel Director. **World Wide Web address:** http://www.tcibr. com. **Description:** Manufactures television and broadcasting equipment and provides services such as DTV, radio broadcasting, communications management, and communications intelligence collection. **Positions advertised include:** Software Engineer. **Corporate headquarters location:** Raymond ME. **Parent company:** Dialectric Communications. **Operations at this facility include:** Manufacturing. **Listed on:** New York Stock Exchange. **Stock exchange symbol:** SPW. **Number of employees at this location:** 160. **Number of employees nationwide:** 3,100.

## TROPIAN

20813 Stevens Creek Boulevard, Cupertino CA 95014. 408/865-1300. **Fax:** 408/865-1596. **Contact:** Debora Jackson. **E-mail address:** jobs@tropian.com. **World Wide Web address:** http://www.tropian. com. **Description:** Provides network equipment to the telecommunication industry. **Positions advertised include:** Senior

PCB Designer; SW Engineer; Program Manager; Configuration Management Engineer; Senior Design Engineer; IC Design Engineer; Hardware Engineer.

## COMPUTER HARDWARE, SOFTWARE, AND SERVICES

You can expect to find the following types of companies in this chapter:
*Computer Components and Hardware Manufacturers • Consultants and Computer Training Companies • Internet and Online Service Providers • Networking and Systems Services • Repair Services/Rental and Leasing • Resellers, Wholesalers, and Distributors • Software Developers/Programming Services • Web Technologies*

### ADI SYSTEMS, INC.
6851 Mowry Avenue, Newark CA 94560. 510/795-6200. **Contact:** Shelly Venegan, Human Resources Manager. **E-mail address:** personnel@adiusa.com. **World Wide Web address:** http://www. adiusa.com. **Description:** Manufactures computer monitors. **Corporate headquarters location:** This location. **Parent company:** ADI Corporation.

### ACMA COMPUTERS
1505 Reliance Way, Fremont CA 94539. 510/623-1212. **Toll-free phone:** 800/786-6888. **Fax:** 510/623-0818. **Contact:** Human Resources. **World Wide Web address:** http://www.acma.com. **Description:** Manufactures personal computers. **Positions advertised include:** Account Manager; Marketing Communications Specialist; In-House Sales Assistant; Technical Support Engineer. **Office hours:** Monday - Friday, 8:30 a.m. - 5:30 p.m. **Corporate headquarters location:** This location.

### ACTEL CORPORATION
955 East Arques Avenue, Sunnyvale CA 94086-4533. 408/739-1010. **Contact:** Barbara McArthur, Vice President of Human Resources. **E-mail address:** talent@actel.com. **World Wide Web address:** http://www.actel.com. **Description:** Manufactures field programmable gate arrays and develops the software to program them. **Positions advertised include:** Software Engineer; Technical Marketing Engineer; Senior Yield Enhancement Engineer; Business Process Analyst; Senior Test Engineer; Product Engineer. **Corporate headquarters location:** This location. **Other U.S. locations:** Nationwide. **International locations:** Canada; France; Germany; Italy; Japan; Korea; United Kingdom. **Number of employees at this location:** 200.

## ACER AMERICA CORPORATION

2641 Orchard Parkway, San Jose CA 95134. 408/432-6200. **Toll-free phone:** 800/SEE-ACER. **Fax:** 408/922-2918. **Contact:** Human Resources. **E-mail address:** careers@acer.com. **World Wide Web address:** http://www.acer.com. **Description:** One of the largest microcomputer manufacturers and OEM suppliers. The company also manufactures a variety of computer peripherals and components including monitors, keyboards, expansion cards, and CD-ROM drives. **Positions advertised include:** Channel Sales Business Coordinator; ISV Programs Manager; Contracts Specialist; Senior Hardware Engineer; Principal Mechanical Engineer; Principal Software Architect. **Parent company:** Acer Group, Inc. **Number of employees at this location:** 700. **Number of employees nationwide:** 1,200. **Number of employees worldwide:** 25,000.

## ADOBE SYSTEMS, INC.

345 Park Avenue, San Jose CA 95110. 408/536-6000. **Contact:** Human Resources. **World Wide Web address:** http://www.adobe. com. **Description:** Develops, markets, and supports computer software products and technologies that enable users to create, display, and print electronic documents for Macintosh, Windows, and OS/2 compatibles. The company distributes its products through a network of original equipment manufacturers, distributors and dealers, value-added resellers, and systems integrators. **Corporate headquarters location:** This location. **Other U.S. locations:** Seattle WA. **International locations:** Australia; Denmark; France; Germany; Ireland; Japan; the Netherlands; Norway; Spain; Sweden. **Listed on:** NASDAQ. **Stock exchange symbol:** ADBE.

## ADVENT SOFTWARE, INC.

301 Brannan Street, 6th Floor, San Francisco CA 94107. 415/543-7696. **Toll-free phone:** 800/678-7005. **Contact:** Human Resources. **E-mail address:** jobs@advent.com. **World Wide Web address:** http://www.advent.com. **Description:** Develops financial planning and investment applications for investment managers, financial planners, and brokerage houses. **Positions advertised include:** Executive Sales and Marketing Assistant; Receptionist; Pricing Analyst. **Corporate headquarters location:** This location. **Other U.S. locations:** Cambridge MA; New York NY. **International locations:** Australia; Europe. **Listed on:** NASDAQ. **Stock exchange symbol:** ADVS. **Annual sales/revenues:** More than $100 million.

## AGILENT TECHNOLOGIES

350-370 West Trimble Road, San Jose CA 95131. 408/435-7400. **Contact:** Human Resources. **World Wide Web address:** http://www. agilent.com. **Description:** Produces test, measurement, and monitoring devices; semiconductor products; and chemical analysis. Agilent Technologies' primary clients are communications equipment manufacturers, Internet service providers, and biopharmaceutical companies. **Positions advertised include:** Finance Representative; Remote Support Engineer. **Corporate headquarters location:** Palo Alto CA. **Listed on:** New York Stock Exchange. **Stock exchange symbol:** A.

## AGILENT TECHNOLOGIES

1400 Fountain Grove Parkway, Santa Rosa CA 95403. 707/577-1400. **Contact:** Human Resources. **World Wide Web address:** http:// www.agilent.com. **Description:** Produces test, measurement, and monitoring devices; semi-conductor products; and chemical analysis. Agilent Technologies' primary clients are communications equipment manufacturers, Internet service providers, and biopharmaceutical companies. **Positions advertised include:** Finance Representative; Remote Support Engineer. **Corporate headquarters location:** Palo Alto CA. **Listed on:** New York Stock Exchange. **Stock exchange symbol:** A.

## AGILENT TECHNOLOGIES

1212 Valley House Drive, Rohnert Park CA 94928. 707/794-1212. **Contact:** Human Resources. **World Wide Web address:** http://www. agilent.com. **Description:** Produces test, measurement, and monitoring devices; semi-conductor products; and chemical analysis. Agilent Technologies' primary clients are communications equipment manufacturers, Internet service providers, and biopharmaceutical companies. **Positions advertised include:** Finance Representative; Remote Support Engineer. **Corporate headquarters location:** Palo Alto CA. **Listed on:** New York Stock Exchange. **Stock exchange symbol:** A.

## AGILENT TECHNOLOGIES

5301 Steven's Creek Boulevard, Santa Clara CA 95051. 408/246-4300. **Contact:** Human Resources. **World Wide Web address:** http:// www.agilent.com. **Description:** Produces test, measurement, and monitoring devices; semi-conductor products; and chemical analysis. Agilent Technologies' primary clients are communications equipment manufacturers, Internet service providers, and biopharmaceutical companies. **Positions advertised include:** Finance Representative; Remote Support Engineer; IT Specialist. **Special programs:** Internships. **Corporate headquarters location:** Palo Alto CA. **Operations at this facility include:** Administration; Manufacturing; Research and Development; Sales; Service. **Listed on:** New York Stock Exchange. **Stock exchange symbol:** A.

## ALCATEL

6385 San Ignacio Avenue, San Jose CA 95119. 408/229-8171. **Contact:** Human Resources. **World Wide Web address:** http://www. alcatel.com. **Description:** Designs computer networks. **Corporate headquarters location:** Plano TX. **Listed on:** New York Stock Exchange. **Stock exchange symbol:** ALA.

## ALIGO, INC.

444 De Haro Street, Suite 211, San Francisco CA 94107. 415/593-8200. **Fax:** 415/553-8896. **Contact:** Human Resources. **E-mail address:** jobs@aligo.com. **World Wide Web address:** http://www. aligo.com. **Description:** A provider of mobile application servers. **Positions advertised include:** Software Engineer.

## ALLDATA CORPORATION

9412 Big Horn Boulevard, Elk Grove CA 95758-1100. 916/684-5200. **Toll-free phone:** 800/859-3282. **Fax:** 916/684-5225. **Contact:** Human Resources. **E-mail address:** hr@alldata.com. **World Wide Web address:** http://www.alldata.com. **Description:** Provides computer-consulting services. **Positions advertised include:** Customer Support Representative; Library Research Specialist; Field Sales Representative; Marketing Campaign Developer. **Corporate headquarters location:** This location. **Number of employees at this location:** 300.

## AMDAHL CORPORATION

1250 East Arques Avenue, Sunnyvale CA 94088. 408/746-6000. **Toll-free phone:** 800/538-8460. **Contact:** Human Resources. **E-mail address:** jobs@amdahl.com. **World Wide Web address:** http://www. amdahl.com. **Description:** Designs, develops, manufactures, markets, and services large-scale, high-performance, general-purpose computer systems. Customers are primarily large corporations, government agencies, and large universities with high-volume data processing requirements. **Special programs:** Internships. **Corporate headquarters location:** This location. **Other U.S. locations:** Nationwide. **International locations:** Germany; Ireland; Italy;

Portugal; Switzerland; United Kingdom. **Parent company:** Fujitsu, Ltd. **Operations at this facility include:** Administration; Manufacturing; Research and Development; Sales; Service. **Listed on:** NASDAQ. **Stock exchange symbol:** FJTSY. **CEO:** David Wright. **Number of employees at this location:** 3,500. **Number of employees nationwide:** 6,000. **Number of employees worldwide:** 9,500.

### AMDOCS LIMITED
2570 Orchard Parkway, San Jose CA 95131. 408/965-7000. **Contact:** Human Resources. **E-mail address:** jobs.web@ amdocs.com. **World Wide Web address:** http://www.amdocs.com. **Description:** Develops customer support management software. **Corporate headquarters location:** Chesterfield MO. **Other U.S. locations:** Stamford CT; Champaign IL. **International locations:** Worldwide. **Listed on:** New York Stock Exchange. **Stock exchange symbol:** DOX.

### AMPRO COMPUTERS INC.
5215 Hellyer Avenue #110, San Jose CA 95138. 408/360-0200. **Toll-free phone:** 800/966-5200. **Fax:** 408/578-8858. **Contact:** Human Resources. **E-mail address:** careers@ampro.com. **World Wide Web address:** http://www.ampro.com. **Description:** A leading ISO 9001 manufacturer of board-level PC and PC/AT compatible computer modules for embedded applications and the originator of the PC/104 and PC/104-Plus standards. **Corporate headquarters location:** This location. **Other U.S. locations:** Nationwide. **International locations:** Worldwide. **Listed on:** Privately held. **Annual sales/revenues:** $21 - $50 million. **Number of employees at this location:** 60.

### ANACOMP, INC.
3855 North Freeway Boulevard, Suite 110, Sacramento CA 95834. 415/285-5771. **Contact:** Human Resources. **World Wide Web address:** http://www.anacomp.com. **Description:** Provides document storage solutions, manufactures computer hardware and software, and develops customized financial software. **Corporate headquarters location:** Poway CA. **Other U.S. locations:** Nationwide. **International locations:** Austria; France; Germany; Italy; Netherlands; Sweden; Switzerland; United Kingdom.

## APPLE COMPUTER, INC.
2511 Laguna Boulevard, Elk Grove CA 95758. 916/394-2600. **Fax:** 916/394-5504. **Contact:** Personnel. **E-mail address:** applejobs@ apple.com. **World Wide Web address:** http://www.apple.com/ employment. **Description:** Apple Computer develops, manufactures, and markets personal computer systems and peripherals. The company's desktop publishing and communications products are marketed internationally. Founded in 1976. **Corporate headquarters location:** Cupertino CA. **Other U.S. locations:** Phoenix AZ; Fountain CO; Austin TX. **Operations at this facility include:** This location is the Sacramento Operations Center, which serves as a systems assembly and distribution site. **Listed on:** NASDAQ. **Stock exchange symbol:** AAPL. **Number of employees at this location:** 650. **Number of employees nationwide:** 8,100.

## APPLE COMPUTER, INC.
One Infinite Loop, Cupertino CA 95014. 408/996-1010. **Fax:** 408/ 996-0275. **Recorded jobline:** 408/974-0529. **Contact:** Personnel. **E-mail address:** applejobs@apple.com. **World Wide Web address:** http://www.apple.com. **Description:** Develops, manufactures, and markets personal computer systems and peripherals. The company's desktop publishing and communications products are marketed internationally. Founded in 1976. **Special programs:** Internships. **Corporate headquarters location:** This location. **Other area locations:** Elk Grove CA. **Other U.S. locations:** Phoenix AZ; Fountain CO; Austin TX. **Operations at this facility include:** Sales. **Listed on:** NASDAQ. **Stock exchange symbol:** AAPL. **Number of employees nationwide:** 8,100.

## APPLIED IMAGING
2380 Walsh Avenue, Building B, Santa Clara CA 95051. 408/562-0264. **Contact:** Human Resources. **World Wide Web address:** http:// www.aicorp.com. **Description:** Develops software used by hospitals and universities for detecting genetic birth defects. **Corporate headquarters location:** Newcastle, England. **Other U.S. locations:** League City TX.

## APPLIED MATERIALS, INC.
3050 Bowers Avenue, Mail Stop 1826, Santa Clara CA 95054. 408/727-5555. **Contact:** Corporate Employment. **World Wide Web address:** http://www.appliedmaterials.com. **Description:** A *Fortune* 500 company that is a leading producer of wafer fabrication systems for the semiconductor industry. The company also sells related spare

parts and services. Applied Materials' products include dry etch systems for the creation of circuit paths in semiconductors and implementation products for silicon wafers. **Positions advertised include:** Finance Manager; Manufacturing Engineer; Mechanical Engineer; Product Marketing Manager; Quality Manager; Technical Support Engineer; User Systems Manager. **Corporate headquarters location:** This location. **Other area locations:** Hayward CA; Irvine CA; Milpitas CA; Ontario CA; Roseville CA. **Other U.S. locations:** Nationwide. **International locations:** Worldwide. **Listed on:** NASDAQ. **Stock exchange symbol:** AMAT. **Number of employees nationwide:** 16,200.

**ASANTE TECHNOLOGIES**
821 Fox Lane, San Jose CA 95131. 408/435-8388. **Contact:** Human Resources Department. **Fax:** 408/891-9150. **E-mail address:** hr@asante.com. **World Wide Web address:** http://www.asante.com. **Description:** Designs, develops, and manufactures Gigabit Ethernet and Fast Ethernet networking systems. **Positions advertised include:** Business Development Manager; Senior Account Executive; Territory Manager, Advanced Systems; Cost Accountant; Software Engineer; Hardware Design Manager. **Corporate headquarters location:** This location. **International locations:** Germany. **Operations at this facility include:** Administration; Research and Development; Sales; Service. **Listed on:** NASDAQ. **Stock exchange symbol:** ASNT. **Annual sales/revenues:** $51 - $100 million. **Number of employees at this location:** 170. **Number of employees nationwide:** 200.

**AUSPEX SYSTEMS, INC.**
2800 Scott Boulevard, Santa Clara CA 95050. 408/566-2000. **Toll-free phone:** 800/735-3177. **Contact:** Senior Recruiter. **E-mail address:** careers@auspex.com. **World Wide Web address:** http://www.auspex.com. **Description:** A leading provider of high-performance network data servers that are optimized to move large amounts of data from central information repositories to users' workstations. Founded in 1987. **Corporate headquarters location:** This location. **International locations:** Worldwide. **Operations at this facility include:** Administration; Manufacturing; Research and Development; Sales; Service. **Listed on:** NASDAQ. **Stock exchange symbol:** ASPX. **Annual sales/revenues:** More than $100 million. **Number of employees worldwide:** 500.

## AUTODESK, INC.
111 McInnis Parkway, San Rafael CA 94903. 415/507-5000. **Contact:** Human Resources. **E-mail address:** resumes@aurodesk. com. **World Wide Web address:** http://www.autodesk.com. **Description:** Designs, develops, markets, and supports a line of computer-aided design (CAD), engineering, and animation software products for desktop computers and workstations. **Positions advertised include:** Programmer/Software Engineer; Transaction Representative; Customer Care Representative; Senior Finance Manager, Business Operations; Executive Assistant; Accounts Payable Analyst; Marketing Manager. **Corporate headquarters location:** This location. **International locations:** Singapore; Switzerland. **Number of employees nationwide:** 1,800. **Listed on:** NASDAQ. **Stock exchange symbol:** ADSK.

## BMC SOFTWARE, INC.
2141 North First Street, San Jose CA 95131. 408/546-9000. **Fax:** 408/546-9001. **Contact:** Human Resources. **E-mail address:** resumes@bmc.com. **World Wide Web address:** http://www. bmc.com. **Description:** Develops, markets, and supports standard systems software products to enhance and increase the performance of large-scale (mainframe) computer database management systems and data communications software systems. **Corporate headquarters location:** Houston TX. **Other area locations:** Costa Mesa CA; Sacramento CA. **Other U.S. locations:** Atlanta GA; Lisle IL; Waltham MA; Farmington Hills MI; Minneapolis MN; Parsippany NJ; New York NY; Charlotte NC; Cincinnati OH; Austin TX; Seattle WA; McLean VA. **International locations:** Worldwide. **Listed on:** New York Stock Exchange. **Stock exchange symbol:** BMC.

## BARRA, INC.
2100 Milvia Street, Berkeley CA 94704. 510/548-5442. **Fax:** 510/548-4374. **Contact:** Human Resources. **E-mail address:** careers@barra.com. **World Wide Web address:** http://www. barra.com. **Description:** Develops, markets, and supports application software and information services used to analyze and manage portfolios of equity, fixed income, and other financial instruments. The company serves more than 750 clients in 30 countries including many of the world's largest portfolio managers, fund sponsors, pension and investment consultants, brokers/dealers, and master trustees. **NOTE:** Entry-level positions are offered. **Positions advertised include:** Derivatives Specialists Project Manager; Course Developer, Consultant; Product marketing Manager; Research

Consultant. **Special programs:** Internships; Training; Summer Jobs. **Corporate headquarters location:** This location. **Other U.S. locations:** Darien CT; Edison NJ; New York NY. **International locations:** Australia; Brazil; England; Germany; Hong Kong; Japan; South Africa. **Operations at this facility include:** Administration; Research and Development; Sales; Service. **Listed on:** NASDAQ. **Stock exchange symbol:** BARZ. **Annual sales/revenues:** More than $100 million. **Number of employees at this location:** 300. **Number of employees nationwide:** 450. **Number of employees worldwide:** 750.

**BELL MICROPRODUCTS INC.**
1941 Ringwood Avenue, San Jose CA 95131. 408/451-9400. **Toll-free phone:** 800/800-1513. **Fax:** 408/451-1600. **Contact:** Human Resources. **World Wide Web address:** http://www.bellmicro.com. **Description:** Markets and distributes a select group of computer products to original equipment manufacturers and value-added resellers. Products include logic microprocessors; disk, tape, and optical drives and subsystems; drive controllers; and board-level products. The company also provides a variety of manufacturing and value-added services to its customers including the supply of board-level products to customer specifications on a turnkey basis; certain types of components and subsystem testing services; systems integration and disk drive formatting and testing; and the packaging of electronic component kits to customer specifications. Founded in 1987. **Positions advertised include:** Inside Sales Representative. **Corporate headquarters location:** This location. **Other U.S. locations:** Nationwide. **International locations:** Argentina; Brazil; Canada; Chile; Italy; Mexico; the Netherlands; United Kingdom. **Listed on:** NASDAQ. **Stock exchange symbol:** BELM.

**BLUE COAT SYSTEMS**
650 Almanor Avenue, Sunnyvale CA 94085. 408/220-2200. **Toll-free phone:** 866/30B-COAT. **Fax:** 408/220-2269. **Contact:** Human Resources. **E-mail address:** careers@bluecoat.com. **World Wide Web address:** http://www.bluecoat.com. **Description:** An Internet security company. **Positions advertised include:** International Accountant and Financial Analyst. **Listed on:** NASDAQ. **Stock exchange symbol:** BCSI.

**BLUEDOT SOFTWARE**
818 Mission Street, 4th Floor, San Francisco CA 94103. 415/979-9550. **Toll-free phone:** 888/391-2583. **Fax:** 415/979-9551. **Contact:**

Human Resources. **E-mail address:** jobs@bluedot.com. **World Wide Web address:** http://www.bluedot.com. **Description:** Designs and manufactures Internet-based software for event planning. Products include EventTools software, which facilitates communication and planning among event participants. **Corporate headquarters location:** This location.

## BRODERBUND LLC
500 Redwood Boulevard, Novato CA 94947. 415/382-4400. **Contact:** Alan Byrne, Vice President of Personnel. **World Wide Web address:** http://www.broderbund.com. **Description:** Develops, publishes, and markets personal computer software for the home, school, and small business markets. Products include personal productivity and education software. **Positions advertised include:** Senior Brand Marketing Manager; Associate Marketing Manager; Sales Director; Marketing Manager, Trade; Managing Editor. **Corporate headquarters location:** This location. **Number of employees at this location:** 340.

## CADENCE DESIGN SYSTEMS, INC.
2655 Seely Avenue, San Jose CA 95134. 408/943-1234. **Fax:** 408/894-2207. **Contact:** Human Resources. **World Wide Web address:** http://www.cadence.com. **Description:** Manufactures electronic design automation software. **Positions advertised include:** Applications Engineer; Architect; Business Development Director; Configuration Management Engineer; Device Engineer; Finance Director; Group Marketing Director; Human Resources Manager; Product Engineer. **Special programs:** Internships. **Corporate headquarters location:** This location. **Other area locations:** Irvine CA; San Diego CA; Santa Barbara CA. **Other U.S. locations:** MD; MA; MS; NJ; NC; OR; PA; TX. **International locations:** Canada; England; France; India; Ireland; Italy; Japan; Scotland; Taiwan. **Operations at this facility include:** Research and Development; Sales. **Listed on:** New York Stock Exchange. **Stock exchange symbol:** CDN.

## CALIFORNIA DIGITAL
47071 Bayside Parkway, Fremont CA 94538. 510/651-8811. **Contact:** Human Resources. **E-mail address:** jobs@californiadigital.com. **World Wide Web address:** http://www.californiadigital.com. **Description:** Sells Linux servers designed by VA Linux systems, and develops new server products. **Positions advertised include:** Sales Account Manager. **Corporate headquarters location:** This location.

## CHRONTEL, INC.
2210 O'Toole Avenue, Suite 100, San Jose CA 95131. 408/383-9328. **Contact:** Human Resources. **E-mail address:** careers@chrontel.com. **World Wide Web address:** http://www.chrontel.com. **Description:** Manufactures computer microchips. **Positions advertised include:** Applications Engineer; Firmware and System Design Engineer; Algorithm Design Engineer. **Corporate headquarters location:** This location.

## CIBER ENTERPRISE SOLUTIONS
77 Battery Street, San Francisco CA 94111. 415/875-1800. **Contact:** Employment Administrator. **World Wide Web address:** http://www.bitcorp.com. **Description:** A leading software-consulting firm serving clients in a variety of industries. The company is engaged in the implementation of HRMS, financial, distribution, manufacturing, and student systems. **Other U.S. locations:** Chicago IL; Philadelphia PA; Dallas TX. **Parent company:** CIBER, Inc. **Listed on:** New York Stock Exchange. **Stock exchange symbol:** CBR. **Number of employees at this location:** 220.

## CISCO SYSTEMS, INC.
P.O. Box 640730, San Jose 95164. 408/526-4000. **Physical address:** 170 West Tasman Drive, San Jose CA 95134. **Fax:** 800/818-9201. **Contact:** Human Resources. **E-mail address:** apply@cisco.com. **World Wide Web address:** http://www.cisco.com. **Description:** Develops, manufactures, markets, and supports high-performance internetworking systems that enable customers to build large-scale integrated computer networks. The company's products connect and manage communications among local and wide area networks that employ a variety of protocols, media interfaces, network topologies, and cable systems. **Corporate headquarters location:** This location. **International locations:** Worldwide. **Listed on:** NASDAQ. **Stock exchange symbol:** CSCO. **Number of employees nationwide:** 15,000.

## CLARINET SYSTEMS, INC.
44040 Fremont Boulevard, Fremont CA 94538. 510/249-9660. **Fax:** 510/249-9661. **Contact:** Sue Cheng, Human Resources. **E-mail address:** hr@clarinetsys.com. **World Wide Web address:** http://www.clarinetsys.com. **Description:** Provides connections for laptops and PC devices. Uses high speed, wireless LAN connectivity. **Positions advertised include:** Sales Contractor.

## COMMUNICATION INTELLIGENCE CORPORATION (CIC)
275 Shoreline Drive, Suite 500, Redwood Shores CA 94065. 650/802-7888. **Fax:** 650/802-7777. **Contact:** Human Resources Department. **World Wide Web address:** http://www.cic.com. **Description:** Develops, markets, and licenses handwriting recognition and related technologies for the emerging pen-based computer market. The company has created a natural input recognition system that allows a computer to recognize hand-printed character input. **Corporate headquarters location:** This location. **International locations:** China. **Listed on:** NASDAQ. **Stock exchange symbol:** CICI.

## COMPUTER ASSOCIATES INTERNATIONAL, INC.
1201 Marina Village Parkway, Alameda CA 94501. 510/769-1400. **Contact:** Human Resources. **World Wide Web address:** http://www.ca.com. **Description:** Computer Associates International is one of the world's leading developers of client/server and distributed computing software. The company develops, markets, and supports enterprise management, database and applications development, business applications, and consumer software products for a broad range of mainframe, midrange, and desktop computers. Computer Associates International serves major business, government, research, and educational organizations. Founded in 1976. **Positions advertised include:** Software Engineer. **Corporate headquarters location:** Islandia NY. **Other U.S. locations:** Nationwide. **International locations:** Worldwide. **Operations at this facility include:** This location is a sales office. **Listed on:** New York Stock Exchange. **Stock exchange symbol:** CA. **Annual sales/revenues:** More than $100 million. **Number of employees worldwide:** 18,000.

## COMPUTER ASSOCIATES INTERNATIONAL, INC.
2044 Concourse Drive, San Jose CA 95131. 408/965-8800. **Contact:** Human Resources. **World Wide Web address:** http://www.ca.com. **Description:** Computer Associates International is one of the world's leading developers of client/server and distributed computing software. The company develops, markets, and supports enterprise management, database and applications development, business applications, and consumer software products for a broad range of mainframe, midrange, and desktop computers. Computer Associates International serves major business, government, research, and educational organizations. Founded in 1976. **Corporate headquarters location:** Islandia NY. **Other U.S. locations:** Nationwide. **Operations at this facility include:** This location is

engaged in the sale, research, and development of software. **Listed on:** New York Stock Exchange. **Stock exchange symbol:** CA. **Annual sales/revenues:** More than $100 million. **Number of employees worldwide:** 18,000.

### COMPUWARE CORPORATION

1300 Clay Street, Suite 700, Oakland CA 94612. 510/251-8900. **Fax:** 877/873-6784. **Contact:** Recruiting. **E-mail address:** compuware.recruiting@compuware.com. **World Wide Web address:** http://www.compuware.com. **Description:** Develops, markets, and supports an integrated line of systems software products that improve the productivity of programmers and analysts in application program testing, test data preparation, error analysis, and maintenance. Compuware also provides a broad range of professional data processing services including business systems analysis, design, and programming, as well as systems planning and consulting. **NOTE:** Please mail resumes to: Human Resources, 31440 Northwestern Highway, Farmington Hills MI 48334. **Corporate headquarters location:** Farmington Hills MI. **Other U.S. locations:** Denver CO; St. Louis MO; Cincinnati OH; Cleveland OH; Columbus OH; Nashville TN; McLean VA; Milwaukee WI. **International locations:** Canada; South Africa; United Kingdom. **Listed on:** NASDAQ. **Stock exchange symbol:** CPWR.

### COMSYS

1400 Fashion Island Boulevard, Suite 303, San Mateo CA 94404. 650/571-0555. **Contact:** Human Resources. **World Wide Web address:** http://www.comsys.com. **Description:** A computer consulting and contracting firm that provides outsourcing, project support, vendor management, and other specialty services. Founded in 1969. **Corporate headquarters location:** Houston TX. **Other area locations:** Fullerton CA; San Diego CA; Santa Monica CA; San Ramon CA. **Other U.S. locations:** Nationwide.

### CONSILIUM, INC.

3535 Garret Drive, Santa Clara CA 95054. 408/727-5555. **Contact:** Human Resources. **World Wide Web address:** http://www. consilium.com. **Description:** One of the world's leading suppliers of integrated manufacturing execution systems software and services. The company's WorkStream and FAB300 product lines allow manufacturers to identify and implement practices in cost, quality, service, and speed. **Positions advertised include:** Finance Manager; Finance Analyst; Manufacturing Engineer; Product Marketing

Manager; Quality Manager; Systems Program Manager; Systems Project Manager; Technical Support Engineer. **Corporate headquarters location:** This location.

## CONSILIUM, INC.

3535 Garret Drive, Santa Clara CA 95054. 408/727-5555. **Contact:** Human Resources. **World Wide Web address:** http://www. consilium.com. **Description:** One of the world's leading suppliers of integrated manufacturing execution systems software and services. The company's WorkStream and FAB300 product lines allow manufacturers to identify and implement practices in cost, quality, service, and speed. **Positions advertised include:** Finance Manager; Finance Analyst; Manufacturing Engineer; Product Marketing Manager; Quality Manager; Systems Program Manager; Systems Project Manager; Technical Support Engineer. **Corporate headquarters location:** This location.

## CORNERSTONE PERIPHERALS TECHNOLOGY, INC.

225 Hammond Avenue, Fremont CA 94539. 510/580-8900. **Fax:** 510/580-8998. **Contact:** Human Resources Representative. **E-mail address:** hr@cptmail.com. **World Wide Web address:** http://www. bigmonitors.com. **Description:** A leader in the design of computer displays and graphics controller cards. Founded in 1986. **Special programs:** Internships. **Corporate headquarters location:** This location. **International locations:** Munich, Germany. **Listed on:** Privately held. **President/CEO:** John Noellert. **Number of employees at this location:** 55. **Number of employees worldwide:** 65.

## CORNERSTONE PERIPHERALS TECHNOLOGY, INC.

225 Hammond Avenue, Fremont CA 94539. 510/580-8900. **Fax:** 510/580-8998. **Contact:** Human Resources Representative. **E-mail address:** hr@cptmail.com. **World Wide Web address:** http://www. bigmonitors.com. **Description:** A leader in the design of computer displays and graphics controller cards. Founded in 1986. **Special programs:** Internships. **Corporate headquarters location:** This location. **International locations:** Munich, Germany. **Listed on:** Privately held. **President/CEO:** John Noellert. **Number of employees at this location:** 55. **Number of employees worldwide:** 65.

## CREATIVE LABS, INC.

1901 McCarthy Boulevard, Milpitas CA 95035. 408/428-6600. **Fax:** 408/546-6305. **Contact:** Human Resources. **E-mail address:** lyee@ creativelabs.com. **World Wide Web address:** http://www.creative.

com. **Description:** Creative Labs provides multimedia products and peripherals for personal computers. Products include graphics and audio cards, multimedia upgrade kits, and speakers. **Corporate headquarters location:** This location. **Other U.S. locations:** Stillwater OK. **International locations:** Canada; Latin America. **Parent company:** Creative Technology, Ltd. **Operations at this facility include:** This location manufactures computer game software. **Listed on:** NASDAQ. **Stock exchange symbol:** CREAF.

**CREATIVE LABS, INC.**
1901 McCarthy Boulevard, Milpitas CA 95035. 408/428-6600. **Fax:** 408/546-6305. **Contact:** Human Resources. **E-mail address:** lyee@ creativelabs.com. **World Wide Web address:** http://www.creative. com. **Description:** Creative Labs provides multimedia products and peripherals for personal computers. Products include graphics and audio cards, multimedia upgrade kits, and speakers. **Corporate headquarters location:** This location. **Other U.S. locations:** Stillwater OK. **International locations:** Canada; Latin America. **Parent company:** Creative Technology, Ltd. **Operations at this facility include:** This location manufactures computer game software. **Listed on:** NASDAQ. **Stock exchange symbol:** CREAF.

**DATA TECHNOLOGY CORPORATION (DTC)**
P.O. Box 6645, Santa Clara CA 95056. 408/745-9320. **Contact:** Human Resources. **Description:** Develops and manufactures computer peripherals including printers, disk drives, terminals, controllers, and supplies. Products are marketed to both original equipment manufacturers and distributors. **Corporate headquarters location:** This location.

**DATA TECHNOLOGY CORPORATION (DTC)**
P.O. Box 6645, Santa Clara CA 95056. 408/745-9320. **Contact:** Human Resources. **Description:** Develops and manufactures computer peripherals including printers, disk drives, terminals, controllers, and supplies. Products are marketed to both original equipment manufacturers and distributors. **Corporate headquarters location:** This location.

**DECISIONONE**
2323 Industrial Parkway West, Hayward CA 94545. 510/266-3000. **Contact:** Human Resources. **E-mail address:** laura.leaverton@ decisionone.com. **World Wide Web address:** http://www. decisionone.com. **Description:** DecisionOne is an international

supplier of plug-compatible computer equipment and accessories. Products include disk and tape storage devices, terminals, intelligent workstations and systems, controllers, printers, airline reservation systems, and a comprehensive range of computer supplies. The company operates in 27 countries around the world. **Corporate headquarters location:** Frazer PA. **Operations at this facility include:** This location repairs computer monitors.

## DECISIONONE

2323 Industrial Parkway West, Hayward CA 94545. 510/266-3000. **Contact:** Human Resources. **E-mail address:** laura.leaverton@ decisionone.com. **World Wide Web address:** http://www. decisionone.com. **Description:** DecisionOne is an international supplier of plug-compatible computer equipment and accessories. Products include disk and tape storage devices, terminals, intelligent workstations and systems, controllers, printers, airline reservation systems, and a comprehensive range of computer supplies. The company operates in 27 countries around the world. **Corporate headquarters location:** Frazer PA. **Operations at this facility include:** This location repairs computer monitors.

## DISCOPYLABS

48641 Milmont Drive, Fremont CA 94538. 510/651-5100. **Contact:** Human Resources. **World Wide Web address:** http://www. discopylabs.com. **Description:** Assembles discs for software developers. **Corporate headquarters location:** This location.

## DISCOPYLABS

48641 Milmont Drive, Fremont CA 94538. 510/651-5100. **Contact:** Human Resources. **World Wide Web address:** http://www. discopylabs.com. **Description:** Assembles discs for software developers. **Corporate headquarters location:** This location.

## E*TRADE

532 Market Street, San Francisco CA 94104. 415/445-0101. **Contact:** Human Resources. **E-mail address:** jobs@etrade.com. **World Wide Web address:** http://www.etrade.com. **Description:** Operates a Website that provides online investing services. **Special programs:** Internships. **International locations:** Worldwide. **Listed on:** New York Stock Exchange. **Stock exchange symbol:** ET.

## EDIFY CORPORATION

2840 San Tomas Expressway, Santa Clara CA 95051. 408/982-2000. **Toll-free phone:** 800/944-0056. **Fax:** 408/982-0777. **Contact:** Human Resources. **E-mail address:** careers@edify.com. **World Wide Web address:** http://www.edify.com. **Description:** Develops software including Electronic Workforce, which provides a company's customers with corporate information through connections using the World Wide Web, telephone, and other interactive media. **Corporate headquarters location:** This location. **Listed on:** NASDAQ. **Stock exchange symbol:** EDFY.

## ELECTRONIC ARTS, INC.

209 Redwood Shore Parkway, Redwood City CA 94065. 650/628-1500. **Contact:** Human Resources. **World Wide Web address:** http://www.ea.com. **Description:** Creates, markets, and distributes interactive entertainment software for use primarily on independent game systems and IBM-compatible PCs. **Positions advertised include:** Accountant; Attorney; Compensation Consultant; Executive Producer; Senior Financial Analyst; Human Resources Technology Program Manager. **Corporate headquarters location:** This location. **Listed on:** NASDAQ. **Stock exchange symbol:** ERTS. **Number of employees worldwide:** 2,500.

## ELECTRONIC DATA SYSTEMS CORPORATION (EDS)

1325 McCandless Drive, Milpitas CA 95035. 408/941-4600. **Fax:** 800/562-6241. **Contact:** Human Resources. **E-mail address:** careers@eds.com. **World Wide Web address:** http://www.eds.com. **Description:** An international supplier of mechanical and engineering software and services. **Listed on:** New York Stock Exchange. **Stock exchange symbol:** EDS. **Number of employees worldwide:** 1,200.

## ELEVON, INC.

303 Second Street, Suite 3N, San Francisco CA 94107. 415/495-8811. **Fax:** 415/281-1573. **Contact:** Recruiter. **E-mail address:** jobs@elevon.com. **World Wide Web address:** http://www.elevon.cc/default.cfm. **Description:** A developer of high-end financial applications software, primarily for *Fortune* 100 companies and government agencies. **Corporate headquarters location:** This location. **Other U.S. locations:** Atlanta GA; Chicago IL; Boston MA. **International locations:** Australia; Singapore; United Kingdom. **Annual sales/revenues:** $51 - $100 million. **Number of employees at this location:** 280.

## ENGAGE-ADKNOWLEDGE TECHNOLOGIES

1808 Embarcadero Road, Palo Alto CA 94303. 650/842-6500. **Fax:** 650/842-0665. **Contact:** Human Resources. **World Wide Web address:** http://www.engage.com. **Description:** Develops software that assists companies in monitoring and improving their Internet advertising campaigns.

## EPLUS, INC.

1900 Point West Way, Suite 120, Sacramento CA 95815. 916/568-1555. **Toll-free phone:** 800/827-5711. **Fax:** 916/568-1590. **Contact:** Human Resources. **World Wide Web address:** http://www. eplus.com. **Description:** Leases and sells computers and other IT equipment. ePlus also develops online software products that provide supply chain management solutions including electronic procurement, e-financing, and e-asset management. **Corporate headquarters location:** Herndon VA. **Other U.S. locations:** Scottsdale AZ; San Diego CA; Lenexa KS; Columbia MD; Minneapolis MN; Greenville NC; Raleigh NC; Waxhaw NC; Wilmington NC; Pottstown PA; West Chester PA; Harrisburg PA; Dallas TX; Austin TX. **Listed on:** NASDAQ. **Stock exchange symbol:** PLUS.

## EVEREX SYSTEMS INC.

5020 Brandin Court, Fremont CA 94538. 510/498-1111. **Fax:** 510/683-2021. **Contact:** Human Resources. **World Wide Web address:** http://www.everex.com. **Description:** Designs, manufactures, and services computer peripheral equipment such as the STEP, EXPLORA, and TEMPO lines. **Corporate headquarters location:** This location. **Operations at this facility include:** Administration; Manufacturing; Sales; Service. **Listed on:** Privately held.

## EXCITE INC.

555 Broadway, Redwood City CA 94063. 650/568-6000. **Contact:** Human Resources Department. **E-mail address:** jobs@staff. excite.com. **World Wide Web address:** http://www.excite.com. **Description:** An Internet search engine that offers Web navigation services and features site reviews, editorial columns, news, and regional information. **Positions advertised include:** Sales Planner. **Corporate headquarters location:** This location. **Listed on:** NASDAQ. **Stock exchange symbol:** XCIT. **Annual sales/revenues:** $5 - $10 million.

## EXODUS COMMUNICATIONS
4650 Old Ironsides Drive, Santa Clara CA 95054. 408/346-2200. **Toll-free phone:** 888/2EXODUS. **Fax:** 408/346-2202. **Contact:** Human Resources. **E-mail address:** inquiry@exodus.com. **World Wide Web address:** http://www.exodus.net. **Description:** Offers Internet server hosting, network solutions, and system management and monitoring services. **Corporate headquarters location:** This location. **Stock exchange symbol:** EXDSQ.

## FILEMAKER INC.
P.O. Box 58168, 5201 Patrick Henry Drive, Santa Clara CA 95054. 408/987-7000. **Contact:** Human Resources. **E-mail address:** filemaker_hr@filemaker.com. **World Wide Web address:** http://www.filemaker.com. **Description:** Develops software including FileMaker Pro 5 and FileMaker Server 5, database systems that are designed for Windows and Macintosh operating systems. **Positions advertised include:** Systems Engineer; Administrative Assistant; Telecomm and Network Administrator. **Corporate headquarters location:** This location.

## FORCE COMPUTERS, INC.
4305 Cushing Parkway, Fremont CA 94538. 510/445-6000. **Toll-free phone:** 800/FORCE99. **Contact:** Human Resources. **E-mail address:** hr@fci.com. **World Wide Web address:** http://www.forcecomputers.com. **Description:** A manufacturer of embedded systems. The company supplies high-performance computer products to a broad range of worldwide telecommunications, industrial, and government customers. **Special programs:** Internships. **Corporate headquarters location:** This location. **International locations:** Germany. **Listed on:** Privately held. **Annual sales/revenues:** More than $100 million. **Number of employees at this location:** 140. **Number of employees nationwide:** 170. **Number of employees worldwide:** 500.

## FORTEL CORPORATION
46832 Lakeview Boulevard, Fremont CA 94538. 510/440-9600. **Fax:** 510/440-9696. **Contact:** Human Resources. **World Wide Web address:** http://www.fortel.com. **Description:** Designs, manufactures, and markets solid-state memory and storage peripherals for mainframe computers. **Corporate headquarters location:** This location.

## FUJITSU COMPUTER PRODUCTS OF AMERICA INC.

2904 Orchard Parkway, San Jose CA 95134. 408/432-6333. **Contact:** Human Resources. **E-mail address:** hr@fcpa.fujitsu.com. **World Wide Web address:** http://www.fcpa.com. **Description:** Fujitsu Computer Products of America manufactures hard drives, magneto-optical drives, printers, scanners, and tape drives. **Positions advertised include:** Senior UNIX Systems Administrator; Technical Support Engineer; Quality Engineer Manager; Service Support Operations Representative. **Corporate headquarters location:** This location. **Other U.S. locations:** Hillsboro CO; Longmont CO. **Parent company:** Fujitsu, Ltd. (Japan). **Operations at this facility include:** This location houses administrative offices.

## FUJITSU MICROELECTRONICS, INC.

3545 North First Street, San Jose CA 95134. 408/922-9000. **Fax:** 408/943-0407. **Contact:** Human Resources. **E-mail address:** careers@fma.fujitsu.com. **World Wide Web address:** http://www. fujitsumicro.com. **Description:** Fujitsu Microelectronics, Inc. manufactures microprocessors, ethernet decoders and encoders, discrete chips, and memory products. **Positions advertised include:** Sales Assistant. **Corporate headquarters location:** This location. **Parent company:** Fujitsu, Ltd. (Japan). **Operations at this facility include:** This location houses administrative offices.

## GENERAL MAGIC, INC.

420 North Mary Avenue, Sunnyvale CA 94085. 408/774-4000. **Fax:** 408/774-4030. **Contact:** Human Resources. **E-mail address:** staffing@generalmagic.com. **World Wide Web address:** http://www. genmagic.com. **Description:** Provides voice application services primarily to telecommunications and Internet companies. The company's magicTalk communications platform allows customers to manage faxes, voicemail, and e-mail with the use of their natural voice. **Corporate headquarters location:** This location. **Listed on:** NASDAQ. **Stock exchange symbol:** GMGC.

## GEOWORKS

6550 Vallejo Street, Suite 102, Emeryville CA 94608. 510/814-1660. **Fax:** 510/597-1821. **Contact:** Human Resources. **E-mail address:** careers@geoworks.com. **World Wide Web address:** http://www. geoworks.com. **Description:** Develops and markets software for the mobile communications device industry. **Corporate headquarters location:** This location. **Listed on:** NASDAQ. **Stock exchange symbol:** GWRX.

## GLOBAL INFORMATION DISTRIBUTION (GID)

2040 Fortune Drive, Suite 101, San Jose CA 95131. 408/232-5500. **Contact:** Personnel. **World Wide Web address:** http://www.gid-it.com. **Description:** Manufactures film-based imaging printers and storage/retrieval hardware. **Parent company:** Softnet.

## GRAPHNET

425 Market Street, Suite 2830, San Francisco CA 94105. 415/543-0300. **Contact:** Human Resources. **E-mail address:** hr@graphnet.com. **World Wide Web address:** http://www.graphnet.com. **Description:** Provides web-enabled message management services. **Positions advertised include:** Sales Executive. **Corporate headquarters location:** New York NY.

## HEWLETT-PACKARD COMPANY

10435 North Tantau Avenue, Cupertino CA 95014-2599. 408/725-6000. **Fax:** 408/285-3960. **Contact:** Human Resources Department. **World Wide Web address:** http://www.hp.com. **Description:** A manufacturer of electronic computer systems and peripherals including laptop and desktop personal computers, PC-based client servers, notebook computers, and tower systems. The company sells its products through retail stores, warehouses, resellers, mail-order catalogs, and telemarketers. **Office hours:** Monday - Friday, 8:00 a.m. - 5:00 p.m. **NOTE:** Resumes should be sent to: P.O. Box 692000, Houston TX 97269. **Positions advertised include:** Administrative Assistant; Solution Architect; Financial Specialist; Sales Expert; Business Development Analyst; Client Manager. **Corporate headquarters location:** Houston TX. **Other U.S. locations:** Nationwide. **International locations:** Worldwide. **Listed on:** New York Stock Exchange. **Stock exchange symbol:** CPQ.

## HEWLETT-PACKARD COMPANY

901 Page Avenue, Fremont CA 94538. 510/354-4000. **Contact:** Human Resources. **World Wide Web address:** http://www.hp.com. **Description:** A manufacturer of electronic computer systems and peripherals including laptop and desktop personal computers, PC-based client servers, notebook computers, and tower systems. The company sells its products through retail stores, warehouses, resellers, mail-order catalogs, and telemarketers. **NOTE:** Resumes should be sent to: P.O. Box 692000, Houston TX 97269. **Positions advertised include:** Solution Architect; Financial Specialist; Strategic Program Manager; Pre-Sales Consultant. **Corporate headquarters location:** Houston TX. **Other U.S. locations:** Nationwide.

**International locations:** Worldwide. **Operations at this facility include:** This location is a manufacturing facility. **Listed on:** New York Stock Exchange. **Stock exchange symbol:** CPQ.

## HEWLETT-PACKARD COMPANY

19111 Pruneridge Avenue, Cupertino CA 95014. 408/725-8900. **Contact:** Human Resources. **World Wide Web address:** http://www.hp.com. **Description:** Hewlett-Packard designs and manufactures measurement and computation products and systems used in business, industry, engineering, science, health care, and education. Principal products include integrated instrument and computer systems such as hardware and software, peripheral products, and electronic medical equipment and systems. **NOTE:** Resumes should be sent to Employment Response Center, Hewlett-Packard Company, Mail Stop 20-APP, 3000 Hanover Street, Palo Alto CA 94304. **Positions advertised include:** Executive Communication Manager; Solution Architect; Financial Specialist; Human Resources Compensation Director; Sales Information Specialist; Information Research Analyst; Commodity Manager. **Corporate headquarters location:** Palo Alto CA. **Other U.S. locations:** Nationwide. **Operations at this facility include:** This location manufactures business computer systems for interactive, online data processing, database management, and distributed data processing. **Listed on:** New York Stock Exchange. **Stock exchange symbol:** HPQ. **Number of employees nationwide:** 93,000.

## HEWLETT-PACKARD COMPANY

8000 Foothills Boulevard, Roseville CA 95747. 916/786-8000. **Contact:** Human Resources. **World Wide Web address:** http://www.hp.com. **Description:** Hewlett-Packard designs and manufactures measurement and computation products and systems used in business, industry, engineering, science, health care, and education. Principal products include integrated instrument and computer systems such as hardware and software, peripheral products, and medical electronic equipment and systems. **NOTE:** Resumes should be sent to Employment Response Center, Hewlett-Packard Company, Mail Stop 20-APP, 3000 Hanover Street, Palo Alto CA 94304. **Positions advertised include:** Solution Architect; Financial Analyst; IT Program Manager; Product Marketing Manager; Software Design Engineer; Workstation Sales Specialist; Client Manager; Remote Applications Engineer. **Corporate headquarters location:** Palo Alto CA. **Other U.S. locations:** Nationwide. **Operations at this facility include:** This location manufactures business computer systems. **Listed on:** New York Stock Exchange. **Stock exchange symbol:** HPQ. **Number of employees nationwide:** 93,000.

## HEWLETT-PACKARD COMPANY
## EMPLOYMENT RESPONSE CENTER

1601 South California Avenue, Palo Alto CA 94304. 650/857-1501. **Fax:** 650/852-8138. **Contact:** Human Resources Department. **World Wide Web address:** http://www.hp.com.¹ **Description:** Hewlett-Packard designs and manufactures measurement and computation products and systems used in business, engineering, science, health care, and education. Principal products include integrated instrument and computer systems such as hardware and software, peripheral products, and electronic medical equipment and systems. **NOTE:** Resumes should be sent to the Employment Response Center, Hewlett-Packard Company, Mail Stop 20-APP, 3000 Hanover Street, Palo Alto CA 94304. **Positions advertised include:** Administrative Assistant; Solution Architect; Communications Administrative Coordinator; Financial Systems Analyst; Internal Audit Manager; Stock Plan Administrator; Shareholder Service Project Manager; Human Resources Compensation Director; Software Engineer. **Special programs:** Internships. **Corporate headquarters location:** This location. **Other U.S. locations:** Nationwide. **Operations at this facility include:** This location is a resume processing center. **Listed on:** New York Stock Exchange. **Stock exchange symbol:** HWP. **Number of employees nationwide:** 93,000.

## HITACHI DATA SYSTEMS

750 Central Expressway, Santa Clara CA 95050. 408/970-1000. **Contact:** Human Resources. **World Wide Web address:** http://www.hds.com. **Description:** Hitachi Data Systems manufactures mainframe computers. **Positions advertised include:** Database Administrator; Business Analyst; Attorney; Global Storage Manager. **Parent company:** Hitachi Ltd. **Corporate headquarters location:** This location. **Operations at this facility include:** This location serves as a sales and marketing office. **Listed on:** New York Stock Exchange. **Stock exchange symbol:** HIT.

## HITACHI DIGITAL GRAPHICS INC.

2325 Paragon Drive, Suite 10, San Jose CA 95131. 408/392-9560. **Contact:** Human Resources. **World Wide Web address:** http://www.hitachidigital.com. **Description:** Manufactures graphics tablets with pressure sensitive pens for computers. **Parent company:** Hitachi

Ltd. **Listed on:** New York Stock Exchange. **Stock exchange symbol:** HIT.

## HOYA CORPORATION USA
101 Metro Drive, San Jose CA 95110. 408/435-1450. **Contact:** Human Resources. **Description:** Develops, produces, and markets glass, thin-film, rigid disks for use in hard drives for mobile computing applications. **NOTE:** Entry-level positions are offered. Resumes should be sent to Human Resources, Hoya Corporation USA, 3400 Edison Way, Fremont CA 94538. **Corporate headquarters location:** This location. **Subsidiaries include:** Continuum; Probe Tech. **Parent company:** Hoya Corporation (Japan). **Listed on:** Privately held. **Number of employees at this location:** 185. **Number of employees worldwide:** 1,000.

## IBM CORPORATION
5600 Cottle Road, San Jose CA 95193. 408/256-1600. **Toll-free phone:** 800/IBM4YOU. **Fax:** 408/256-8888. **Contact:** Personnel Department. **World Wide Web address:** http://www.ibm.com. **Description:** IBM is a developer, manufacturer, and marketer of advanced information processing products including computers and microelectronic technology, software, networking systems and information technology-related services. **Positions at this facility include:** Account Analyst; Administrative Assistant; Customer Engineer; Circuit Design Engineer; General Supply Technician; Executive Assistant; Manager; Research Staff Member; Software Engineer; Staff Counselor. **Corporate headquarters location:** White Plains NY. **Subsidiaries include:** IBM Credit Corporation; IBM Instruments, Inc.; IBM World Trade Corporation. **Operations at this facility include:** This location is engaged in the development of data access and storage devices. **Listed on:** New York Stock Exchange. **Stock exchange symbol:** IBM.

## IAMBIC SOFTWARE
12 South First Street, Suite 300, San Jose CA 95113. 408/882-0390. **Contact:** Vidal Graupera, President. **E-mail address:** jobs@iambic.com. **World Wide Web address:** http://www.iambic.com. **Description:** Develops and manufactures software applications for the handheld computing market. **Positions advertised include:** Technical Support Engineer; Graphic Designer. **Corporate headquarters location:** This location.

## IKOS SYSTEMS, INC.
79 Great Oaks Boulevard, San Jose 95119. 408/284-0400. **Fax:** 408/284-0401. **Contact:** Human Resources. **World Wide Web address:** http://www.ikos.com. **Description:** Designs, manufactures, markets, and supports logic simulation software and compatible hardware accelerators. IKOS's simulators are used in the design of Application Specific Integrated Circuits (ASIC) and ASIC-based systems. **Corporate headquarters location:** This location. **Listed on:** NASDAQ. **Stock exchange symbol:** IKOS.

## INCYTE GENOMICS
3160 Porter Drive, Palo Alto CA 94304. 650/855-0555. **Contact:** Human Resources. **E-mail address:** careers@incyte.com. **World Wide Web address:** http://www.incyte.com. **Description:** Designs and develops genomic software. **Corporate headquarters location:** This location. **Listed on:** NASDAQ. **Stock exchange symbol:** INCY.

## INFORMATION BUILDERS INC.
224 Airport Parkway, Suite 310, San Jose CA 95110-1022. 408/453-7600. **Contact:** Human Resources. **E-mail address:** employment_opportunities@ibi.com. **World Wide Web address:** http://www.ibi.com. **Description:** A software development firm. Products include WebFOCUS, FOCUS Solutions, EDA Middleware, and SmartMart Data Warehouse. Other services include software support and sales. **Positions advertised include:** Senior Webfocus Programmer Consultant. **Corporate headquarters location:** New York NY. **Other U.S. locations:** Nationwide. **Number of employees nationwide:** 1,500.

## INFORMATION SYSTEMS SUPPORT
4151 Middlefield Road, Suite 101, Palo Alto CA 94303. 650/496-2400. **Contact:** Human Resources. **World Wide Web address:** http://www.iss-md.com. **Description:** Provides computer consulting services including information technology and facility management support. **Corporate headquarters location:** Bethesda MD.

## INFORMIX SOFTWARE, INC.
4100 Bohannon Drive, Menlo Park CA 94025. 650/926-6300. **Contact:** Human Resources. **World Wide Web address:** http://www.informix.com. **Description:** Provides database technology to build, deploy, run, and evolve applications. Informix products include distributed database management systems, application development tools, and graphical- and character-based productivity

software. **Corporate headquarters location:** This location. **Other U.S. locations:** Englewood CO; Downers Grove IL; Lenexa KS; Portland OR. **International locations:** England; Singapore. **Parent company:** IBM. **Operations at this facility include:** Administration; Research and Development; Sales. **Listed on:** New York Stock Exchange. **Stock exchange symbol:** IBM. **Number of employees at this location:** 800. **Number of employees nationwide:** 1,300.

## INKTOMI CORPORATION
4100 East Third Avenue, Foster City CA 94404. 650/653-2800. **Toll-free phone:** 888/INKTOMI. **Contact:** Human Resources. **E-mail address:** jobs@inktomi.com. **World Wide Web address:** http://www. inktomi.com. **Description:** Creator and operator of HotBot, a search engine on the World Wide Web. **Corporate headquarters location:** This location. **Listed on:** NASDAQ. **Stock exchange symbol:** INKT.

## INTEL CORPORATION
1900 Prairie City Road, Folsom CA 95630. 916/356-8080. **Contact:** Human Resources. **World Wide Web address:** http://www.intel.com. **Description:** Intel Corporation is one of the largest semiconductor manufacturers in the world. Other products include supercomputers; embedded control chips and flash memories; motherboards; multimedia hardware; personal computer enhancement products; and design and marketing of microcomputer components, modules, and systems. Intel sells its products to original equipment manufacturers and other companies that incorporate them into their products. **Positions advertised include:** Audit Specialist; Consulting Engineer; Human Resources Senior Researcher; Patent Attorney; Principal Storage Architect; Senior IT Auditor; Tax Benefits Attorney. **Corporate headquarters location:** Santa Clara CA. **Operations at this facility include:** This location develops semiconductors that provide silicon connectivity, LAN switching, and WAN access solutions for telecommunications and network applications. **Listed on:** NASDAQ. **Stock exchange symbol:** INTC. **Annual sales/revenues:** More than $100 million.

## INTELLICORP
1975 West El Camino Real, Suite 101, Mountain View CA 94040-2216. 650/965-5500. **Fax:** 650/965-5647. **Contact:** Human Resources Department. **E-mail address:** jobs@intellicorp.com. **World Wide Web address:** http://www.intellicorp.com. **Description:** Designs, develops, and markets software development tools and provides related training, customer support, and consulting services.

IntelliCorp provides its customers with object-oriented software tools for the design, development, and delivery of scalable client/server applications. **Positions advertised include:** Regional Sales Manager. **Corporate headquarters location:** This location. **Other U.S. locations:** Nationwide. **International locations:** Europe.

### INTERNATIONAL MICROCOMPUTER SOFTWARE, INC. (IMSI)

75 Rowland Way, Suite 340, Novato CA 94945. 415/257-3000. **Fax:** 415/897-0043. **Contact:** Jackie Wandrey, Human Resources. **World Wide Web address:** http://www.imsisoft.com. **Description:** A leading developer of productivity software for business and home use. The company's Home Living Media division focuses on CD-ROM multimedia software for learning and education. IMSI's three primary product lines are business, consumer productivity, and multimedia learning software. **Corporate headquarters location:** This location.

### INTUIT, INC.

2632 Marine Way, Mountain View CA 94043. 650/944-6000. **Contact:** Human Resources. **World Wide Web address:** http://www. intuit.com. **Description:** Develops and markets personal finance and small business accounting software and also offers support services. Products include Quicken, which allows users to organize and manage personal finances. **Positions advertised include:** Marketing and Sales Leader; Director of Engineering Services; Senior Software Engineer; Web Application Configurator; Director of Engineering Services; Process Excellence Leader; Director of In-Product Marketing; Group Manager; Senior Brand Manager, Verticals; Senior Business Operations Manager; Senior Information Architect; Senior Web Development Manager. **Corporate headquarters location:** This location. **Other U.S. locations:** AZ; MA; MI; NV; NY; TX; UT; VA. **International locations:** Canada; Japan; United Kingdom. **Listed on:** NASDAQ. **Stock exchange symbol:** INTU. **Number of employees nationwide:** 500.

### KENSINGTON TECHNOLOGY GROUP

2000 Alameda de las Pusgas, Suite 200, San Mateo CA 94403. 650/572-2700. **Toll-free phone:** 800/243-2972. **Fax:** 650/572-9675. **Contact:** Human Resources. **E-mail address:** jobs@kensington.com. **World Wide Web address:** http://www.kensington.com. **Description:** Designs and markets computer accessories, peripherals, and software for the computer aftermarket. Products include mice and trackballs, joysticks, gamepads, surge suppressor systems, cable and lock security devices, and carrying cases. **NOTE:** Entry-level positions are offered. **Positions advertised include:** Controller; Web Project Manager. **Special programs:** Internships. **Office hours:** Monday - Friday, 8:00 a.m. - 5:00 p.m. **Corporate headquarters location:** This location. **Parent company:** ACCO Brands, Inc. **Listed on:** New York Stock Exchange. **Stock exchange symbol:** FO. **Number of employees at this location:** 120. **Number of employees nationwide:** 145.

## LSI LOGIC

1778 McCarthy Boulevard, Milpitas CA 95035. 408/944-6300. **Fax:** 408/433-8918. **Contact:** Human Resources. **World Wide Web address:** http://www.lsilogic.com. **Description:** Designs and markets integrated circuits that implement the compression, decompression, and transmission of digital full-motion video and still images for consumer electronics, communications, and computer applications such as video CD players, direct broadcast of television programming by satellites, and multimedia computing. Founded in 1988. **Corporate headquarters location:** This location. **Other area locations:** Irvine CA; Los Angeles CA; San Diego CA. **U.S. locations:** Nationwide. **International locations:** China; France; Germany; Italy; the Netherlands; Sweden; United Kingdom. **Number of employees worldwide:** 600. **Listed on:** New York Stock Exchange. **Stock exchange symbol:** LSI.

## THE LEARNING COMPANY

6493 Kaiser Drive, Fremont CA 94555. 510/792-2101. **Contact:** Human Resources. **World Wide Web address:** http://www. learningco.com. **Description:** The Learning Company uses emerging technologies to create a system of easy-to-use software products that help build lifelong learning and communications skills. The company has developed families of educational software products in key subject areas that are appropriate for different age groups. Most of the company's products are available in home editions, and certain products are also available in school editions that include network, site license, and stand-alone configurations. Product families include the Rabbit Family (ages 3 to 7), the Treasure Family (ages 6 to 8), the Writing Tools Family and The Children's Writing & Publishing Center (ages 8 and up), and The Foreign Languages Family (ages 15 and up). **Corporate headquarters location:** Cambridge MA. **Other U.S. locations:** Nationwide. **Parent company:** Broderbund LLC. **Operations at this facility include:** This location develops and markets software. **Number of employees at this location:** 190. **Number of employees nationwide:** 480.

## LEGEND INFORMATION TECHNOLOGY

46401 Landing Parkway, Fremont CA 94538. 510/668-4933. **Contact:** Human Resources. **World Wide Web address:** http://www. legend.com. **Description:** A manufacturer of computer components and motherboards. **Corporate headquarters location:** Beijing, China.

## LOGICA, INC.

505 Montgomery Street, 11th Floor, San Francisco CA 94111. 415/288-5200. **Contact:** Human Resources. **World Wide Web address:** http://www.logica.com. **Description:** Provides computer programming systems, design, and consulting services for the banking, insurance, and telecommunications industries. **Corporate headquarters location:** Lexington MA.

## LOGITECH, INC.

6505 Kaiser Drive, Fremont CA 94555. 510/795-8500. **Fax:** 510/ 792-8901. **Contact:** Human Resources Manager. **World Wide Web address:** http://www.logitech.com. **Description:** Designs, develops, manufactures, and markets computer hardware and software products. Logitech is a leading worldwide manufacturer of computer pointing devices including mice, trackballs, and joysticks, and imaging devices such as scanners and cameras for PC, MAC, and other platforms. **Special programs:** Internships. **Corporate headquarters location:** This location. **Other U.S. locations:** Framingham MA; Dallas TX. **Parent company:** Logitech International S.A. **Operations at this facility include:** Administration; Research and Development; Sales. **Listed on:** NASDAQ. **Stock exchange symbol:** LOGI. **Number of employees at this location:** 350.

## LOTUS DEVELOPMENT CORPORATION

425 Market Street, 25th Floor, San Francisco CA 94105. 415/545-3800. **Contact:** Human Resources. **World Wide Web address:** http:// www.lotus.com/jobs. **Description:** Develops, manufactures, and markets applications software and services that meet the evolving technology and business applications requirements of individuals, work groups, and entire organizations. **Corporate headquarters location:** Cambridge MA. **Parent company:** IBM Corporation. **Listed on:** New York Stock Exchange. **Stock exchange symbol:** IBM.

## LUCAS ARTS ENTERTAINMENT COMPANY

P.O. Box 10307, San Rafael CA 94912. 415/472-3400. **Fax:** 415/ 444-8438. **Contact:** Human Resources. **World Wide Web address:** http://www.lucasarts.com. **Description:** An international developer and publisher of entertainment software, some of which incorporate a Star Wars theme. **Positions advertised include:** International Accountant; Software Engineer; Animator; Artist; Programmer. **Corporate headquarters location:** This location.

## LUCENT TECHNOLOGIES INTERNETWORKING SYSTEMS
1001 Murphy Ranch Road, Milpitas CA 95035. 408/321-2000. **Contact:** Human Resources. **World Wide Web address:** http://www. lucent.com. **Description:** Develops, manufactures, markets, and supports a family of high-performance, multiservice wide area network (WAN) switches that enable public carrier providers and private network managers to provide cost-effective, high-speed, enhanced data communications services. These products direct and manage data communications across wide area networks that utilize different network architectures and services, and are designed to support, on a single platform, the major high-speed packet data communications services. These services include frame relay, switched multimegabit data service, and asynchronous transfer mode. The company markets its products to interexchange carriers, local exchange carriers, competitive access providers, other public network providers, and private network managers. **Positions advertised include:** Director, IT Security Counseling Services; Senior Professional Services Account Manager. **Corporate headquarters location:** Murray Hill NJ. **Listed on:** New York Stock Exchange. **Stock exchange symbol:** LU.

## MACROMEDIA, INC.
600 Townsend Street, Suite 310 West, San Francisco CA 94103. 415/252-2000. **Contact:** Personnel. **World Wide Web address:** http://www.macromedia.com. **Description:** Develops multimedia software for the Web. **Special programs:** Internships. **Corporate headquarters location:** This location. **Listed on:** NASDAQ. **Stock exchange symbol:** MACR. **Number of employees worldwide:** 1,200.

## MAXTOR CORPORATION
500 McCarthy Boulevard, Milpitas Ca 95035. 408/432-1700. **Contact:** Human Resources. **E-mail address:** staffing_ca@ maxtor.com. **World Wide Web address:** http://www.maxtor.com. **Description:** Manufactures hard disk drives and related electronic data storage equipment for computers, as well as related components for original equipment manufacturers. **Positions advertised include:** Accountant; Principal Mechanical Engineer; Senior Staff Mechanical Engineer. **Corporate headquarters location:**

This location. **International locations:** Hong Kong; Singapore. **Listed on:** New York Stock Exchange. **Stock exchange symbol:** MXO.

**MENTOR GRAPHICS**
1001 Ridder Park Drive, San Jose CA 95131. 408/487-7000. **Toll-free phone:** 800/547-3000. **Contact:** Human Resources Department. **World Wide Web address:** http://www.mentor.com. **Description:** A developer and marketer of logic synthesis software and EDA software tools. **Positions advertised include:** Software Engineer; Technical Marketing Engineer; HR Business Partner; Senior Marcom Manager; Software Engineer; Technical Marketing Engineer. **Corporate headquarters location:** Wilsonville OR. **Listed on:** NASDAQ. **Stock exchange symbol:** MENT.

**MERCURY INTERACTIVE CORPORATION**
1325 Borregas Avenue, Sunnyvale CA 94089. 408/822-5200. **Fax:** 408/822-5300. **Contact:** Personnel. **World Wide Web address:** http://www.mercuryinteractive.com. **Description:** Develops automated software quality tools for enterprise applications testing. The company's products are used to isolate software and system errors prior to application deployment. **Positions advertised include:** Senior Product Manager; Director of Product Marketing. **Corporate headquarters location:** This location. **Listed on:** NASDAQ. **Stock exchange symbol:** MERQ. **Annual sales/revenues:** More than $100 million.

**MICROSOFT CORPORATION**
1065 Lavenida Street, Mountain View CA 94043. 650/693-4000. **Contact:** Human Resources Department. **E-mail address:** jobs@microsoft.com. **World Wide Web address:** http://www. microsoft.com. **Description:** Microsoft designs, sells and supports a product line of microcomputer software for business, home, and professional use. Microsoft also manufactures related books and hardware products. Software products include spreadsheets, desktop publishing, project management, graphics, word processing, and database applications, as well as operating systems and programming languages. **Positions advertised include:** Program Manager; Software Development Engineer; Business Development Manager; Lead Systems; Technologist. **Corporate headquarters location:** Redmond WA. **Operations at this facility include:** This location is a research and design office. **Listed on:** NASDAQ. **Stock exchange symbol:** MSFT.

## MIDWAY GAMES WEST

675 Sycamore Drive, Milpitas CA 95035. 408/434-3700. **Contact:** Human Resources. **World Wide Web address:** http://www. midway.com. **Description:** Atari Games Corporation develops video game software. **Corporate headquarters location:** This location. **Operations at this facility include:** This location is a research and development facility. **Listed on:** New York Stock Exchange. **Stock exchange symbol:** MWY.

## MIPS TECHNOLOGIES, INC.

1225 Charleston Road, Mountain View CA 94043. 650/567-5052. **Fax:** 650/567-5150. **Contact:** Human Resources. **E-mail address:** getajob@mips.com. **World Wide Web address:** http://www.mips. com. **Description:** Designs 32- and 64-bit RISC processors for license to semiconductor suppliers. The company's products are then embedded in such items as digital cameras, handheld computing devices, and video game systems. **Positions advertised include:** Design Verification Engineer; Marketing Manager; Solutions Architect; Senior Product Support Engineer; Training and Technological Documentation Specialist. **Corporate headquarters location:** This location. **Listed on:** NASDAQ. **Stock exchange symbol:** MIPS. **Annual sales/revenues:** $51 - $100 million.

## MYLEX CORPORATION

6607 Kaiser Street, Fremont CA 94555. 510/796-6100. **Contact:** Human Resources. **World Wide Web address:** http://www.mylex. com. **Description:** Designs and manufactures disk array controllers, system boards, and network interface cards. The company also supports proprietary software for a wide range of personal computers, workstations, and servers. Mylex is a world leader in RAID (Redundant Array of Independent Disks) technology. **Corporate headquarters location:** This location. **Parent company:** IBM. **Listed on:** New York Stock Exchange. **Stock exchange symbol:** IBM.

## NAVIGATION TECHNOLOGIES (NAVTECH)

740 East Arques Avenue, Sunnyvale CA 94086-3839. 408/737-3200. **Toll-free phone:** 888/NAV-MAPS. **Fax:** 408/730-0691. **Contact:** Human Resources. **E-mail address:** career@navtech.com. **World Wide Web address:** http://www.navtech.com. **Description:** Develops digital databases for in-vehicle navigation systems. **NOTE:** Entry-level positions are offered. **Corporate headquarters location:** Rosemont IL. **International locations:** Canada; Europe; Japan. **Listed**

on: Privately held. **Annual sales/revenues:** Less than $5 million. **Number of employees at this location:** 150. **Number of employees nationwide:** 400. **Number of employees worldwide:** 800.

## NETIS TECHNOLOGY, INC.
1606 Centre Pointe Drive, Milpitas CA 95035. 408/263-0368. **Fax:** 408/263-4624. **Contact:** Human Resources. **E-mail address:** hr@netistech.com. **World Wide Web address:** http://www.netistech. com. **Description:** Provides systems integration and networking services. The company also manufactures personal computers and offers a network consulting service. Founded in 1989. **Corporate headquarters location:** This location. **Listed on:** Privately held. **Number of employees at this location:** 20.

## NETSCAPE COMMUNICATIONS CORPORATION
P.O. Box 7050, Mountain View CA 94039. 650/254-1900. **Physical address:** 466 Ellis Street, Mountain View CA 94043. **Contact:** Human Resources. **World Wide Web address:** http://www.home. netscape.com. **Description:** An Internet service provider. The company also provides developmental tools, commercial applications, and client/server software. **Positions advertised include:** Technical Support Engineer; Communications Manager; QA Engineer; Senior Software Engineer. **Corporate headquarters location:** This location. **Other area locations:** Manhattan Beach CA. **Other U.S. locations:** Washington DC; Atlanta GA; Chicago IL; New York NY; Dallas TX. **Parent company:** AOL Time Warner. **Listed on:** New York Stock Exchange. **Stock exchange symbol:** AOL. **Annual sales/revenues:** More than $100 million.

## NETWORK APPLIANCE, INC.
495 East Java Drive, Sunnyvale CA 94089. 408/822-6000. **Fax:** 408/ 822-4501. **Contact:** Human Resources. **E-mail address:** ntapjobs@ netapp.com. **World Wide Web address:** http://www.netapp.com. **Description:** Develops data storage equipment for corporate networks. **Positions advertised include:** Corporate Service Manager; Customer Operations Manager; Data Quality Administrator; Desktop Systems Administrator; Director of Tax; Facilities Manager; Learning and Development Manager; Manager of Platform Hardware; Marketing Manager, Technical Applications; Member of Technical Staff; Product Manager; Product Marketing Manager. **Corporate headquarters location:** This location. **Listed on:** NASDAQ. **Stock exchange symbol:** NTAP. **Annual sales/revenues:** More than $100 million.

## NETWORK ASSOCIATES, INC.
3965 Freedom Circle, Santa Clara CA 95054. 408/988-3832. **Contact:** Human Resources. **World Wide Web address:** http://www.nai.com. **Description:** Designs, manufactures, markets, and supports software-based analysis and monitoring tools primarily for managing enterprisewide computer networks. The company's product line consists of software and network interface cards used with portable PC-compatible computers to monitor and analyze individual local area network (LAN) or wide area network (WAN) segments. Products include VirusScan, an antivirus software. **Positions advertised include:** Senior QA Director; Strategic Account Manager; Software Sales Territory Manager; Marketing Data Analyst; Interwoven Teamsite Web Developer; Product Manager; Global Marketing Manager; Security Product manager; Web Editor; Product Marketing Engineer; Networking Technical Writer. **Corporate headquarters location:** This location. **Listed on:** New York Stock Exchange. **Stock exchange symbol:** NET.

## NETWORK COMPUTING DEVICES, INC.
301 Ravendale Drive, Mountain View CA 94043. 650/694-0650. **Contact:** Human Resources Department. **E-mail address:** resumes@ncd.com. **World Wide Web address:** http://www.ncd.com. **Description:** Provides desktop information access solutions for network computing environments. The company is a leading worldwide supplier of X Window System terminals and PC-X server software products that integrate Microsoft Windows- and DOS-based PCs into X/UNIX networks. The company also supplies the Z-Mail family of cross-platform electronic mail and messaging software for open systems environments, as well as Mariner, an Internet access and navigation software tool that provides a unified interface to all Internet resources. Founded in 1988. **Corporate headquarters location:** This location. **Listed on:** NASDAQ. **Stock exchange symbol:** NCDI.

## NORTEL NETWORKS
4401 Great America Parkway, Santa Clara CA 95052. 408/988-2400. **Contact:** Staffing. **World Wide Web address:** http://www.nortelnetworks.com. **Description:** Designs, produces, and supports multimedia access devices for use in building corporate, public, and Internet networks. The primary focus of the company's services is the consolidation of voice, fax, video, and data and multimedia traffic into a single network link. **Corporate headquarters location:** Ontario, Canada. **Other U.S. locations:** Nationwide. **Listed on:** New

York Stock Exchange; Toronto Stock Exchange. **Stock exchange symbol:** NT. **Annual sales/revenues:** More than $100 million. **Number of employees worldwide:** 70,000.

## NOVELL, INC.
1900 Guadalupe Street, San Jose CA 95131. 408/967-5000. **Recorded jobline:** 800/624-4520. **Contact:** Human Resources. **World Wide Web address:** http://www.novell.com. **Description:** Novell, Inc. develops software tools and systems, works in partnership with other companies, and provides computer network management services. **Corporate headquarters location:** Orem UT. **Other U.S. locations:** Nationwide. **International locations:** Worldwide. **Operations at this facility include:** This location is involved in marketing, software engineering, and administration. **Listed on:** NASDAQ. **Stock exchange symbol:** NOVL. **Number of employees nationwide:** 7,900.

## NOVELLUS SYSTEMS, INC.
4000 North First Street, San Jose CA 95134. 408/943-9700. **Fax:** 408/943-3422. **Contact:** Matt Moscovich, Professional Staffing. **World Wide Web address:** http://www.novellus.com. **Description:** Manufactures semiconductor capital equipment. **NOTE:** Entry-level positions are offered. **Corporate headquarters location:** This location. **Other U.S. locations:** Nationwide. **International locations:** Worldwide. **Operations at this facility include:** Administration; Manufacturing; Research and Development; Sales; Service. **Listed on:** NASDAQ. **Stock exchange symbol:** NVLS. **Annual sales/revenues:** More than $100 million. **Number of employees at this location:** 650. **Number of employees nationwide:** 800. **Number of employees worldwide:** 1,050.

## OBJECTIVITY, INC.
301-B East Evelyn Avenue, Mountain View CA 94041. 650/254-7100. **Contact:** Human Resources. **E-mail address:** hr@objectivity.com. **World Wide Web address:** http://www.objectivity.com. **Description:** Manufactures computer database software. **Corporate headquarters location:** This location.

## ORACLE CORPORATION
500 Oracle Parkway, LTN-1, Redwood Shores CA 94065. 650/506-7000. **Contact:** Recruiting. **E-mail address:** resumes_us@oracle.com. **World Wide Web address:** http://www.oracle.com. **Description:** Designs and manufactures database and information management

software for business, and provides consulting services. **Corporate headquarters location:** This location. **Other U.S. locations:** Nationwide. **Operations at this facility include:** Administration; Sales. **Listed on:** NASDAQ. **Stock exchange symbol:** ORCL. **Number of employees nationwide:** 12,000.

## PC PROFESSIONAL INC.

1615 Webster Street, Oakland CA 94612. 510/465-5700. **Contact:** Human Resources. **E-mail address:** resume@pcprofessional.com. **World Wide Web address:** http://www.pcprofessional.com. **Description:** A value-added reseller of various types of computer hardware to corporate and consumer customers. **Positions advertised include:** Sales Account Manager; Field Service Engineer. **Corporate headquarters location:** This location.

## PEOPLESOFT, INC.

2525 Augustine Drive, Santa Clara CA 95054. 408/982-5700. **Contact:** Human Resources. **E-mail address:** jobs@peoplesoft.com. **World Wide Web address:** http://www.peoplesoft.com. **Description:** Provides client/server applications and software solutions for businesses worldwide. PeopleSoft develops, markets, and supports a variety of enterprise solutions for accounting, materials management, distribution, manufacturing, and human resources. The company also offers industry-specific enterprise solutions to markets including financial services, health care, manufacturing, higher education, the public sector, and the federal government. **Corporate headquarters location:** Pleasanton CA. **Other area locations:** Irvine CA. **Other U.S. locations:** Miami FL; Atlanta GA; Chicago IL; Boston MA; Bethesda MD; Dallas TX. **International locations:** Worldwide. **Listed on:** NASDAQ. **Stock exchange symbol:** PSFT. **Annual sales/revenues:** More than $100 million. **Number of employees nationwide:** 2,500. **Number of employees worldwide:** 3,000.

## PERSONIFY INC.

114 Sansome Street, San Francisco CA 94104. 415/782-2050. **Fax:** 415/544-0318. **Contact:** Carey Simon, Human Resources. **E-mail address:** jobs@personify.com. **World Wide Web address:** http://www.personify.com. **Description:** Develops software that assists companies in monitoring and improving their Internet advertising campaigns. **Corporate headquarters location:** This location.

## PHILIPS ADAC

540 Alder Drive, Milpitas CA 95035. 408/321-9100. **Contact:** Vice President of Human Resources. **E-mail address:** recruit@adaclabs. com. **World Wide Web address:** http://www.adaclabs.com. **Description:** Produces medical diagnostic computer systems and components including state-of-the-art digital radiography image processing, nuclear medicine image processing, and radiation therapy planning systems. **Corporate headquarters location:** This location. **Other U.S. locations:** Washington DC; Philadelphia PA.

## PHOTRONICS INC.

1913 Tarob Court, Milpitas CA 95035. 408/262-0102. **Contact:** Human Resources. **World Wide Web address:** http://www. photronics.com. **Description:** A manufacturer of photomasks for the semiconductor industry. **Corporate headquarters location:** This location.

## PINNACLE SYSTEMS

280 North Bernardo Avenue, Mountain View CA 94043. 650/526-1600. **Contact:** Human Resources. **E-mail address:** resume@ pinnaclesys.com. **World Wide Web address:** http://www. pinnaclesys.com. **Description:** Develops digital and video-editing tools for both professional and consumer markets. Products include DVExtreme, a digital special effects system; and Studio 400, a video-editing system for consumers. **Positions advertised include:** Inventory Control Manager; QA Tester; Technical Writer; Web Editorial Manager; Workgroup Performance Manager. **Corporate headquarters location:** This location. **Listed on:** NASDAQ. **Stock exchange symbol:** PCLE.

## PROMISE TECHNOLOGY INC.

1745 McCandless Drive, Milpitas CA 95035. 408/228-6300. **Fax:** 408/228-6407. **Contact:** Human Resources. **E-mail address:** hr@promise.com. **World Wide Web address:** http://www.promise. com. **Description:** Manufactures high-performance hard drive controller cards for use in IBM computers. **Positions advertised include:** Senior Lab Technician; Senior Engineer; Channel Marketing Manager; Competitive Analysis Technician; Senior Sales OEM Account Executive. **Corporate headquarters location:** This location.

## QANTEL TECHNOLOGIES

3506 Breakwater Court, Hayward CA 94545-3611. 510/731-2080. **Toll-free phone:** 800/666-3686. **Fax:** 510/731-2075. **Contact:**

Human Resources. **E-mail address:** jobs@qantel.com. **World Wide Web address:** http://www.qantel.com. **Description:** Manufactures coprocessor systems and related peripherals. **Positions advertised include:** Applications Software Developer; Java/Web Developer; Manufacturing Software Product Manager; Software Development Project Manager. **Corporate headquarters location:** This location.

## QUADRAMED
22 Pelican Way, San Rafael CA 94901. 415/482-2100. **Contact:** Human Resources Department. **E-mail address:** resume@ quadramed.com. **World Wide Web address:** http://www. quadramed.com. **Description:** Develops and markets specialized decision support software designed to improve the organizational and clinical effectiveness of hospitals, academic medical centers, managed care providers, large physician groups, and other health care providers. **Corporate headquarters location:** This location. **Listed on:** NASDAQ. **Stock exchange symbol:** QMDC.

## QUANTUM CORPORATION
501 Sycamore Drive, Milpitas CA 95035. 408/894-4000. **Contact:** Human Resources. **E-mail address:** jobs@quantum.com. **World Wide Web address:** http://www.quantum.com. **Description:** Designs, manufactures, and markets small hard disk drives used in desktop PCs, workstations, and notebook computers. **Corporate headquarters location:** This location. **Listed on:** New York Stock Exchange. **Stock exchange symbol:** DSS. **Annual sales/revenues:** More than $100 million. **Number of employees nationwide:** 2,455.

## QUICK EAGLE NETWORKS
217 Humboldt Court, Sunnyvale CA 94089-1300. 408/745-6200. **Fax:** 408/745-4516. **E-mail address:** jobs@quickeagle.com. **Contact:** Human Resources. **World Wide Web address:** http://www. quickeagle.com. **Description:** Develops, manufactures, and markets high-speed digital access products for the WAN marketplace. **Corporate headquarters location:** This location.

## QUICKLOGIC CORPORATION
1277 Orleans Drive, Sunnyvale CA 94089-1138. 408/990-4000. **Contact:** Human Resources. **E-mail address:** employment@ quicklogic.com. **World Wide Web address:** http://www.quicklogic. com. **Description:** Manufactures and distributes field programmable logic units. **Corporate headquarters location:** This location. **Listed on:** NASDAQ. **Stock exchange symbol:** QUIK.

## QUICKTURN DESIGN SYSTEMS, INC.
2670 Sealy Avenue, San Jose CA 95134. 408/914-6000. **Contact:** Human Resources. **World Wide Web address:** http://www. quickturn.com. **Description:** A manufacturer of emulation systems, a design verification tool. **Corporate headquarters location:** This location. **Parent company:** Cadence Design Systems, Inc. **Listed on:** New York Stock Exchange. **Stock exchange symbol:** CDN.

## RATIONAL SOFTWARE CORPORATION
18880 Homestead Road, Cupertino CA 95014. 408/863-9900. **Contact:** Human Resources. **World Wide Web address:** http://www.rational.com. **Description:** Develops, markets, and supports embedded software products for Web and e-commerce applications. The company's products operate on both Windows and UNIX systems. **Corporate headquarters location:** This location. **International locations:** Worldwide. **Listed on:** NASDAQ. **Stock exchange symbol:** RATL.

## READ-RITE CORPORATION
44100 Osgood Road, Fremont CA 94539. 408/262-6700. **Contact:** Recruiting Manager. **E-mail address:** rrcstaffing@readrite.com. **World Wide Web address:** http://www.readrite.com. **Description:** An independent supplier of thin-film magnetic recording heads for Winchester disk drives. **Positions advertised include:** Engineering Manager. **Number of employees nationwide:** 2,500. **Corporate headquarters location:** This location. **Listed on:** NASDAQ. **Stock exchange symbol:** RDRT.

## SAP AMERICA, INC.
950 Tower Lane, 12th Floor, Foster City CA 94404. 650/637-1655. **Contact:** Human Resources. **World Wide Web address:** http://www. sap.com. **Description:** Develops a variety of client/server computer software packages including programs for finance, human resources, and materials management applications. **Corporate headquarters location:** Newtown Square PA. **Other U.S. locations:** Nationwide. **International locations:** Germany. **Parent company:** SAP AG. **Listed on:** New York Stock Exchange. **Stock exchange symbol:** SAP. **Number of employees nationwide:** 3,000. **Number of employees worldwide:** 13,000.

## SANDISK CORPORATION
140 Caspian Court, Sunnyvale CA 94089. 408/542-0500. **Fax:** 408/542-0604. **Contact:** Human Resources. **E-mail address:**

careers@sandisk.com. **World Wide Web address:** http://www. sandisk.com. **Description:** Manufactures computer components including memory cards. **Corporate headquarters location:** This location. **Listed on:** NASDAQ. **Stock exchange symbol:** SNDK. **Annual sales/revenues:** More than $100 million.

## SAPIENT CORPORATION
101 California Street, 5th Floor, San Francisco CA 94111. 415/263-4000. **Contact:** Director of Hiring. **World Wide Web address:** http://www.sapient.com. **Description:** Provides systems integration, consulting, and software integration services. Founded in 1991. **Corporate headquarters location:** Cambridge MA. **Other area locations:** Los Angeles CA. **Other U.S. locations:** Denver CO; Washington DC; Chicago IL; Portland ME; Minneapolis MN; Jersey City NJ; Austin TX; Dallas TX. **International locations:** Australia; England; Germany; India; Italy; Japan. **Listed on:** NASDAQ. **Stock exchange symbol:** SAPE. **Annual sales/revenues:** More than $100 million.

## SIEBEL SYSTEMS, INC.
2207 Bridgepoint Parkway, San Mateo CA 94404. 650/295-5000. **Toll-free phone:** 800/647-4300. **Contact:** Human Resources. **World Wide Web address:** http://www.siebel.com. **Description:** A leading provider of e-commerce application software. **Positions advertised include:** International Tax Analyst; Human Resources Call Center Specialist; Principal Analyst; Senior Compensation Analyst; Principal Consultant; Product Manager, Interactive Selling; Analyst Relations Manager. **Corporate headquarters location:** This location. **Listed on:** NASDAQ. **Stock exchange symbol:** SEBL. **Annual sales/revenues:** More than $100 million. **Number of employees worldwide:** 4,500.

## SILICON GRAPHICS INC. (SGI)
1600 Amphitheatre Parkway, Mountain View CA 94043. 650/960-1980. **Contact:** Human Resources. **World Wide Web address:** http://www.sgi.com. **Description:** Manufactures a family of workstation and server systems that are used by engineers, scientists, and other creative professionals to develop, analyze, and simulate complex, three-dimensional objects. **Positions advertised include:** GUI Software Engineer; MTS Designer. **Corporate headquarters location:** This location. **Listed on:** New York Stock Exchange. **Stock exchange symbol:** SGI.

## SMART MODULAR TECHNOLOGIES
4305 Cushing Parkway, Fremont CA 94538. 510/623-1231. **Contact:** Human Resources Department. **E-mail address:** career@ smartm.com. **World Wide Web address:** http://www.smartm.com. **Description:** Manufactures and distributes computer components including PC cards and memory modules. **Corporate headquarters location:** This location. **Parent company:** Selectron. **Listed on:** New York Stock Exchange. **Stock exchange symbol:** SLR.

## SONICBLUE
2841 Mission College Boulevard, Santa Clara CA 95054. 408/588-8000. **Contact:** Human Resources. **E-mail address:** jobs@sonicblue.com. **World Wide Web address:** http://www.sonicblue.com. **Description:** An Internet appliance company that designs graphics subsystems, network connectivity products, and sound accelerators. Founded in 1989. **Positions advertised include:** Senior Staff Engineer. **Corporate headquarters location:** This location. **Listed on:** NASDAQ. **Stock exchange symbol:** SBLU.

## SPEAR TECHNOLOGIES
436 14th Street, Suite 200, Oakland CA 94612. 510/267-3333. **Contact:** Human Resources. **E-mail address:** jobs@ speartechnologies.com. **World Wide Web address:** http://www. speartechnologies.com. **Description:** Develops, markets, and supports a line of maintenance management software for the transportation industry. **Positions advertised include:** Project Implementation Manager; Senior Software Engineer; Software Engineer; Proposal Manager. **Corporate headquarters location:** This location. **Other U.S. locations:** Hartford CT. **International locations:** Netherlands. **Number of employees at this location:** 225.

## SPECTRAL DYNAMICS INC.
1010 Timothy Drive, San Jose CA 95133. 408/918-2500. **Contact:** Personnel. **World Wide Web address:** http://www.sd-corp.com. **Description:** Specializes in the design and manufacture of computer-controlled test, measurement, and development systems and software for a wide variety of customers in three high-tech markets: electronic equipment manufacturers, mechanical equipment manufacturers, and semiconductor manufacturers. Products are used for design verification testing and process improvement. **Corporate headquarters location:** This location. **Parent company:** Carrier Corporation.

## SUN MICROSYSTEMS, INC.
100 California Street, Suite 800, San Francisco CA 94111. 415/781-8140. **Toll-free phone:** 800/555-9786. **Contact:** Human Resources Department. **E-mail address:** resumes@sun.com. **World Wide Web address:** http://www.sun.com. **Description:** Produces high-performance computer systems, workstations, servers, CPUs, peripherals, and operating system software. The company developed its own microprocessor called SPARC. Most products are sold to engineering, scientific, technical, and commercial markets worldwide. **NOTE:** Please send all employment-related correspondence to: 901 San Antonio Road, UMIL 15-106, Palo Alto CA 94303. **Corporate headquarters location:** Palo Alto CA. **Subsidiaries include:** Forte Software Inc. manufactures enterprise application integration software. **Listed on:** NASDAQ. **Stock exchange symbol:** SUNW.

## SUN MICROSYSTEMS, INC.
901 San Antonio Road, UMIL 15-106, Palo Alto CA 94303. 650/960-1300. **Toll-free phone:** 800/555-9786. **Contact:** Human Resources. **World Wide Web address:** http://www.sun.com. **Description:** Produces high-performance computer systems, workstations, servers, CPUs, peripherals, and operating systems software. Products are sold to engineering, scientific, technical, and commercial markets worldwide. **Corporate headquarters location:** This location. **Subsidiaries include:** Forte Software Inc. manufactures enterprise application integration software. **Listed on:** NASDAQ. **Stock exchange symbol:** SUNW. **Number of employees nationwide:** 26,300.

## SYBASE, INC.
5000 Hacienda Drive, Dublin CA 94568. 510/922-3500. **Contact:** Human Resources. **World Wide Web address:** http://www.sybase.com. **Description:** Develops, markets, and supports a full line of relational database management software products and services for integrated, enterprisewide information management systems. **Positions advertised include:** Senior Executive Administrative Associate; Senior HR Manager; Senior Information Security Analyst; Senior Systems Manager; Systems Consultant; Senior Product Manager. **Corporate headquarters location:** This location. **Listed on:** New York Stock Exchange. **Stock exchange symbol:** SY. **Number of employees at this location:** 2,350.

## SYMANTEC CORPORATION

20300 Stevens Creek Boulevard, Cupertino CA 95014. 408/253-9600. **Contact:** Human Resources Staffing. **E-mail address:** jobs@symantec.com. **World Wide Web address:** http://www.symantec.com. **Description:** Symantec Corporation is a global organization that develops, manufactures, and markets software products for individuals and businesses. The company is a vendor of utility software for stand-alone and networked personal computers. In addition, the company offers a wide range of project management products, productivity applications, and development languages and tools. The company is organized into several product groups that are devoted to product marketing, engineering, technical support, quality assurance, and documentation. Founded in 1982. **Special programs:** Internships. **Corporate headquarters location:** This location. **Operations at this facility include:** This location houses finance, sales, and marketing operations. **Listed on:** NASDAQ. **Stock exchange symbol:** SYMC. **Number of employees nationwide:** 1,200.

## SYMBOL TECHNOLOGIES, INC.

6480 Via Del Oro, Mail Stop 21-B, San Jose CA 95119. 408/528-2700. **Contact:** Human Resources. **E-mail address:** jobopps@symbol.com. **World Wide Web address:** http://www.symbol.com. **Description:** Designs, manufactures, and sells various lines of portable and nonportable computers and systems for business information and bill collection applications. Clients include retail food stores, drug stores, and hardware stores. **NOTE:** Resumes should be sent to Human Resources Department, Symbol Technologies, Inc., One Symbol Plaza, Holtsville NY 11742-1300. **Positions advertised include:** Senior Systems Verification Manager; Software Development Manager; Senior Software Engineer; Wireless Systems Analyst; Field Service Representative; Software Engineer; Director of Product Development. **Corporate headquarters location:** Holtsville NY. **Operations at this facility include:** Education; Repairs; Sales; Systems/Software Services. **Listed on:** New York Stock Exchange. **Stock exchange symbol:** SBL.

## SYNOPSYS INC.

700 East Middlefield Road, Mountain View CA 94043. 650/962-5000. **Toll-free phone:** 800/541-7737. **Contact:** Human Resources Department. **E-mail address:** employment@synopsys.com. **World Wide Web address:** http://www.synopsys.com. **Description:** Develops, markets, and supports high-level design automation software for designers of integrated circuits and electronic systems.

**Positions advertised include:** Staff R&D Engineer; Vice President, Merging and Acquisitions; Senior Member of Technical Staff; Senior Applications Consultant; Senior Credit Advisor; Sales Analyst. **Corporate headquarters location:** This location. **Listed on:** NASDAQ. **Stock exchange symbol:** SNPS. **Number of employees at this location:** 415.

## TELEATLAS NORTH AMERICA

1605 Adams Drive, Menlo Park CA 94025. 650/328-3825. **Contact:** Human Resources. **E-mail address:** hr-na@na.teleatlas.com. **World Wide Web address:** http://www.teleatlas.com. **Description:** Develops digital mapping software for the automotive and transportation industries. **Corporate headquarters location:** Hertogenbosch, the Netherlands.

## TERADYNE, INC.

880 Fox Lane, San Jose CA 95131-1685. 408/437-9700. **Contact:** Personnel Department. **E-mail address:** resume@teradyne.com. **World Wide Web address:** http://www.teradyne.com. **Description:** Teradyne manufactures in-circuit testers, automated inspection systems (optical), and probe testers for printed circuit board manufacturers. **Corporate headquarters location:** Boston MA.

## THERMA-WAVE, INC.

1250 Reliance Way, Fremont CA 94539. 510/490-3663. **Fax:** 510/661-6836. **Recorded jobline:** 510/668-2JOB. **Contact:** Julie Venierakis, Manager of Human Resources. **E-mail address:** careers@ thermawave.com. **World Wide Web address:** http://www. thermawave.com. **Description:** Manufactures semiconductor testing equipment. **Corporate headquarters location:** This location. **Other U.S. locations:** AZ; CO; FL; MA; OR; TX. **International locations:** England; France; Italy; Japan; Korea; Scotland; Taiwan. **Listed on:** NASDAQ. **Stock exchange symbol:** TWAV. **Annual sales/revenues:** $51 - $100 million. **Number of employees at this location:** 200.

## 3COM CORPORATION

5400 Bayfront Plaza, Santa Clara CA 95052. 408/326-5000. **Contact:** Human Resources. **World Wide Web address:** http:// www.3com.com. **Description:** 3Com is a *Fortune* 500 company delivering global data networking solutions to organizations around the world. 3Com designs, manufactures, markets, and supports a broad range of ISO 9000-compliant global data networking solutions including routers, hubs, remote access servers, switches, and adapters for Ethernet, Token Ring, and high-speed networks. These products enable computers to communicate at high speeds and share resources including printers, disk drives, modems, and minicomputers. **Corporate headquarters location:** This location. **Listed on:** NASDAQ. **Stock exchange symbol:** COMS.

**3DO COMPANY**
100 Cardinal Way, Redwood City CA 94063-4746. 650/385-3000. **Contact:** Human Resources Manager. **World Wide Web address:** http://www.3do.com. **Description:** Develops video game software for multiple platforms. Products include Legend of Might and Magic, Heroes Chronicles, World Destruction League, and Army Men. **Positions advertised include:** Senior Artist; Senior Engineer; Physics Engineer. **Corporate headquarters location:** This location. **Listed on:** NASDAQ. **Stock exchange symbol:** THDO.

**TRIDENT MICROSYSTEMS**
1090 East Arques Avenue, Sunnyvale CA 94085. 408/991-8800. **Fax:** 408/733-2087. **Contact:** Staffing Representative. **E-mail address:** hr@tridentmicro.com. **World Wide Web address:** http://www.tridentmicro.com. **Description:** Designs, develops, and markets integrated graphics ICs and multimedia audio/visual chips for PCs. Founded in 1987. **Positions advertised include:** Financial Analyst; Design Engineer; Hardware Design Engineer; Logic Design Engineer; Senior Design Engineer; Senior Software Engineer; Software Manager; Application Engineer; Network Engineer. **Corporate headquarters location:** This location. **Other U.S. locations:** Chandler AZ. **Operations at this facility include:** Sales; Technical Support. **Listed on:** NASDAQ. **Stock exchange symbol:** TRID. **Number of employees at this location:** 300. **Number of employees nationwide:** 400.

**VERIFONE, INC.**
2455 Augustine Drive, Santa Clara CA 95054. 408/330-6300. **Contact:** Human Resources. **E-mail address:** jobs@verifone.com. **World Wide Web address:** http://www.verifone.com. **Description:** VeriFone develops, manufactures, and services software for electronic payment systems that are used in a variety of industries including consumer, financial, and health care. **Positions advertised include:** Hardware Design Engineer; Software Engineer; Sales Account Manager. **Corporate headquarters location:** This location. **Parent company:** Hewlett-Packard Company.

## VERITAS SOFTWARE CORPORATION

350 Ellis Street, Mountain View CA 94043. 650/527-8000. **Contact:** Human Resources. **E-mail address:** jobs@veritas.com. **World Wide Web address:** http://www.veritas.com. **Description:** Designs, develops, and markets enterprise data and storage management software. The company's products are designed to improve system performance and to reduce administration costs. **Positions advertised include:** Call Center Technology Engineer; Commission Analyst; Director of Pricing; Contracts Manager; Media Specialist; Finance Manager. **Corporate headquarters location:** This location. **Listed on:** NASDAQ. **Stock exchange symbol:** VRTS.

## VERITY INC.

894 Ross Drive, Sunnyvale CA 94089. 408/541-1500. **Contact:** Human Resources Department. **E-mail address:** resumes@verity.com. **World Wide Web address:** http://www.verity.com. **Description:** Develops and markets software tools and applications for searching, retrieving, and filtering information on the Internet. **Positions advertised include:** Product Manager; Sales Development Representative; Systems Engineer; Software Engineer. **Corporate headquarters location:** This location. **Listed on:** NASDAQ. **Stock exchange symbol:** VRTY.

## WIND RIVER SYSTEMS

500 Wind River Way, Alameda CA 94501. 510/748-4100. **Contact:** Human Resources. **World Wide Web address:** http://www.wrs.com. **Description:** A software engineering and development firm. **Corporate headquarters location:** This location. **Listed on:** NASDAQ. **Stock exchange symbol:** WIND.

## WYSE TECHNOLOGY

3471 North First Street, San Jose CA 95134. 408/473-1200. **Contact:** Human Resources. **E-mail address:** careers@wyse.com. **World Wide Web address:** http://www.wyse.com. **Description:** Manufactures workstations that access information from a server rather than from a hard drive. **Corporate headquarters location:** This location. **CEO:** Douglas Chance. **Facilities Manager:** Lee Perry.

## XILINX, INC.

2100 Logic Drive, San Jose CA 95124. 408/559-7778. **Contact:** Ms. Chris Taylor, Vice President of Human Resources. **E-mail address:** jobs@xilinx.com. **World Wide Web address:** http://www.xilinx.com. **Description:** A leading supplier of field programmable gate arrays and related development system software used by electronic systems manufacturers. **Special programs:** Internships. **Corporate headquarters location:** This location. **Operations at this facility include:** Administration; Manufacturing; Research and Development; Sales; Service. **Listed on:** NASDAQ. **Stock exchange symbol:** XLNX. **Number of employees at this location:** 850. **Number of employees nationwide:** 900.

### YAHOO! INC.
701 First Avenue, Sunnyvale CA 94089. 408/731-3300. **Fax:** 408/349-3301. **Contact:** Nancy Larocca, Staffing Manager. **World Wide Web address:** http://www.yahoo.com. **Description:** A global Internet communications, commerce, and media company that offers a comprehensive branded network of services to millions of users each month. Founded in 1994. **NOTE:** The company does not accept phone calls regarding employment. **Positions advertised include:** Senior Financial Analyst; Yahoo! Personals Media Performance Analyst; US Market Research Analyst; Staffing Assistant; Product Manager; International Human Resources Program Manager; Campaign Manager. **Special programs:** Internships. **Office hours:** Monday - Friday, 8:00 a.m. - 6:00 p.m. **Corporate headquarters location:** This location. **Other U.S. locations:** Nationwide. **International locations:** Asia; Central America; Europe; South America. **Listed on:** NASDAQ. **Stock exchange symbol:** YHOO. **Number of employees at this location:** 1,300. **Number of employees nationwide:** 1,600. **Number of employees worldwide:** 2,000.

## EDUCATIONAL SERVICES

**You can expect to find the following types of facilities in this chapter:**
*Business/Secretarial/Data Processing Schools •*
*Colleges/Universities/Professional Schools • Community Colleges/Technical*
*Schools/Vocational Schools • Elementary and Secondary Schools •*
*Preschool and Child Daycare Services*

### ALLIANT INTERNATIONAL UNIVERSITY
1000 South Fremont Avenue, Alhambra CA 91803. 415/346-4500. **Contact:** Human Resources. **E-mail address:** jobs@alliant.edu. **World Wide Web address:** http://www.alliant.edu. **Description:** Offers undergraduate and graduate degree programs in liberal arts, education, business, and behavioral and social sciences. **Positions advertised include:** Assistant to the Vice Provost and Dean; Director of Clinical Training; Receptionist; Math Learning Specialist; Major Gifts Director; Reference and Instruction Librarian; Writing and Reading Learning Specialist. **Corporate headquarters location:** This location. **Other area locations:** Fresno CA; Irvine CA; Los Angeles CA; Sacramento CA; San Diego CA; San Francisco CA. **International locations:** Nairobi, Kenya; Mexico City, Mexico. **Number of employees at this location:** 30. **Number of employees nationwide:** 1,100.

### CALIFORNIA COLLEGE OF PODIATRIC MEDICINE
370 Hawthorne Avenue, Oakland CA 94609. 510/869-6511. **Contact:** Director of Human Resources. **World Wide Web address:** http://www.ccpm.edu. **Description:** A college/teaching hospital offering postgraduate programs in the field of podiatry.

### CALIFORNIA CULINARY ACADEMY, INC.
625 Polk Street, San Francisco CA 94102. 415/771-3536. **Contact:** Human Resources. **World Wide Web address:** http://www. baychef.com. **Description:** One of the largest accredited schools for professional chef training in the United States. The academy offers instruction in classic and modern methods of food preparation in its core degree program, specialized baking and pastry certificate programs, and a full range of classes for cooking and wine enthusiasts. Founded in 1977. **Corporate headquarters location:** This location. **Listed on:** NASDAQ. **Stock exchange symbol:** COOK.

## CALIFORNIA STATE UNIVERSITY, HAYWARD

25800 Carlos Bee Boulevard, Hayward CA 94542-3026. 510/885-3000. **Contact:** Dr. Elinor Nelson, Director of Personnel. **E-mail address:** enelson@csuhayward.com. **World Wide Web address:** http://www.csuhayward.edu. **Description:** One of 23 campuses of the California State University System. California State University, Hayward offers 37 bachelor's degree programs and 26 master's degree programs. **Positions advertised include:** Assistant and Associate Professors of Agriculture, Business, Communication, Computer Science, Education, along with others. **Other area locations:** Concord CA.

## ERNEST ORLANDO LAWRENCE BERKELEY NATIONAL LABORATORY

One Cyclotron Road, Mail Stop 937-600, Berkeley CA 94720. 510/486-7950. **Contact:** Lori Fong, Recruitment Manager. **E-mail address:** employment@lbl.gov. **World Wide Web address:** http://www.lbl.gov. **Description:** A multiprogram national research facility operated by the University of California for the Department of Energy. The oldest of the nine national laboratories, the company's major activities include the Advanced Light Source, Human Genome Center, California Institute for Energy Efficiency, and the Center for Advanced Materials. **Positions advertised include:** Administrative Assistant; Scientist; Engineer. **Special programs:** Internships. **Corporate headquarters location:** This location. **Operations at this facility include:** Administration; Research and Development. **Number of employees at this location:** 3,000.

## FOOTHILL - DE ANZA COMMUNITY COLLEGE DISTRICT

12345 El Monte Road, Los Altos Hills CA 94022. 650/949-6217. **Recorded jobline:** 650/949-6218. **Contact:** Personnel. **E-mail address:** employment@fhda.edu. **World Wide Web address:** http://www.fhda.edu. **Description:** A nonprofit community college district comprised of Foothill College (also at this location) and De Anza College (Cupertino CA). Foothill College offers associate in arts, associate in science, certificate, and transfer programs in over 80 areas of study. De Anza Community College offers two-year degrees and certificate programs in approximately 100 areas of study. **NOTE:** Entry-level positions and part-time jobs are offered. **Positions advertised include:** Vice Chancellor of Business Services; Medical Laboratory Technician Coordinator; Automotive Machining and Engines Instructor; Automotive Powertrain Instructor; Police Officer; Theatre Fine Arts Faculties Assistant. **Corporate headquarters**

**location:** This location. **Annual sales/revenues:** More than $100 million. **Number of employees at this location:** 2,500.

## FREMONT UNIFIED SCHOOL DISTRICT (FUSD)
4210 Technology Drive, Fremont CA 94538. 510/657-2350. **Contact:** Human Resources. **World Wide Web address:** http://www.fremont.k12.ca.us. **Description:** A school district comprised of 31 elementary schools, 6 junior high schools, and 12 high schools. **Number of employees nationwide:** 1,250.

## KNOWLEDGE LEARNING CORPORATION (KLC)
4340 Redwood Highway, Building B, San Rafael CA 94903-2121. 415/444-1600. **Contact:** Human Resources. **E-mail address:** familyservices@klcorp.com. **World Wide Web address:** http://www.knowledgelearning.com. **Description:** Operates one of the largest chains of childcare centers in the United States with more than 150 childcare centers in 15 states. KLC's community schools operate under the names Children's Discovery Centers, Magic Years, Learning Universe, and Hildebrandt Learning Centers. **Corporate headquarters location:** This location. **Parent company:** Knowledge Universe.

## LA PETITE ACADEMY
3891 Lakeside Drive, Richmond CA 94806. 916/276-3766. **Toll-free phone:** 800/LAPETITE. **Fax:** 916/721-1884. **Contact:** Human Resources. **World Wide Web address:** http://www.lapetite.com. **Description:** A provider of preschool and elementary school education. **Positions advertised include:** Academy Director.

## MARIN COMMUNITY COLLEGE (COLLEGE OF MARIN)
835 College Avenue, Kentfield CA 94904. 415/485-9340. **Fax:** 415/485-0135. **Recorded jobline:** 415/485-9693. **E-mail address:** hrjobs@marin.cc.ca.us. **World Wide Web address:** http://www.marin.cc.ca.us. **Description:** A community college. **Positions advertised include:** Police Officer.

## MILLS COLLEGE
5000 MacArthur Boulevard, Oakland CA 94613. 510/430-2282. **Fax:** 510/430-3314. **Recorded jobline:** 510/430-2012. **Contact:** Personnel Department. **E-mail address:** hire@mills.edu. **World Wide Web address:** http://www.mills.edu. **Description:** An independent liberal arts college for women offering bachelors and master's degrees. Founded in 1852. **Positions advertised include:** Head

Teacher of Kindergarten; Financial Aide Counselor and Systems Specialist; On-Call Cook; Area Coordinator; Relief Public Safety Officer; Relief Van Driver.

**OHLONE COLLEGE**
43600 Mission Boulevard, P.O. Box 3909, Fremont CA 94539. 510/659-6088. **Fax:** 510/659-6025. **Recorded jobline:** 510/656-8295. **Contact:** Human Resources. **World Wide Web address:** http://www.ohlone.cc.ca.us. **Description:** A college offering both undergraduate and graduate degrees. **Positions advertised include:** Executive Director of College Advancement; Skilled Maintenance Mechanic; Collaboration Specialist; Health Sciences Skills Lab Coordinator. **Other area locations:** Newark CA. **Number of employees at this location:** 550.

**SAN FRANCISCO STATE UNIVERSITY**
1600 Holloway Avenue, ADM 252, San Francisco CA 94132. 415/338-1872. **Contact:** Human Resources. **World Wide Web address:** http://www.sfsu.edu. **Description:** A four-year, state university. San Francisco State University offers 115 bachelor's degree programs, 93 master's degree programs, a Ph.D. and Ed.D. in education with University of California Berkeley, a master's of science in physical therapy with University of California San Francisco, 28 credential programs, and 22 certificate programs. **NOTE:** Entry-level positions are offered. **Special programs:** Internships. **Parent company:** California State University System. **Number of employees at this location:** 3,000.

**SANTA CLARA UNIVERSITY**
500 El Camino Real, Santa Clara CA 95053. 408/554-4000. **Contact:** Director of Personnel. **World Wide Web address:** http://www.scu.edu. **Description:** A four-year university offering undergraduate programs through its schools of Arts and Sciences, Business, Engineering, and Education. The university also offers graduate programs through its schools of Law, Engineering, Business, Agricultural Business, and Counseling Psychology. **Positions advertised include:** Administrative Assistant; Assistant Dean of Finance and Operation; Associate Campus Minister; Campus Safety Officer; Resident Minister; Substitute Pre-School Teacher; Assistant Director. **Corporate headquarters location:** This location.

## SIERRA COMMUNITY COLLEGE

5000 Rocklin Road, Rocklin CA 95677. 916/781-0520. **Toll-free phone:** 800/242-4004. **Contact:** Peter Kolster, Associate Vice President of Human Resources. **World Wide Web address:** http://www.sierra.cc.ca.us. **Description:** A community college. **Positions advertised include:** Organic Chemistry Instructor; Part Time Anthropology Instructor; ESL Faculty Member. **Operations at this facility include:** Administration; Divisional Headquarters. **Number of employees at this location:** 450.

## STANFORD UNIVERSITY

300 Pasteor Drive, Stanford CA 94305. 650/723-1888. **Contact:** Human Resources. **E-mail address:** empwebsite@forsythe. stanford. edu. **World Wide Web address:** http://www.stanford.edu. **Description:** A private university offering undergraduate programs through its schools of Humanities and Sciences, Engineering, and Earth Sciences. Stanford University also offers graduate programs through its professional schools of Law, Medicine, Business, and Education. Founded in 1885.

## UNIVERSITY OF CALIFORNIA, BERKELEY

2200 University Avenue, #3540, Berkeley CA 94720. 510/642-1011. **Contact:** Campus Personnel. **E-mail address:** applyucb@uclink.berkeley.edu. **World Wide Web address:** http://www.berkeley.edu. **Description:** A university offering undergraduate and graduate programs in various liberal arts and professional fields. The university is a leader in teaching, research, and public service. Undergraduate divisions include the colleges of Chemistry, Engineering, Environmental Design, Letters and Science, and Natural Resources. Founded in 1868. **NOTE:** Please be sure to include the job number in the subject heading of your e-mail. **Positions advertised include:** Lead Parking Representative; Senior Automotive Equipment Operator; Police Officer; Junior Development Engineer; Associate Development Engineer; Senior Administrative Analyst. **Operations at this facility include:** Administration; Research and Development.

## UNIVERSITY OF CALIFORNIA, DAVIS

Employment Office, One Shields Avenue, Davis CA 95616. 530/752-0530. **Recorded jobline:** 530/752-1760. **Contact:** Personnel. **E-mail address:** apply@ucdavis.edu. **World Wide Web address:** http://www.ucdavis.edu. **Description:** A university offering various degrees through its colleges of Agricultural and Environmental Sciences,

Engineering, and Letters and Science; Graduate School of Management; School of Law; School of Medicine; and School of Veterinary Medicine. **Positions advertised include:** Admissions Support Assistant; Student Loan Exit Interview Counselor; Purchasing Assistant; Undergraduate and Graduate Advising Assistant; Programmatic Assistant; Front Desk and Admissions Assistant; Material Expeditor.

## UNIVERSITY OF SAN FRANCISCO
2130 Fulton Street, San Francisco CA 94117-1080. 415/422-6707. **Fax:** 415/386-1074. **Recorded jobline:** 415/422-5600. **Contact:** Ingrid Coco, Human Resources. **E-mail address:** resumes@usfca.edu. **World Wide Web address:** http://www.usfca.edu. **Description:** Established as one of San Francisco's first universities, the University of San Francisco serves approximately 8,000 students in the schools of arts and sciences, business, education, nursing, law, and professional studies. The university is a nonprofit, private, Catholic and Jesuit institution. Founded in 1855. **Positions advertised include:** Assistant Librarian; Dean; Director of Graduate Admission. **Corporate headquarters location:** This location. **Other area locations:** Cupertino CA; Sacramento CA; San Ramon CA; Santa Rosa CA. **Operations at this facility include:** Administration. **President/CEO/Owner:** Father Schlegel, S.J. **Number of employees at this location:** 1,100.

## WESTED
730 Harrison Street, San Francisco CA 94107. 415/565-3000. **Toll-free phone:** 877/4-WESTED. **Fax:** 415/565-3012. **Contact:** Personnel Manager. **E-mail address:** jobs@wested.org. **World Wide Web address:** http://www.wested.org. **Description:** WestEd is a nonprofit educational agency focused on improving the quality of education by helping policy makers and practitioners apply knowledge from research, development, and practice. Founded in 1966. **NOTE:** Jobseekers should send resumes to Ann Williams, Personnel Manager, 4665 Lampson Avenue, Los Alamitos CA 90720. **Positions advertised include:** Senior Development Associate; Senior Assessment Manager. **Corporate headquarters location:** This location. **Other U.S. locations:** Tucson AZ. **Number of employees at this location:** 145. **Number of employees nationwide:** 165.

## ELECTRONIC/INDUSTRIAL ELECTRICAL EQUIPMENT

**You can expect to find the following types of companies in this chapter:**
*Electronic Machines and Systems • Semiconductor Manufacturers*

### ADT SECURITY SERVICES
3551 Arden Road, Hayward CA 94545-3922. 510/785-2912. **Toll-free phone:** 800/228-0530. **Contact:** Human Resources Department. **World Wide Web address:** http://www.adtsecurityservices.com. **Description:** Designs, programs, markets, and installs protective systems to safeguard life and property from hazards such as burglary, hold-up, and fire. ADT Security Services has over 180,000 customers in the United States, Canada, and Western Europe. **Corporate headquarters location:** Boca Raton FL.

### ADVANCED MICRO DEVICES, INC. (AMD)
One AMD Place, P.O. Box 3453, Sunnyvale CA 94088-3453. 408/732-2400. **Contact:** Human Resources Department. **E-mail address:** jobs@amd.com. **World Wide Web address:** http://www. amd.com. **Description:** Advanced Micro Devices, Inc. designs, develops, manufactures, and markets complex, monolithic integrated circuits for use by electronic equipment and systems manufacturers in instrument applications and products involved in computation and communications. **Positions advertised include:** Auditor; Customer Marketing Manager; Executive Assistant; Lead Source Manager; Senior Administrative Assistant; Senior Customer Marketing Analyst. **Corporate headquarters location:** This location. **Other area locations:** Los Angeles CA; Pleasanton CA; Sacramento CA; San Diego CA; San Jose CA. **International locations:** Worldwide. **Number of employees nationwide:** 13,000.

### ALTERA CORPORATION
101 Innovation Drive, San Jose CA 95134-1941. 408/544-7000. **Fax:** 408/544-8303. **Contact:** Staffing. **E-mail address:** hr@altera.com. **World Wide Web address:** http://www.altera.com. **Description:** Designs and develops high-performance, high-density programmable logic devices (PLDs) and associated computer-aided engineering (CAE) logic development tools. These products are used in a variety of areas including telecommunications, data communications, computers, and industrial applications. Founded in 1983. **Positions advertised include:** Administrative Assistant; Applications Engineer; Buyer; Customer Marketing Manager; Customer Quality Senior

Engineer; Layout Designer; Quality Engineer; Technical Account Engineer; Senior Training Engineer. **Special programs:** Internships. **Corporate headquarters location:** This location. **International locations:** Canada; Japan; Malaysia; United Kingdom. **Listed on:** NASDAQ. **Stock exchange symbol:** ALTR. **Annual sales/revenues:** More than $100 million. **Number of employees at this location:** 700. **Number of employees worldwide:** 1,100.

### AMPEX CORPORATION
1228 Douglas Avenue, Redwood City CA 94063. 650/367-4111. **Contact:** Human Resources. **E-mail address:** info@ampex.com. **World Wide Web address:** http://www.ampex.com. **Description:** A manufacturer of video technology for the professional television, mass data storage, and instrumentation industries. Products include recorders, editors, switchers, special effects, robotic libraries, tapes, and interconnect equipment. **Subsidiaries include:** iNEXTV; Ampex Data Systems; MicroNet Technologies. **Corporate headquarters location:** This location. **Operations at this facility include:** Administration; Divisional Headquarters; Research and Development; Sales; Service. **Listed on:** American Stock Exchange. **Stock exchange symbol:** AXC.

### ANALOG DEVICES, INC.
1500 Space Park Drive, Santa Clara CA 95052. 408/727-9222. **Toll-free phone:** 800/446-6212. **Contact:** Personnel. **E-mail address:** candidates.hr@analog.com. **World Wide Web address:** http://www.analog.com. **Description:** Analog Devices is a *Fortune* 500 company that designs, manufactures, and markets a broad line of high-performance analog, mixed-signal, and digital integrated circuits (ICs) that address a wide range of real-world signal processing applications. The company's principal product is the general purpose, standard linear ICs. The company's largest communications application is the pan-European GSM (Global System for Mobile Communications) digital cellular telephone system. The company has direct sales offices in 17 countries including the United States. **Corporate headquarters location:** Norwood MA. **Other U.S. locations:** Greensboro NC; Austin TX. **International locations:** Worldwide. **Operations at this facility include:** This location is a sales office.

### ARROW CMS DISTRIBUTION GROUP
1680 McCandless Drive, Milpitas CA 95035. 408/441-4050. **Contact:** Human Resources. **World Wide Web address:** http://www.

arrow.com. **Description:** An industrial distributor of electronic products. Products are distributed through 24 distribution centers and 5 sales offices throughout the United States. The company focuses on advanced technology, semiconductors, and disk drive products, and also provides materials and manufacturing management services to its customers. **Parent company:** Arrow Electronics, Inc. **Other area locations:** Statewide. **Other U.S. locations:** Nationwide. **Operations at this facility include:** Administration; Sales; Service. **Listed on:** New York Stock Exchange. **Stock exchange symbol:** ARW. **Number of employees at this location:** 300.

### ARROW ELECTRONICS
3000 Bowers Avenue, Santa Clara CA 95051. 408/764-7750. **Contact:** Personnel Department. **World Wide Web address:** http://www.arrow.com. **Description:** Engaged in the distribution of selected lines of electronic supplies and components primarily to the electronics and computer industries, as well as to military and aerospace industries. Principal products include semiconductors, capacitors, resistors, and various computer products such as printers, video display terminals, and other products supplied by major computer manufacturing firms. **Corporate headquarters location:** Melville NY. **Operations at this facility include:** Administration; Sales; Service. **Listed on:** New York Stock Exchange. **Stock exchange symbol:** ARW.

### ARTESYN TECHNOLOGIES
47173 Benecia Street, Fremont CA 94538. 510/657-6700. **Contact:** Human Resources. **World Wide Web address:** http://www.artesyn.com. **Description:** Manufactures both standard and custom electronic products used in an array of applications including powering communications networks, controlling the manufacture of fiber optics, enabling voice messaging, providing multimedia power for global Internet servers, and operating traffic signals with real-time embedded computers. **Corporate headquarters location:** Boca Raton FL. **Other U.S. locations:** Eden Prairie MN; Redwood Falls MN. **International locations:** Germany. **Listed on:** NASDAQ. **Stock exchange symbol:** ATSN. **Number of employees worldwide:** 6,500.

### ATMEL CORPORATION
2325 Orchard Parkway, San Jose CA 95131. 408/441-0311. **Contact:** Human Resources. **E-mail address:** hr@atmel.com. **World Wide Web address:** http://www.atmel.com. **Description:**

Manufactures semiconductors including integrated microcircuits. **Positions advertised include:** Finance Accountant; Design Engineer; Product Marketing Engineer; Quality/Reliability Engineer. **Corporate headquarters location:** This location. **Other U.S. locations:** Colorado Springs CO; Irving TX. **International locations:** England; France; Germany. **Listed on:** NASDAQ. **Stock exchange symbol:** ATML.

### AVNET, INC.
2105 Lundey Avenue, San Jose CA 95131. 408/435-7770. **Contact:** Human Resources. **E-mail address:** human-resources@avnet.com. **World Wide Web address:** http://www.avnet.com. **Description:** A multiregional distributor of a wide variety of electronic products including wire and cable, connectors, and other passive and electromechanical products and interconnect assemblies used by customers in assembling and manufacturing electronic equipment. Kent Electronics Corporation also manufactures electronic interconnect assemblies that are built to customers' specifications. **Corporate headquarters location:** Phoenix AZ. **Listed on:** New York Stock Exchange. **Stock exchange symbol:** AVT.

### CALIFORNIA MICRO DEVICES CORPORATION
430 North McCarthy Boulevard, Milpitas CA 95035. **Toll-free phone:** 800/325-4966. **Fax:** 408/263-7846. **Contact:** Personnel. **E-mail address:** hr@calmicro.com. **World Wide Web address:** http://www.calmicro.com. **Description:** Manufactures integrated thin film, silicon-based termination and filtering components. The company specializes in combining thin film, passive electronic components, and semiconductor devices into single-chip solutions for various electronic applications. **Positions advertised include:** Analog IC Design Engineer; Director of Marketing. **Corporate headquarters location:** This location. **Other U.S. locations:** Tempe AZ. **Listed on:** NASDAQ. **Stock exchange symbol:** CAMD. **President/CEO:** Robert V. Dickinson. **Annual sales/revenues:** $21 - $50 million. **Number of employees at this location:** 150. **Number of employees nationwide:** 280.

### CATALYST SEMICONDUCTOR, INC.
1250 Borregas Avenue, Sunnyvale CA 94089. 408/542-1000. **Fax:** 408/542-1410. **Contact:** Human Resources. **World Wide Web address:** http://www.catsemi.com. **Description:** Supplies nonvolatile semiconductors that provide design solutions for a broad range of applications including computers, wireless communications,

networks, instrumentation, and automotive systems. The company's devices include FLASH, mixed signal devices, Serial and Parallel EEPROMs (electrically erasable programmable read-only memory), and NVRAMs. Founded in 1985. **Corporate headquarters location:** This location. **International locations:** Japan; Philippines; Singapore; Thailand. **Operations at this facility include:** Development; Engineering and Design; Marketing; Sales. **Listed on:** NASDAQ. **Stock exchange symbol:** CATS.

## CHIP EXPRESS

2323 Owen Street, Santa Clara CA 95054. 408/988-2445. **Toll-free phone:** 800/95-CHIPX. **Fax:** 408/988-0513. **Contact:** Personnel. **E-mail address:** hr@chipx.com. **World Wide Web address:** http://www.chipexpress.com. **Description:** Manufactures semiconductor chips. **Positions advertised include:** ASIC Physical Design Engineer. **Corporate headquarters location:** This location. **International locations:** Haifa, Israel. **Listed on:** Privately held.

## CIRRUS LOGIC, INC.

46831 Lakeview Boulevard, Fremont CA 94538. 510/623-8300. **Contact:** Employment Manager. **World Wide Web address:** http://www.cirrus.com. **Description:** Develops innovative architectures for analog and digital systems functions and implements these architectures in very large scale integrated (VLSI) circuits for applications that include mass storage, user interface (graphics, audio, and video), communications, and data acquisition. **Positions advertised include:** Applications Engineer. **Corporate headquarters location:** Austin TX. **Other U.S. locations:** Broomfield CO; Boulder CO; Boca Raton FL; Fort Wayne IN; Nashua NH. **International locations:** England; Hong Kong; Japan. **Operations at this facility include:** Administration; Divisional Headquarters; Manufacturing; Research and Development; Sales. **Listed on:** NASDAQ. **Stock exchange symbol:** CRUS. **Annual sales/revenues:** More than $100 million. **Number of employees at this location:** 1,400. **Number of employees nationwide:** 2,850. **Number of employees worldwide:** 3,000.

## COGNEX CORPORATION

1001 North Rengstorff Avenue, Mountain View CA 94043. 650/969-4812. **Contact:** Human Resources. **E-mail address:** hr@cognex.com. **World Wide Web address:** http://www.cognex.com. **Description:** Cognex Corporation designs, develops, manufactures, and markets machine vision systems used to automate a wide range of manufacturing processes. Machine vision systems are used in the electronics, semiconductor, pharmaceutical, health care, aerospace, automotive, packaging, and graphic arts industries to gauge, guide, inspect, and identify products in manufacturing operations. **NOTE:** Send resumes to Human Resources, One Vision Drive, Natick MA 01760. **Corporate headquarters location:** Natick MA. **Other U.S. locations:** IL, MI, OR, PA, TX, WI. **International locations:** France; Germany; Japan; Singapore; United Kingdom. **Operations at this facility include:** This location is the West Coast regional technology center. **Listed on:** NASDAQ. **Stock exchange symbol:** CGNX.

### COHERENT INC.
2303 Lindbergh Street, Auburn CA 95602. 530/823-9550. **Contact:** Human Resources. **World Wide Web address:** http://www.cohr. com. **Description:** the company produces laser-related instruments for a variety of applications. Founded in 1966. **Positions advertised include:** Corporate Exercise Instructor; Product Support Engineer. **Corporate headquarters location:** Santa Clara CA. **Operations at this facility include:** This location is a supplier of optics, diodes, and laser instrumentation. **Listed on:** NASDAQ. **Stock exchange symbol:** COHR.

### COMMUNICATIONS & POWER INDUSTRIES (CPI)
811 Hansen Way, P.O. Box 50750, Palo Alto CA 94303-0750. 650/846-3700. **Contact:** Human Resources. **World Wide Web address:** http://www.cpii.com/satcom. **Description:** CPI is engaged in the research, development, manufacture, and marketing of various products and services in the fields of communications, industrial equipment, medicine, and scientific research. **Positions advertised include:** Senior RF Design Engineer; Digital Design Engineer. **Corporate headquarters location:** This location. **Other U.S. locations:** Nationwide. **International locations:** Worldwide. **Operations at this facility include:** This location manufactures satellite communications equipment.

### CONDUCTUS, INC.
969 West Maude Avenue, Sunnyvale CA 94085. 408/523-9950. **Fax:** 408/532-9499. **Contact:** Human Resources. **E-mail address:** jobs@conductus.com. **World Wide Web address:** http://www. conductus.com. **Description:** Develops, manufactures, and markets electronics systems and components based on superconductor technology. Conductus has developed high-temperature, thin-film superconducting materials and devices for wireless communications

and magnetic resonance instruments. **Positions advertised include:** Senior Payroll Administrator; Senior Staff Engineer; Design Engineer; Material Handler; Senior Staff Engineer. **Corporate headquarters location:** This location. **Listed on:** NASDAQ. **Stock exchange symbol:** CDTS.

## CREDENCE SYSTEMS CORPORATION
215 Fourier Avenue, Fremont CA 94539. 510/657-7400. **Contact:** Human Resources. **E-mail address:** yourfuture@credence.com. **World Wide Web address:** http://www.credence.com. **Description:** Manufactures automatic testing equipment for digital and mixed-signal integrated circuits. **Positions advertised include:** Senior Software QA Engineer; System Performance Engineer. **Corporate headquarters location:** This location. **Listed on:** NASDAQ. **Stock exchange symbol:** CMOS.

## CYPRESS SEMICONDUCTOR CORPORATION
198 Champion Court, San Jose CA 95134. 408/943-2600. **Contact:** Personnel. **World Wide Web address:** http://www.cypress.com. **Description:** Manufactures high-performance digital integrated circuits. **Positions advertised include:** Senior Accountant; Senior Internal Accountant; Training Manager; Process Integration Engineer Staff Member; Financial Analyst; Product Marketing Engineer. **Corporate headquarters location:** This location. **Listed on:** New York Stock Exchange. **Stock exchange symbol:** CY.

## DSP GROUP, INC.
3120 Scott Boulevard, Santa Clara CA 95054. 408/986-4300. **Fax:** 408/986-4323. **Contact:** Human Resources. **E-mail address:** hr@dspg.com. **World Wide Web address:** http://www.dspg.com. **Description:** Develops, licenses, and markets digital signal processing software and digital signal processor technologies for use in digital speech products. DSP Group offers a wide range of products and licensed technologies to major original equipment manufacturers in the personal computer, telecommunications, and consumer electronics markets. Products include digital speech processors for telephone answering machines. **Corporate headquarters location:** This location. **International locations:** Israel; France; Japan. **Listed on:** NASDAQ. **Stock exchange symbol:** DSPG.

## DATUM INC.
230 Orchard Parkway, San Jose CA 95131. 408/433-0910. **Contact:** Human Resources. **World Wide Web address:** http://www.datum.

com. **Description:** Designs, develops, manufactures, and markets precision frequency and timing instrumentation products. Datum's principal products are cesium and quartz crystal frequency standards that produce or stabilize frequencies. Datum's timing instrumentation products use a stable frequency standard to generate, encode, translate, and distribute precise time information. These products are used in a broad range of applications including accurate synchronization of telecommunications networks, synchronization of computers in local area networks, generation of precise time information, and control of global navigation satellite systems. **Positions advertised include:** Administrative Assistant; Accounting Assistant. **Corporate headquarters location:** Irvine CA. **Listed on:** NASDAQ. **Stock exchange symbol:** DATM.

### DIGIDESIGN INC.
2001 Junipero Serra Boulevard, Daly City CA 94014-3886. 650/731-6300. **Contact:** Human Resources. **E-mail address:** jobs@digidesign. com. **World Wide Web address:** http://www.digidesign.com. **Description:** Digidesign manufactures electronic audio and video equipment for the home and automobiles, public address systems, and music distribution apparatus. **Corporate headquarters location:** This location. **Operations at this facility include:** This location manufactures audio workstations for sound editing.

### ELECTROGLAS, INC.
6024 Silver Creek Valley Road, San Jose CA 95138. 408/528-3000. **Contact:** Human Resources. **E-mail address:** staffing@electroglas. com. **World Wide Web address:** http://www.electroglas.com. **Description:** Develops, manufactures, markets, and services automatic wafer probing equipment for use in the fabrication of semiconductor devices. Founded in 1960. **Corporate headquarters location:** This location. **Listed on:** NASDAQ. **Stock exchange symbol:** EGLS.

### ELECTRONICS FOR IMAGING, INC.
303 Velocity Way, Foster City CA 94404. 650/357-3500. **Fax:** 650/357-3907. **Contact:** Human Resources. **E-mail address:** enghr@ efi.com. **World Wide Web address:** http://www.efi.com. **Description:** Designs and markets products that enable high-quality color printing in short production runs. The company's Fiery Color Servers incorporate hardware and software technologies that transform digital color copiers into fast, high-quality color printers. **Positions advertised include:** Program Managing; Senior Software

Engineer; Human Resources Analyst; Business Development Manager; Customer Service Representative; Director of Software Marketing; Field Sales Engineer; Inside Sales Representative; eBeam Sales Representative. **Corporate headquarters location:** This location. **Listed on:** NASDAQ. **Stock exchange symbol:** EFII.

### EUPHONIX INC.

220 Portage Avenue, Palo Alto CA 94306-2242. 650/855-0400. **Contact:** Human Resources Manager. **E-mail address:** hr@euphonix. com. **World Wide Web address:** http://www.euphonix.com. **Description:** A manufacturer of digitally controlled mixing consoles and audio components. **Corporate headquarters location:** This location.

### EXAR CORPORATION

48720 Kato Road, Fremont CA 94538. 510/668-7000. **Contact:** Human Resources. **World Wide Web address:** http://www.exar.com. **Description:** Engaged in the design, manufacture, and marketing of analog and mixed signal integrated circuits and subsystems, primarily for use in telecommunications, data communications, microperipherals, and consumer electronics products. **Positions advertised include:** Accounting Supervisor; Test Engineering Group Manager. **Corporate headquarters location:** This location. **Listed on:** NASDAQ. **Stock exchange symbol:** EXAR. **Number of employees at this location:** 500.

### FAIRCHILD IMAGING

1801 McCarthy Boulevard, Milpitas CA 95035. 408/433-2500. **Fax:** 408/433-2604. **Contact:** Human Resources. **E-mail address:** hr@ fcimg.com. **World Wide Web address:** http://www.fairchildimaging. com. **Description:** Produces visible and infrared CCDs and cameras for use in military, space, and commercial applications. **Corporate headquarters location:** This location.

### FAIRCHILD SEMICONDUCTOR CORPORATION

3001 Orchard Parkway, San Jose CA 95134. 408/822-2000. **Toll-free phone:** 800/341-0392. **Contact:** Recruitment. **E-mail address:** corporate.resume@fairchildsemi.com. **World Wide Web address:** http://www.fairchildsemi.com. **Note:** Jobseekers should apply to 333 Western Avenue, MS 10-04, South Portland ME 04106. **Description:** Manufactures semiconductors for use in telecommunications, personal computing, and digital video applications. **Corporate**

**headquarters location:** South Portland ME. **Listed on:** New York Stock Exchange. **Stock exchange symbol:** FCS.

### FLEXTRONICS INTERNATIONAL
2090 Fortune Drive, San Jose CA 95131. 408/428-1300. **Contact:** Human Resources. **World Wide Web address:** http://www. flextronics.com. **Description:** Provides electronic design, engineering, and manufacturing services to OEMs in various industries. **Positions advertised include:** Desktop Support Analyst; Division Controller; Sales Coordinator; Senior Program Manager; Materials Manager; Staff Financial Analyst; Quality Engineer; Director of QA Engineering; Senior Accountant; Supply Chain Analyst. **Corporate headquarters location:** This location. **Listed on:** NASDAQ. **Stock exchange symbol:** FLEX.

### FORTREND ENGINEERING COMPANY
404 Tasman Drive, Sunnyvale CA 94089. 408/734-9311. **Fax:** 408/734-4299. **Contact:** Human Resources. **E-mail address:** hr@ fortrend.com. **World Wide Web address:** http://www.fortrend.com. **Description:** Designs and manufactures automated equipment for wafer and disk handling in the semiconductor industry. **Corporate headquarters location:** This location. **International locations:** Worldwide. **Listed on:** Privately held. **Annual sales/revenues:** $5 - $10 million. **Number of employees at this location:** 50.

### GENERAL DYNAMICS ELECTRONIC SYSTEMS
P.O. Box 7188, Mountain View CA 94039. 650/966-2995. **Physical address:** 100 Ferguson Drive, Mountain View CA 94039. **Contact:** Millie A. Miller, Vice President of Human Resources. **E-mail address:** resumes@gd-es.com. **World Wide Web address:** http://www.gd-es.com. **Description:** Engaged in the advancement of information systems and command, control, communications, computer, and intelligence technology. General Dynamics Electronic Systems designs and produces customized systems for defense, government, and industry clients. **Positions advertised include:** Security Force Assistant; Contracts Manager; Security Force Assistant; Lead Engineer; Principal Systems Engineer; Hardware Engineer; Software Engineer. **Corporate headquarters location:** This location. **Parent company:** General Dynamics Corporation. **Listed on:** New York Stock Exchange. **Stock exchange symbol:** GD. **Number of employees at this location:** 1,200.

## GENUS, INC.

1139 Karlstad Drive, Sunnyvale CA 94089. 408/747-7120. **Fax:** 408/ 752-2009. **Contact:** Human Resources. **World Wide Web address:** http://www.genus.com. **Description:** Designs, manufactures, markets, and services advanced systems for thin film deposition used in the fabrication of complex ultra-large-scale integration semiconductor devices. Genus's products are used for several critical process steps required to produce integrated circuits for the computer, aerospace, communications, data processing, medical, military, aeronautical, automotive, and consumer electronics industries. **Positions advertised include:** Senior Software Engineer; Field Process Engineer. **Corporate headquarters location:** This location. **International locations:** Korea. **Listed on:** NASDAQ. **Stock exchange symbol:** GGNS.

## HONEYWELL-MEASUREX CORPORATION

One Results Way, Mail Stop 8109, Cupertino CA 95014-5991. 408/ 255-1500. **Fax:** 408/864-7570. **World Wide Web address:** http:// www.honeywell.com. **Contact:** Professional Staffing. **Description:** Honeywell-Measurex is a leading supplier of measurement, control, and information systems and services for continuous and batch manufacturing processes. Industries served by the company include pulp and paper, plastic, nonwoven, aluminum, and rubber. **Corporate headquarters location:** This location. **International locations:** Worldwide. **Listed on:** New York Stock Exchange. **Stock exchange symbol:** HON. **Number of employees worldwide:** 2,000.

## IMP, INC.

2830 North First Street, San Jose CA 95134. 408/432-9100. **Fax:** 408/434-0335. **Contact:** Human Resources. **E-mail address:** hr@ impinc.com. **World Wide Web address:** http://www.impweb.com. **Description:** Develops and manufactures application-specific standard integrated circuits for mass storage and power management applications. **Positions advertised include:** Senior Staff Design Engineer; Senior Test Engineer; Test Engineer; Management Information Systems Manager. **Corporate headquarters location:** Tokyo, Japan. **Listed on:** NASDAQ. **Stock exchange symbol:** IMPXC.

## ISE LABS, INC.

2095 Ringwood Avenue, San Jose CA 95131. 408/954-8378. **Contact:** Manager of Administrative Operations. **World Wide Web address:** http://www.iselabs.com. **Description:** Provides electrical and environmental testing services for integrated circuits. Founded in

1983. **Corporate headquarters location:** Fremont CA. **Other U.S. locations:** Manteca CA; Santa Clara CA. **International locations:** Hong Kong; Singapore. **Listed on:** Privately held. **Parent company:** ASE Test Ltd. **Listed on:** NASDAQ. **Stock exchange symbol:** ASTSF. **Annual sales/revenues:** $51 - $100 million. **Number of employees at this location:** 140. **Number of employees nationwide:** 415. **Number of employees worldwide:** 550.

## IMPACT VOITH PAPER AUTOMATION

14600 Winchester Boulevard, Los Gatos CA 95032. 408/379-0910. **Contact:** Susan Rice, Human Resources. **E-mail address:** susan.rice@voith.com. **World Wide Web address:** http://www.voithpaper.com. **Description:** Develops, manufactures, sells, and services a wide variety of computer-based measurement and control systems to the paper industry. Impact's cross-direction (CD) measurement and control systems reduce CD variations in key variables occurring in the production of virtually all grades of paper. Founded in 1980. **Corporate headquarters location:** This location.

## INFINEON TECHNOLOGIES CORPORATION

1730 North First Street, San Jose CA 95112. 408/501-6000. **Contact:** Personnel Manager. **E-mail address:** careers@infineon.com. **World Wide Web address:** http://www.infineon.com. **Description:** Infineon Technologies Corporation is one of the world's largest semiconductor manufacturers. The company operates in five major business units. Automotive & Industrial develops and manufactures power semiconductors, optoelectronic components, microcontrollers, sensors, and discrete semiconductors for automotive and industrial applications. Communications & Peripherals develops and manufactures semiconductors, systems, and components for use in wire communications applications including cable television, LANs, and WANs. Wireless Products designs and manufactures semiconductors and complete wireless systems for such applications as cellular and cordless telephone networks and devices. Memory Products designs and manufactures memory components for computers and electronics. Security & Chip Card ICs develops and manufactures semiconductors and security components for use in applications requiring security, such as credit card systems, pay-per-view television, and traffic control. **Positions advertised include:** Tactical Marketing Analyst; Director of Marketing, Fiber Optics. **Corporate headquarters location:** Munich, Germany. **Operations at this facility include:** This location is a research and development center. **Listed on:** New York Stock Exchange. **Stock exchange symbol:** IFX.

## INTEGRATED SILICON SOLUTION, INC. (ISSI)

2231 Lawson Lane, Santa Clara CA 95054. 408/588-0800. **Contact:** Human Resources. **E-mail address:** jobs@issi.com. **World Wide Web address:** http://www.issiusa.com. **Description:** Designs, develops, and markets high-performance SRAM and nonvolatile memory integrated circuits used in personal computers, data communications, telecommunications, instrumentation, and consumer products. **Positions advertised include:** Bluetooth Product Marketing Manager; Circuit Design Engineer; Test Engineer; Database Programmer; Senior Reliability Engineer. **Corporate headquarters location:** This location. **International locations:** Taiwan. **Listed on:** NASDAQ. **Stock exchange symbol:** ISSI. **Number of employees nationwide:** 220.

## INTEL CORPORATION

2200 Mission College Boulevard, P.O. Box 58119, Santa Clara CA 95052-8119. 408/765-8080. **Contact:** Staffing Department. **World Wide Web address:** http://www.intel.com. **Description:** One of the largest semiconductor manufacturers in the world. Other products include supercomputers; embedded control chips and flash memories; motherboards; multimedia hardware; personal computer enhancement products; and the design and marketing of microcomputer components, modules, and systems. Intel sells its products to original equipment manufacturers and other companies that incorporate them into their products. **Positions advertised include:** Audit Specialist; CAD Engineer; Consulting Engineer; Hardware Test Engineer; Human Resources Senior Researcher; IP Attorney; Patent Attorney; Principal Storage Architect; Senior Media Analyst; Software Engineer; Tax Benefits Attorney. **Corporate headquarters location:** This location. **Subsidiaries include:** Shiva produces a line of direct-dial products and remote access servers. **Listed on:** NASDAQ. **Stock exchange symbol:** INTC.

## INTERNATIONAL RECTIFIER

2270 Martin Avenue, Santa Clara CA 95050. 408/727-0500. **Fax:** 408/988-3952. **Contact:** Human Resources Director. **E-mail address:** resume@AA-M3.com. **World Wide Web address:** http://www. irf.com. **Description:** Designs and manufactures hybrid, DC-DC converters, and VHF and HF communication systems used in space and military products. **Positions advertised include:** Component

Engineer. **Corporate headquarters location:** El Segundo CA. **Listed on:** New York Stock Exchange. **Stock exchange symbol:** IRF.

### INVIVO CORPORATION
42025 Osgood Avenue, Fremont CA 94539. 510/226-9600. **Contact:** Human Resources. **World Wide Web address:** http://www.invivo.com. **Description:** Manufactures sensor-based instrumentation such as pressure transducers and calibration sensors. **Positions advertised include:** Network Integration Engineer; Switch Technician; Provisioner. **Corporate headquarters location:** Pleasanton CA. **Listed on:** NASDAQ. **Stock exchange symbol:** SAFE.

### JDS UNIPHASE CORPORATION
80 Rose Orchard Way, San Jose CA 95134. 408/943-9411. **Toll-free phone:** 888/883-SDLI. **Contact:** Human Resources. **World Wide Web address:** http://www.jdsu.com. **Description:** Develops, manufactures, and distributes fiber-optic products including cable assemblies, fusion splicers, couplers, and lasers. **Listed on:** NASDAQ. **Stock exchange symbol:** JDSU. **Annual sales/revenues:** More than $100 million.

### KLA-TENCOR CORPORATION
160 Rio Robles, San Jose CA 95134. 408/875-3000. **Contact:** Human Resources. **World Wide Web address:** http://www.kla-tencor.com. **Description:** Manufactures high-speed, image-processing systems for the semiconductor industry. **Special programs:** Internships. **Corporate headquarters location:** This location. **Listed on:** NASDAQ. **Stock exchange symbol:** KLAC.

### KULICKE AND SOFFA INDUSTRIES, INC. (K&S)
2210 Martin Avenue, Santa Clara CA 95050. 408/727-5040. **Contact:** Human Resources. **World Wide Web address:** http://www.kns.com. **Description:** Engaged in semiconductor assembly and services. The company designs, manufactures, markets, and supports equipment for IC and MCM/hybrid semiconductor manufacturers worldwide. Product lines include wafer and hard materials dicing, die bonding and wire bonding equipment, service and spare parts, and the Micro-Swiss line of bonding and dicing tools and production accessories. Founded in 1951. **Special programs:** Co-ops; Internships. **Corporate headquarters location:** Willow Grove PA. **Operations at this facility include:** Regional Headquarters. **Listed on:** NASDAQ. **Stock exchange symbol:** KLIC.

## L3 COMMUNICATIONS, INC.
130 Constitution Drive, Menlo Park CA 94025. 650/326-9500. **Contact:** Paula Moroney, Human Resources Representative. **E-mail address:** cooljobs@l-3com.com. **World Wide Web address:** http://www.l-3com.com. **Description:** Designs and manufactures integrated microwave antenna subassemblies and low-radar cross-section antenna designs and measurements. **Corporate headquarters location:** New York NY. **Number of employees at this location:** 235. **Listed on:** New York Stock Exchange. **Stock exchange symbol:** LLL.

## LINEAR TECHNOLOGY CORPORATION
1630 McCarthy Boulevard, Milpitas CA 95035-7487. 408/432-1900. **Contact:** Human Resources. **E-mail address:** hr@linear.com. **World Wide Web address:** http://www.linear.com. **Description:** Designs and manufactures a broad line of standard high-performance linear integrated circuits. These circuits monitor, condition, amplify, or transform continuous analog signals. **Positions advertised include:** Analog IC Design Engineer; Credit Accountant; High Frequency Product Marketing Engineer; Inside Sales Representative; Mixed Signal Test Engineer; Production Control Planner; Quality Assurance Test Engineer. **Corporate headquarters location:** This location. **Listed on:** NASDAQ. **Stock exchange symbol:** LLTC. **Number of employees at this location:** 1,000.

## MATTSON TECHNOLOGY
2800 Bayview Drive, Fremont CA 94538. 510/657-5900. **Toll-free phone:** 800/635-2250. **Contact:** Human Resources. **E-mail address:** hr@matson.com. **World Wide Web address:** http://www.mattson.com. **Description:** Manufactures rapid thermal processing systems for the semiconductor industry. **Positions advertised include:** Financial Analyst. **Office hours:** Monday - Friday, 8:00 a.m. - 5:00 p.m. **Corporate headquarters location:** Fremont CA. **International locations:** Worldwide. **Parent company:** Mattson Technology, Inc. **Listed on:** NASDAQ. **Stock exchange symbol:** MTSN. **Annual sales/revenues:** More than $100 million. **Number of employees at this location:** 200.

## MICREL
2180 Fortune Drive, San Jose CA 95131. 408/944-0800. **Contact:** Recruiting. **E-mail address:** recruit@micrel.com. **World Wide Web address:** http://www.micrel.com. **Description:** Designs and manufactures analog integrated circuits. Founded in 1978. **Positions**

178/The San Francisco JobBank

**advertised include:** Applications Engineer; Product Engineer; Senior Analog Design Engineer; Senior Design Engineer. **Corporate headquarters location:** This location. **Listed on:** NASDAQ. **Stock exchange symbol:** MCRL. **Annual sales/revenues:** More than $100 million.

### MICRO LINEAR CORPORATION
2050 Concourse Drive, San Jose CA 95131. 408/433-5200. **Contact:** Human Resources. **E-mail address:** jobs@microlinear.com. **World Wide Web address:** http://www.microlinear.com. **Description:** Designs, develops, and markets high-performance analog and mixed-signal integrated circuits for a broad range of applications in the communications, computer, and industrial markets. The company's products provide highly integrated systems-level solutions for a variety of applications including local area networks, mass storage, telecommunications, power management, motor control, and data conversion. The company uses its proprietary design methodology and bipolar, CMOS, and BiCMOS manufacturing processes to produce standard and semistandard products. **Positions advertised include:** Field Applications Engineer; Design Engineer; Senior Applications Engineer. **Corporate headquarters location:** This location. **Listed on:** NASDAQ. **Stock exchange symbol:** MLIN.

### MICROCHIP TECHNOLOGY INC.
2107 North First Street, Suite 590, San Jose CA 95134. 408/436-7950. **Contact:** Personnel. **World Wide Web address:** http://www. microchip.com. **Description:** A semiconductor manufacturer. Microchip Technology specializes in eight-bit micro controllers, eproms, eeproms, and other nonvolatile memory products. **NOTE:** Please send resumes to Microchip Technology Inc., Human Resources, 2355 West Chandler Boulevard, Chandler AZ 85224. **Positions advertised include:** Engineer's Assistant. **Corporate headquarters location:** Chandler AZ. **Listed on:** NASDAQ. **Stock exchange symbol:** MCHP.

### MORGAN ADVANCED CERAMICS
477 Harbor Boulevard, Belmont CA 94002. 650/592-9440. **Contact:** Human Resources. **World Wide Web address:** http://www. morganadvancedceramics.com. **Description:** Manufactures technical ceramics. **Corporate headquarters location:** This location. **Operations at this facility include:** Administration; Manufacturing; Research and Development; Sales.

## MOTOROLA, INC.
1150 Kifer Road, Suite 100, Sunnyvale CA 94086. 408/749-0510. **Contact:** Human Resources. **World Wide Web address:** http://www.motorola.com. **Description:** Designs and manufactures semiconductors and integrated circuits for the computing, communications, electronics, and transportation industries. **Corporate headquarters location:** Austin TX. **Operations at this facility include:** Divisional Headquarters. **Listed on:** New York Stock Exchange. **Stock exchange symbol:** MEU.

## MULTICHIP ASSEMBLY
1598 Monterey Road, San Jose CA 95110. 408/271-2740. **Fax:** 408/324-1036. **Contact:** Human Resources. **E-mail address:** hr@multichipassy.com. **World Wide Web address:** http://www.multichipassy.com. **Description:** A contract manufacturer of tab devices and other assembly processes for the electronics industry. Founded in 1991. **Corporate headquarters location:** This location. **Listed on:** Privately held. **Annual sales/revenues:** Less than $5 million. **Number of employees at this location:** 45.

## NATIONAL SEMICONDUCTOR CORPORATION
P.O. Box 58090, Santa Clara CA 95052-8090. 408/721-5000. **Physical address:** 2900 Semiconductor Drive, Santa Clara CA 95051. **Contact:** Staffing. **World Wide Web address:** http://www.nsc.com. **Description:** Designs, develops, and manufactures microprocessors, consumer products, integrated circuits, memory systems, computer products, telecommunications systems, and high-speed bipolar circuits. **Positions advertised include:** Principal Applications Engineer, Power Management. **Special programs:** Internships. **Corporate headquarters location:** This location. **International locations:** Scotland. **Operations at this facility include:** Administration; Manufacturing; Research and Development; Sales; Service. **Listed on:** New York Stock Exchange. **Stock exchange symbol:** NSM.

## NEXWATCH
47102 Mission Falls Court, Fremont CA 94539-7818. 510/360-7800. **Fax:** 510/360-7827. **Contact:** Human Resources. **E-mail address:** resume.hr@nciaccess.com. **World Wide Web address:** http://www.nexwatch.com. **Description:** Manufactures access control systems. **Corporate headquarters location:** This location. **Parent company:** Honeywell, Inc. **Listed on:** New York Stock Exchange. **Stock exchange symbol:** HON.

## NORTHROP GRUMMAN ELECTRONIC SYSTEMS

P.O. Box 7012, San Jose CA 95150-7012. 408/365-4747. **Physical address:** 5225 Hellyer Avenue, Suite 100, San Jose CA 95138. **Contact:** Professional Recruiting Department. **World Wide Web address:** http://www.sensor.northgrum.com. **Description:** Designs and manufactures electronic defense systems used by the U.S. Department of Defense, other U.S. government agencies, and U.S. allies. Products include radar warning receiving systems, cover and deception systems, and surveillance systems. **Positions advertised include:** Senior Scientist; Principal Design Specialist; Software Specialist; Production Master Scheduler; Government Property Administrator. **Corporate headquarters location:** Los Angeles CA. **Operations at this facility include:** Administration; Divisional Headquarters; Engineering and Design; Financial Offices; Manufacturing; Marketing; Research and Development; Sales; Service. **Listed on:** New York Stock Exchange. **Stock exchange symbol:** NOC.

## NORTHOP GRUMMAN ELECTRONIC SYSTEMS

960 Industrial Road, San Carlos CA 94070. 650/591-8411. **Contact:** Human Resources Recruiter. **E-mail address:** jobs_esss@ md.northgrum.com. **World Wide Web address:** http://sensor. northgrum.com. **Description:** Serves worldwide markets with commercial, consumer, industrial, professional, and defense-related products. A major business area for the division is advanced microwave components and subsystems for military radar, communications, and electronic countermeasure markets. Product technologies are focused in high-power vacuum tubes, microwave semiconductors, amplifiers and oscillators, night vision and optical devices, and military switching power supplies. **Corporate headquarters location:** Woodland Hills CA. **Operations at this facility include:** Administration; Divisional Headquarters; Manufacturing; Research and Development; Sales. **Listed on:** New York Stock Exchange. **Stock exchange symbol:** NOC.

## NORTHROP GRUMMAN INTEGRATED SYSTEMS

5225 Hellyer Avenue, San Jose CA 95138. 408/365-4747. **Contact:** Human Resources. **World Wide Web address:** http://www.northop-grummann.com. **Description:** Manufactures radar warning systems. **Corporate headquarters location:** Woodland Hills CA. **Listed on:** New York Stock Exchange. **Stock exchange symbol:** NOC.

## NOVELLUS SYSTEMS, INC.

4000 North First Street, San Jose CA 95134. 408/943-9700. **Toll-free phone:** 888/321-4272. **Contact:** Human Resources Department. **World Wide Web address:** http://www.novellus.com. **Description:** Novellus Systems is a leading supplier of process systems used in the fabrication of advanced integrated circuits. The company is one of the world's largest suppliers of equipment for dry removal of photoresist and other mask layer materials applied to semiconductor wafers during fabrication. Novellus also offers systems for related phases of semiconductor manufacturing including thermal growth of oxide layers and selective cleaning applications. The company's products feature proprietary technologies that help semiconductor manufacturers increase fabrication throughput and reduce wafer damage, which in turn raise production yields. **Positions advertised include:** Technical Publications Director; Spare Parts Manager; Accounting Clerk; Technologist; Financial Analyst; Engineer Trainee; Senior Process Applications Technologist. **Corporate headquarters location:** This location. **Listed on:** NASDAQ. **Stock exchange symbol:** NVLS.

## PERKINELMER OPTOELECTRONICS

44370 Christy Street, Fremont CA 94538-3180. 510/979-6500. **Toll-free phone:** 800/775-6786. **Contact:** Cris Wilbur, Director of Human Resources Department. **E-mail address:** cris.wilbur@perkinelmer.com. **World Wide Web address:** http://www.perkinelmer.com. **Description:** PerkinElmer designs and manufactures a variety of image sensors, multiplexors, and camera systems for use in medical, scientific, and document scanning applications. **Corporate headquarters location:** This location. **Operations at this facility include:** This location manufactures solid-state image sensors for electronics applications. **Listed on:** New York Stock Exchange. **Stock exchange symbol:** PKI.

## PHILLIPS SEMICONDUCTORS

1151 McKay Drive, San Jose CA 95131. 408/434-3000. **Contact:** Human Resources. **World Wide Web address:** http://www.semiconductors.phillips.com. **Description:** Designs and manufactures application-specific and application-standard integrated circuits for computer, telecommunications, consumer, and industrial uses. **Positions advertised include:** Senior Design Engineer. **Special programs:** Internships. **Corporate headquarters location:** Eindhoven, the Netherlands. **Other U.S. locations:** Tempe AZ; San Antonio TX. **Listed on:** New York Stock Exchange. **Stock** exchange symbol: PHG. **Number of employees at this location:** 1,500. **Number of employees nationwide:** 3,000.

## PRESCOLITE, INC.

1251 Doolittle Drive, San Leandro CA 94577. 510/562-3500. **Contact:** Renee Green, Human Resources Manager. **World Wide Web address:** http://www.prescolite.com. **Description:** Manufactures incandescent and high-intensity discharge lighting fixtures.

## SAE ENGINEERING

282 Brokaw Road, Santa Clara CA 95050. 408/988-0700. **Contact:** Personnel. **World Wide Web address:** http://www.saeintl.com. **Description:** An international manufacturer of interconnection hardware and systems for the original equipment market. The company is a minority manufacturer of a broad line of edgeboard connectors, flat ribbon cable interconnection systems, and wire wrapping services. **Corporate headquarters location:** This location. **Number of employees nationwide:** 1,200.

## SANMINA-SCI CORPORATION

445 El Camino Real, Santa Clara CA 95050. 408/241-9900. **Contact:** Jackie Iten, Human Resources. **World Wide Web address:** http:// www.sanmina.com. **Description:** Sanmina-SCI designs, develops, manufactures, markets, distributes, and services electronic products for the computer, aerospace, defense, telecommunications, medical, and banking industries, as well as for the United States government. Sanmina-SCI is one of the world's largest contract electronics manufacturers and operates one of the largest surface mount technology production capacities in the merchant market. Operations are conducted through a Commercial Division and a Government Division. The Commercial Division operates in five geographically organized business units: Eastern, Central, and Western North America; Europe; and Asia. Each unit operates multiple plants that manufacture components, subassemblies, and finished products primarily for original equipment manufacturers. Design, engineering, purchasing, manufacturing, distribution, and support services are also offered. The Governmental Division provides data management, instrumentation, communication, and computer subsystems to the U.S. government and several foreign governments. **International locations:** Canada; France; Ireland; Mexico; Scotland; Singapore; Thailand. **Operations at this facility include:** This location Manufactures printed circuit boards and back

panel assemblies. **Listed on:** NASDAQ. **Stock exchange symbol:** SANM.

### SCIENTIFIC TECHNOLOGIES INC. (STI)

6550 Dumbarton Circle, Fremont CA 94555-3611. 510/608-3400. **Fax:** 510/744-1309. **Contact:** Human Resources. **E-mail address:** employment@sti.com. **World Wide Web address:** http://www.sti. com. **Description:** Designs, manufactures, and distributes electrical and electronic controls for the industrial market. **Positions advertised include:** Electrical Engineer; Field Service Engineer; Manufacturing Engineer; Technical Staff Member; Reliability Engineer. **Corporate headquarters location:** This location. **Listed on:** NASDAQ. **Stock exchange symbol:** STIZ. **President/CEO:** Joseph J. Lazzara.

### SIGNAL TECHNOLOGY CORPORATION

975 Benecia Avenue, Sunnyvale CA 94086. 408/730-6300. **Contact:** Woody Boyles, Human Resources Manager. **E-mail address:** wood.boyles@sigtech-ca.com. **World Wide Web address:** http:// www.sigtech.com. **Description:** Manufactures a wide variety of microwave and electronics components in four product areas: solid state devices including test equipment and microwave assemblies and subsystems; microwave components including isofilters and multiplexers; semiconductor products including solid state RF switches and double-balanced mixers; and YIG Products including harmonic generators and tracking filter-oscillator sets. **Corporate headquarters location:** Danvers MA. **Operations at this facility include:** Administration; Manufacturing; Research and Development; Sales; Service. **Listed on:** NASDAQ. **Stock exchange symbol:** STCO.

### SIMCO ELECTRONICS

1178 Bordeaux Drive, Sunnyvale CA 94089. 408/734-9750. **Contact:** Lisa Clark, Manager of Human Resources. **E-mail address:** resumes@simco.com. **World Wide Web address:** http://www.simco. com. **Description:** Engaged in the calibration and repair of electronic test and measuring equipment; electrical and physical standards; physical, dimensional, mechanical gauges and tools; and the calibration and validation of biomedical process equipment. **Corporate headquarters location:** This location. **Other area locations:** Anaheim, CA; Burbank, CA; San Diego, CA; Santa Fe Springs, CA. **Other U.S. locations:** Huntsville AL; Naperville IL; St. Louis MO; Greensboro NC; Springboro OH; Allentown PA; Austin TX; Dallas TX; Sterling VA. **Listed on:** Privately held. **CEO:** Lee McKenna. **Annual sales/revenues:** $11 - $20 million. **Number of**

**employees at this location:** 70. **Number of employees nationwide:** 300.

## SOLECTRON CORPORATION

847 Gibraltar Drive, Milpitas CA 95035. 408/957-8500. **Contact:** Human Resources. **World Wide Web address:** http://www. solectron.com. **Description:** Manufactures complex printed circuit boards using surface mount technology and pin-through-hole interconnection technology. The company also provides electronic subsystem testing and assembly services for OEMs in the electronics industry. **Corporate headquarters location:** This location. **Listed on:** New York Stock Exchange. **Stock exchange symbol:** SLR. **Annual sales/revenues:** More than $100 million.

## SUPERTEX INC.

1235 Bordeaux Drive, Sunnyvale CA 94089. 408/744-0100. **Fax:** 408/422-4805. **Contact:** Human Resources. **E-mail address:** jobopps@supertex.com. **World Wide Web address:** http://www. supertex.com. **Description:** Produces integrated silicon circuits and other microelectronic products for computer and electronics original equipment manufacturers. **Positions advertised include:** Accounts Payable Support; Applications Engineer; Design Engineer; Electrical Test Engineer; Senior Product Engineer; Senior Foundry Engineer; Technical Marketing Manager. **Corporate headquarters location:** This location. **Operations at this facility include:** Administration; Manufacturing; Research and Development; Sales; Service. **Listed on:** NASDAQ. **Stock exchange symbol:** SUPX.

## TRW ELECTROMAGNETIC SYSTEMS

1330 Geneva Drive, Sunnyvale CA 94088-3510. 408/738-2888. **Contact:** Professional Employment. **World Wide Web address:** http://www.trw.com. **Description:** Designs, develops, and implements specialized direction-finding equipment with reconnaissance applications. **Corporate headquarters location:** Cleveland OH. **Other U.S. locations:** Sacramento CA; Reston VA. **Listed on:** New York Stock Exchange. **Stock exchange symbol:** TRW.

## TRW LUCAS NOVASENSOR

1055 Mission Court, Fremont CA 94539. 510/661-6000. **Fax:** 510/657-6420. **Contact:** Personnel. **World Wide Web address:** http://www.novasensor.com. **Corporate headquarters location:** Cleveland OH. **Description:** Manufactures pressure sensors for all types of applications. **Positions advertised include:** Customer Service

Representative. **Listed on:** New York Stock Exchange. **Stock exchange symbol:** TRW.

## TELEDYNE ELECTRONIC TECHNOLOGIES
1274 Terra Bella Avenue, Mountain View CA 94043. 650/691-9800. **Contact:** Human Resources. **World Wide Web address:** http://www. tet.com. **Description:** Engaged in the design and manufacture of passive and active devices, power supplies, and scientific instruments. Products include MMIC devices; amplifiers; integrated subsystems; voltage-controlled oscillators; microwave switches, filters, and ferrite devices; and mass spectrometry scientific instruments. **Corporate headquarters location:** Los Angeles CA. **Parent company:** Teledyne Technologies. **Listed on:** New York Stock Exchange. **Stock exchange symbol:** TDY. **Number of employees at this location:** 250. **Number of employees nationwide:** 5,800.

## VISHAY SILICONIX INC.
2201 Laurelwood Road, Santa Clara CA 95054. 408/988-8000. **Contact:** Human Resources. **World Wide Web address:** http://www.vishay.com/brands/siliconix. **Description:** Manufactures semiconductor products. **Corporate headquarters location:** Melbourn PA. **Listed on:** New York Stock Exchange. **Stock exchange symbol:** VSH.

## WINBOND ELECTRONICS
2727 North First Street, San Jose CA 95134. 408/943-6666. **Fax:** 408/544-1784. **Contact:** Human Resources. **E-mail address:** usresume@winbond.com. **World Wide Web address:** http://www. winbond.com. **Description:** Designs, develops, and markets integrated circuit products for voice recording and playback using the company's proprietary ChipCorder high-density storage technology and mixed signal expertise. The company's products offer voice reproduction, low-power consumption, and batteryless storage in a single-chip solution. **Positions advertised include:** DRAM Design Engineer; Senior System Design Engineer; Senior Test Engineer; Technology Development Engineer; Marketing Director; Operations Manager; Sales Engineer. **Corporate headquarters location:** This location.

## ZETA
17680 Butterfield Boulevard, Suite 100, Morgan Hill CA 95037. 408/852-0800. **Contact:** Human Resources. **E-mail address:**

hr@zeta-idt.com. **World Wide Web address:** http://www.zeta-idt.com. **Description:** Manufactures and distributes microwave equipment and RF and signal intercept and location systems. **Corporate headquarters location:** Buffalo NY. **Operations at this facility include:** Administration. **Annual sales/revenues:** $11 - $20 million. **Number of employees at this location:** 90.

**ZILOG, INC.**
532 Race Street, San Jose CA 95126. 408/558-8500. **Contact:** Tony S. Perez, Human Resources Representative. **E-mail address:** jobs@zilog.com. **World Wide Web address:** http://www.zilog.com. **Description:** Designs, develops, manufactures, and markets application-specific standard integrated circuits products (ASSPs) for the data communications, intelligent peripheral controller, consumer product controller, and memory markets. **Positions advertised include:** IR Wireless Program Manager; CAD Manager; Software Applications Engineer; Staff Field Applications Engineer. **Corporate headquarters location:** This location. **Other U.S. locations:** Nampa ID. **Operations at this facility include:** Administration; Research and Development; Sales. **Number of employees at this location:** 250. **Number of employees nationwide:** 1,500.

## ENVIRONMENTAL AND WASTE MANAGEMENT SERVICES

**You can expect to find the following types of companies in this chapter:**
*Environmental Engineering Firms • Sanitary Services*

### CATALYTICA ENERGY SYSTEMS, INC.

430 Ferguson Drive, Mountain View CA 94043. 650/960-3000. **Contact:** Regina Machado, Human Resources. **E-mail address:** hr@ catalyticaenergy.com. **World Wide Web address:** http://www. catalyticaenergy.com. **Description:** Develops catalytic technologies for the prevention of pollution in combustion systems, advanced process technologies, and chemical products. The company also develops an ultraslow emission-combustion system for natural gas turbines. Catalytica provides contract research, development, and consulting services to the petroleum refining and chemical industries. Additional programs include the development of a process for manufacturing gasoline alkylate to eliminate the use of liquid acid catalysts, the conversion of methane to transportation fuels, and the application of nanotechnology for new catalysts and materials. The company also manufactures fine chemical products. **Positions advertised include:** Chemist; Chemical Engineer; Test Engineer. **Corporate headquarters location:** This location. **Other U.S. locations:** Gilbert AZ. **Subsidiaries include:** Advanced Sensor Devices develops environmental monitoring devices including a continuous emissions monitor. **Listed on:** NASDAQ. **Stock exchange symbol:** CESI.

### EARTH TECH

2101 Webster Street, Oakland CA 94612. 510/419-6000. **Contact:** Personnel Department. **World Wide Web address:** http://www. earthtech.com. **Description:** Provides global water management, environmental, and transportation services. **Corporate headquarters location:** Long Beach CA. **Parent company:** Tyco International Ltd. **Listed on:** New York Stock Exchange. **Stock exchange symbol:** TYC.

### EBERLINE SERVICES

P.O. Box 4040, Richmond CA 94804-0040. 510/235-2633. **Physical address:** 2030 Wright Avenue, Richmond CA 94804. **Contact:** Human Resources Administrator. **E-mail address:** hr@ eberlineservices.com. **World Wide Web address:** http://www. eberlineservices.com. **Description:** Engaged in hazardous, radiological, and mixed-waste testing of soil and water. The company's work is related to regulatory compliance, and each of their laboratories is extensively licensed and qualified to accept radioactive samples. **Corporate headquarters location:** Albuquerque NM.

## ENVIRON CORPORATION

5820 Shellmound Street, Suite 700, Emeryville CA 94608. 510/655-7400. **Fax:** 510/655-9517. **Contact:** Mary Eichler, Director of Human Resources. **World Wide Web address:** http://www. environcorp.com. **Description:** A multidisciplinary environmental and health sciences consulting firm that provides a broad range of services relating to the presence of hazardous substances in the environment, consumer products, and the workplace. Services provided by ENVIRON are concentrated in the assessment and management of chemical risk. **Positions advertised include:** Engineering Associate; Air Science Manager; Associate, Human Health Risk Assessment; Manager, RWA Compliance. **Corporate headquarters location:** Arlington VA. **Other area locations:** Irvine CA; Novato CA. **Other U.S. locations:** Princeton NJ; Houston TX. **Parent company:** Applied BioScience International Inc.

## ENVIRON CORPORATION

101 Rowland Way, Suite 220, Novato CA 94945. 415/899-0700. **Fax:** 415/899-0707. **Contact:** Human Resources. **World Wide Web address:** http://www.environcorp.com. **Description:** A multidisciplinary environmental and health sciences consulting firm that provides a broad range of services relating to the presence of hazardous substances in the environment, consumer products, and the workplace. Services provided by ENVIRON are concentrated in the assessment and management of chemical risk. **Corporate headquarters location:** Arlington VA. **Other area locations:** Emeryville CA; Irvine CA. **Other U.S. locations:** Princeton NJ; Houston TX. **Parent company:** Applied BioScience International Inc.

## NORCAL WASTE SYSTEMS INC.

160 Pacific Avenue, Suite 200, San Francisco CA 94111. 415/875-1000. **Fax:** 415/875-1217. **Contact:** Human Resources Department. **World Wide Web address:** http://www.norcalwaste.com. **Description:** Engaged in waste management and recycling services. **Corporate headquarters location:** This location. **Number of employees at this location:** 1,375.

## SEVERN TRENT LABORATORIES, INC.
880 Riverside Parkway, West Sacramento CA 95605. 916/373-5600. **Fax:** 916/372-1059. **Contact:** Joseph Schrairer, Human Resources Representative. **E-mail address:** jschairer@stl-inc.com. **World Wide Web address:** http://www.stl-inc.com. **Description:** Provides a complete range of environmental testing services to private industry, engineering consultants, and government agencies in support of federal and state environmental regulations. The company also possesses analytical capabilities in the fields of air toxins, field analytical services, radiochemistry/mixed waste, and advanced technology.

## SHAW ENVIRONMENTAL AND INFASTRUCTURE
1921 Ringwood Avenue, San Jose CA 95131. 408/453-7300. **Contact:** Human Resources. **World Wide Web address:** http://www.theitgroup.com. **Description:** Provides environmental engineering, consulting, and construction services to a variety of public and private sector clients. Shaw is a leader in the design and remediation of solid and hazardous waste, transfer, storage, and disposal facilities. Shaw's waste facility services include site selection and evaluation, facility design, development of preprocessing and operating plans, assistance in regulatory compliance and permitting, final closures, and end use planning and design. The company's services also include the development of programs dealing with environmental assessments and remediation of contaminated sites, as well as services related to applied sciences such as marine fate-and-effect studies and fuel spill and natural resource damage assessments. **NOTE:** Entry-level positions are offered. **Office hours:** Monday - Friday, 8:00 a.m. - 5:00 p.m. **Corporate headquarters location:** Baton Rouge LA. **Parent company:** Shaw Group. **Listed on:** New York Stock Exchange. **Stock exchange symbol:** SGR.

## SIMSMETAL AMERICA
130 North 12th Street, Sacramento CA 95814. 916/444-3380. **Contact:** Human Resources. **World Wide Web address:** http://www.simsmetal.com. **Description:** A multifaceted company involved in metals recycling and related ventures. **Corporate headquarters location:** Richmond CA. **Parent company:** Simsmetal Limited (Australia).

## SIMSMETAL AMERICA
699 Seaport Boulevard, Redwood City CA 94063-2712. 650/369-4161. **Contact:** Human Resources. **World Wide Web address:** http://

www.sims-group.com. **Description:** A multifaceted company involved in metals recycling and related ventures. **Corporate headquarters location:** Richmond CA. **Parent company:** Simsmetal Limited (Australia).

## THE TRUST FOR PUBLIC LAND
116 New Montgomery, Fourth Floor, San Francisco CA 94105. 415/495-4014. **Fax:** 415/495-0540. **Contact:** Human Resources. **E-mail address:** jobs@tpl.org. **World Wide Web address:** http://www.tpl.org. **Description:** A national, not-for-profit organization that focuses on protecting land for human enjoyment. Land is conserved for recreation, spiritualization, and improvement of quality of life. **Positions advertised include:** Field Representative; Project Manager; Computer Support Specialist; Senior Project Manager; Staff Accountant; Legal Assistant.

## WASTE MANAGEMENT, INC.
715 Comstock Street, Santa Clara CA 95054-3403. 408/980-9900. **Contact:** Human Resources. **E-mail address:** careers@wm.com. **World Wide Web address:** http://www.wastemanagement.com. **Description:** Engaged in commercial and residential refuse removal. **Corporate headquarters location:** Oak Brook IL. **Listed on:** New York Stock Exchange. **Stock exchange symbol:** WMI.

# FABRICATED/PRIMARY METALS AND PRODUCTS

**You can expect to find the following types of companies in this chapter:**
*Aluminum and Copper Foundries • Die-Castings • Iron and Steel Foundries • Steel Works, Blast Furnaces, and Rolling Mills*

## AB&I FOUNDRY

7825 San Leandro Street, Oakland CA 94621. 510/632-3467. **Toll-free phone:** 800/GOT-IRON. **Fax:** 510/632-8035. **Contact:** Michael Lowe, Human Resources Manager. **World Wide Web address:** http://www.abifoundry.com. **Description:** A manufacturer of cast iron soil pipe, fittings, and custom castings. Founded in 1906. **Positions advertised include:** Vice President Trainee, Sales and Marketing. **Corporate headquarters location:** This location. **Annual sales/revenues:** $21 - $50 million. **Number of employees at this location:** 190.

## COORSTEK

8455 Cabot Court, Newark CA 94560. 510/793-9100. **Toll-free phone:** 800/821-6110. **Contact:** Human Resources. **E-mail address:** staffing@coorstek.com. **World Wide Web address:** http://www.coorstek.com. **Description:** The company engineers parts from ceramics, metals, and plastics. **Positions advertised include:** Lead Mechanic.

## PACIFIC STEEL CASTING COMPANY

1333 Second Street, Berkeley CA 94710. 510/525-9200. **Fax:** 510/524-9135. **Contact:** Ralph Hoover, Controller. **World Wide Web address:** http://www.pacificsteel.com. **Description:** Produces steel castings and is engaged in the heat-treating of metals. **Corporate headquarters location:** This location.

## SIMSMETAL AMERICA

600 South Fourth Street, Richmond CA 94804-3504. 510/236-0606. **Contact:** Jimmie Buckland, Senior Vice President. **E-mail address:** jbuckland@worldnet.att.net. **World Wide Web address:** http://www.simsmetal.com. **Description:** A multifaceted company involved in metals recycling and related ventures. **Corporate headquarters location:** This location. **Parent company:** Simsmetal Limited (Australia).

## C.E. TOLAND & SON

5300 Industrial Way, Benicia CA 94510. 707/747-1000. **Contact:** Office Manager. **Description:** Engaged in the fabrication of metal and metal products. Products include stairs, railings, and toilet partitions. **NOTE:** Jobseekers interested in working in the shop or field must be union members. **Corporate headquarters location:** This location.

## FINANCIAL SERVICES

**You can expect to find the following types of companies in this chapter:**
*Consumer Finance and Credit Agencies • Investment Specialists •*
*Mortgage Bankers and Loan Brokers •*
*Security and Commodity Brokers, Dealers, and Exchanges*

### ALLIANCE FINANCIAL CAPITOL, INC.

700 Airport Road, Burlingame CA 94010. 650/343-4400. **Fax:** 650/343-6977. **Contact:** Human Resources. **E-mail address:** bob@ alliancefinancialcap.com. **World Wide Web address:** http://www. alliancefinancialcap.com. **Description:** A financing company. **Positions advertised include:** Account Manager.

### AMERICAN EXPRESS COMPANY

455 Market Street, San Francisco CA 94105. 415/536-2600. **Toll-free phone:** 800/554-AMEX. **Contact:** Human Resources Department. **World Wide Web address:** http://www.americanexpress.com. **Description:** A diversified travel and financial services company operating in 160 countries around the world. American Express Travel Related Services offers consumers the Personal, Gold, and Platinum Cards, as well as revolving credit products such as Optima Cards, which allow customers to extend payments. Other products include the American Express Corporate Card and the Corporate Purchasing Card. Travel Related Services also offers American Express Traveler's Cheques and travel services including trip planning, reservations, ticketing, and management information. American Express Financial Advisors offers financial planning, annuities, mutual funds, insurance, investment certificates, institutional investment advisory trust services, tax preparation, and retail securities brokerage services. Founded in 1850. **Corporate headquarters location:** New York NY. **Other U.S. locations:** Nationwide. **International locations:** Worldwide. **Listed on:** New York Stock Exchange. **Stock exchange symbol:** AXP. **Annual sales/revenues:** More than $100 million. **Number of employees nationwide:** 95,000.

### BARCLAYS GLOBAL INVESTORS

45 Fremont Street, San Francisco CA 94105. 415/597-2000. **Fax:** 415/597-2492. **Contact:** Human Resources. **E-mail address:** staffing@barclaysglobal.com. **World Wide Web address:** http:// www.barclaysglobal.com. **Description:** An investment banking company. **Positions advertised include:** Equity Trading Researcher;

Quantitative International Equity Trader; Senior Systems Developer, Team Leader; Project Manager, Performance Measurement Counsel; Administrative Assistant/Program Assistant; Senior Business Planning and Reporting Analyst; Senior Systems Engineer; Systems Developer; Client Technology Lead Developer; Securities Lending Trader; Assistant Portfolio Manager. **Other U.S. locations:** Chicago IL; Boston MA. **International locations:** China; India; Indonesia; Korea; Malaysia; Mexico; New Zealand; Philippines; Taiwan; Thailand.

## BEAR, STEARNS & COMPANY, INC.

One Sansome Street, 41st Floor, Citicorp Center, San Francisco CA 94104. 415/772-2924. **Toll-free phone:** 800/688-2327. **Fax:** 415/772-3201. **Contact:** Personnel Manager. **E-mail address:** hresources_internet@bear.com. **World Wide Web address:** http://www.bearstearns.com. **Description:** A leading investment banking and securities trading and brokerage firm serving governments, corporations, institutions, and individuals worldwide. The company offers services in corporate finance, mergers and acquisitions, institutional equities, fixed income sales and trading, derivatives, futures sales and trading, asset management, and custody. **NOTE:** Please submit resume through the on-line application process. **Special programs:** Internships. **Internship information:** The company offers internships year-round. Applicants should mail or fax a resume to the Personnel Department. **Corporate headquarters location:** New York NY. **Other U.S. locations:** Nationwide. **International locations:** Worldwide. **Parent company:** The Bear Stearns Companies Inc. also operate Bear Stearns Securities Corporation, which provides professional and correspondent clearing services, including securities lending, and Custodial Trust Company, which provides master trust, custody, and government securities services. **Listed on:** New York Stock Exchange. **Stock exchange symbol:** BSC. **Annual sales/revenues:** More than $100 million. **Number of employees at this location:** 200. **Number of employees nationwide:** 7,800.

## BOWNE OF SAN FRANCISCO, INC.

343 Sansome Street, 15th Floor, San Francisco CA 94104. 415/362-2300. **Contact:** Human Resources. **World Wide Web address:** http://www.bowne.com. **Description:** Provides financial and corporate printing services. **Positions advertised include:** Office Service Associate; Strategic Account Manager. **Corporate headquarters location:** New York NY. **Other U.S. locations:** Nationwide. **International locations:** Worldwide. **Parent company:** Bowne &

Company, Inc. **Listed on:** New York Stock Exchange. **Stock exchange symbol:** BNE.

## CHARLES SCHWAB & CO., INC.

101 Montgomery Street, San Francisco CA 94104. 415/627-7000. **Fax:** 415/636-8018. **Recorded jobline:** 415/627-7227. **Contact:** Human Resources. **World Wide Web address:** http://www.schwab. com. **Description:** One of the largest discount brokerage companies in the United States. The firm has more than 200 branches and over 2.5 million active customer accounts. **NOTE:** All resumes received will be scanned into a recruiting database. Resumes should be sent on white or light-colored paper without any bullets, boldface print, italics, or underlines. **Special programs:** Internships. **Corporate headquarters location:** This location. **Other U.S. locations:** Nationwide. **International locations:** Worldwide. **Parent company:** Charles Schwab Corporation. **Operations at this facility include:** Administration; Sales; Service. **Listed on:** New York Stock Exchange. **Stock exchange symbol:** SCH. **Number of employees at this location:** 2,200.

## CITICORP
## CITIBANK

One Sansome Street, San Francisco CA 94104-4448. 415/627-6000. **Recorded jobline:** 415/658-4562. **Contact:** Human Resources Department. **E-mail address:** hr-resumes@citicorp.com. **World Wide Web address:** http://www.citybank.com. **Description:** Provides investment and financial services to individuals, businesses, governments, and financial institutions in approximately 3,000 locations. **Corporate headquarters location:** New York NY. **Parent company:** Citigroup. **Operations at this facility include:** Administration; Regional Headquarters; Sales; Service. **Listed on:** New York Stock Exchange. **Stock exchange symbol:** CIH-A. **Number of employees worldwide:** 85,000.

## FRANKLIN RESOURCES, INC.

One Franklin Parkway, San Mateo CA 94403. 650/312-2578. **Fax:** 650/312-3655. **Contact:** Human Resources. **E-mail address:** careers@frk.com. **World Wide Web address:** http://www. franklintempleton.com/public/corporate. **Description:** Provides mutual fund and money market services. **Positions advertised include:** Financial Analyst; Product Manager; Administrative Assistant; Sales Associate; Compliance Analyst; Account Administrator; Campaign Project Manager; Paralegal; Performance

Consultant; Relationship Manager. **Corporate headquarters location:** This location. **Subsidiaries include:** Franklin Templeton Group. **Listed on:** New York Stock Exchange. **Stock exchange symbol:** BEN.

## GATX CAPITAL CORPORATION

4 Embarcadero Center, Suite 2200, San Francisco CA 94111. 415/955-3200. **Fax:** 415/403-3517. **Contact:** Human Resources. **E-mail address:** jobs@gatxcapital.com. **World Wide Web address:** http://www.gatxcap.com. **Description:** GATX Capital is a diversified, international financial services company providing asset-based financing for transportation and industrial equipment. The company arranges full payout financing leases, secured loans, operating leases, and other structured financing both as an investing principal and with institutional partners. **Positions advertised include:** Senior Contract Specialist; Senior Portfolio Accountant. **Corporate headquarters location:** This location. **Subsidiaries include:** GATX Rail acquires, leases, and sells railcars and locomotives for GATX Capital's own portfolio and for managed portfolios. **Parent company:** GATX Corporation. **Listed on:** New York Stock Exchange. **Stock exchange symbol:** GMT. **Number of employees at this location:** 190.

## HOUSEHOLD FINANCE CORPORATION

388 Market Street, Suite 850, San Francisco CA 94111. 415/362-4542. **Fax:** 415/362-4548. **Contact:** Branch Manager. **World Wide Web address:** http://www.hfc.com. **Description:** Offers real estate, home equity, and personal loans. **Corporate headquarters location:** Prospect Heights IL. **Parent company:** Household International. **Operations at this facility include:** Sales; Service. **Listed on:** New York Stock Exchange. **Stock exchange symbol:** HI. **Number of employees at this location:** 5. **Number of employees nationwide:** 5,000.

## ITEX CORPORATION

3400 Cottage Way, Sacramento CA 95825. 916/679-1111. **Contact:** Human Resources. **World Wide Web address:** http://www.itex.com. **Description:** ITEX Corporation operates one of the nation's largest barter exchanges with over 130 offices nationwide. ITEX operates an internationally accessible electronic trading and communications system known as BarterWire, which allows ITEX members coast-to-coast to market and purchase goods and services. The company publishes *alt.finance*, which focuses on the barter industry. All goods and services advertised within its pages are sold for ITEX trade dollars. The company also has the ITEX Express Card, the first debit/credit card in the barter industry. **Corporate headquarters location:** This location.

### JEFFERIES & COMPANY, INC.
650 California Street, 30th Floor, San Francisco CA 94108. 415/229-1500. **Contact:** Dee Dee Bird, Recruiting Coordinator. **E-mail address:** dbird@jefco.com. **World Wide Web address:** http://www.jefco.com. **Description:** Jefferies & Company is engaged in equity, convertible debt and taxable fixed income securities brokerage and trading, and corporate finance. Founded in 1962. **NOTE:** Resumes should be sent to Human Resources, Jefferies & Company, Inc., 11100 Santa Monica Boulevard, Los Angeles CA 90025. **Corporate headquarters location:** Los Angeles CA. **Parent company:** Jefferies Group, Inc. is a holding company that, through Jefferies & Company, Inc.; Investment Technology Group, Inc.; Jefferies International Limited; and Jefferies Pacific Limited, is engaged in securities brokerage and trading, corporate finance, and other financial services. **Listed on:** New York Stock Exchange. **Stock exchange symbol:** JEF.

### MERRILL LYNCH
600 California Street, 8th Floor, San Francisco CA 94108. 415/955-3700. **Contact:** Human Resources. **World Wide Web address:** http://www.ml.com. **Description:** Merrill Lynch provides financial services in the following areas: securities, extensive insurance, and real estate. One of the largest securities brokerage firms in the United States, the company also brokers commodity futures and options and corporate and municipal securities and is engaged in investment banking activities. The company operates three offices in San Francisco. **Positions advertised include:** Finance Manager; Administrative Assistant; Director, Cash Flow; Vice President, Due Diligence; Senior Underwriter; Investment Officer. **Corporate headquarters location:** New York NY. **Operations at this facility include:** Sales. **Listed on:** New York Stock Exchange. **Stock exchange symbol:** MITT.

### MORGAN STANLEY DEAN WITTER & COMPANY
101 California Street, 7th Floor, San Francisco CA 94111. 415/693-6000. **Contact:** Renee Minnis, Personnel Manager. **E-mail address:** imrecruiting@morganstanley.com (for Investment Management positions); instsecrecruiting@morganstanley.com (for Institutional Securities Information Technology positions). **World Wide Web**

**address:** http://www.morganstanley.com. **Description:** Offers diversified financial services including equities, fixed income securities, commodities, money market instruments, and investment banking services. **Corporate headquarters location:** New York NY. **Listed on:** New York Stock Exchange. **Stock exchange symbol:** BDJ.

### MORGAN STANLEY DEAN WITTER & COMPANY

555 California Street, Suite 2200, San Francisco CA 94104. 415/576-2000. **Contact:** Human Resources Manager. **E-mail address:** imrecruiting@morganstanley.com (for investment management positions); instsecrecruiting@morganstanley.com (for institutional securities information technology positions). **World Wide Web address:** http://www.morganstanley.com. **Description:** Offers diversified financial services including equities, fixed income securities, commodities, money market instruments, and investment banking services. **Corporate headquarters location:** New York NY. **Listed on:** New York Stock Exchange. **Stock exchange symbol:** BDJ.

### NORTH AMERICAN MORTGAGE

3883 Airway Drive, Santa Rosa CA 95403. 707/523-5000. **Contact:** Human Resources. **World Wide Web address:** http://www.namc. com. **Description:** Originates, acquires, sells, and services mortgage loans, principally first lien mortgage loans secured by single-family residences. North American Mortgage also sells servicing rights associated with a portion of such loans. The company operates through a network of 50 loan origination offices in 14 states, primarily in California and Texas. **Parent company:** Washington Mutual Bank. **Listed on:** New York Stock Exchange. **Stock exchange symbol:** WM.

### PROVIDIAN FINANCIAL

201 Mission Street, San Francisco CA 94105. 415/543-0404. **Toll-free phone:** 800/918-9101. **Contact:** Human Resources. **World Wide Web address:** http://www.providian.com. **Description:** Provides lending, deposit, bankcard issuing, and other related financial services. **Positions advertised include:** Auditor; Administrative Assistant; Compliance Officer; Credit Analyst; Credit Manager; Director; Project Manager. **Corporate headquarters location:** This location. **Listed on:** New York Stock Exchange. **Stock exchange symbol:** PVN.

## PRUDENTIAL SECURITIES

4 Embarcadero Center, Suite 2400, San Francisco CA 94111. 415/395-9888. **Contact:** Personnel. **World Wide Web address:** http://www.prudentialsecurities.com. **Description:** An international securities brokerage and investment firm. The company offers clients more than 70 investment products including stocks, options, bonds, commodities, tax-favored investments, and insurance, as well as several specialized financial services. Prudential Securities operates more than 240 offices in 17 countries. **Corporate headquarters location:** New York NY. **Parent company:** Prudential Insurance Company. **Listed on:** New York Stock Exchange. **Stock exchange symbol:** PRU.

## RBC DAIN RAUCHER

201 California Street, San Francisco CA 94111. 415/445-8500. **Fax:** 415/421-7632. **Contact:** Tony Schultz, Manager of Human Resources. **World Wide Web address:** http://www.rbcdain.com. **Description:** A full-service, regional investment brokerage firm. Founded in 1858. **Corporate headquarters location:** This location. **Parent company:** Royal Bank of Canada. **Operations at this facility include:** Administration; Research and Development; Sales; Service. **Listed on:** New York Stock Exchange. **Stock exchange symbol:** RY.

## SEI INVESTMENTS COMPANY

300 Montgomery Street, Suite 930, San Francisco CA 94104. 415/627-1900. **Contact:** Human Resources. **E-mail address:** careers@seic.com. **World Wide Web address:** http://www.seic.com. **Description:** An investment services firm that operates in two business markets: trust and banking, and fund/sponsor investments. The company also provides an online investment accounting system for trust departments. **Corporate headquarters location:** Wayne PA. **Listed on:** NASDAQ. **Stock exchange symbol:** SEIC.

## TRANSAMERICA CORPORATION

600 Montgomery Street, 23rd Floor, San Francisco CA 94111. 415/983-4000. **Contact:** Human Resources. **World Wide Web address:** http://www.transamerica.com. **Description:** Operates diversified financial services and insurance companies. **Corporate headquarters location:** This location. **Operations at this facility include:** Administration. **Listed on:** New York Stock Exchange. **Stock exchange symbol:** TFD.

## UBS PAINEWEBBER INC.
555 California Street, Suite 3200, San Francisco CA 94104-1501. 415/398-6400. **Contact:** Mr. Tony Tarrab, Branch Manager. **World Wide Web address:** http://www.ubspainewebber.com. **Description:** A full-service securities firm with over 300 offices nationwide. Services include investment banking, asset management, merger and acquisition consulting, municipal securities underwriting, estate planning, retirement programs, and transaction management. UBS PaineWebber offers its services to corporations, governments, institutions, and individuals. Founded in 1879. **Corporate headquarters location:** New York NY. **Other U.S. locations:** Nationwide. **Annual sales/revenues:** More than $100 million.

## UBS PAINEWEBBER INC.
One California Street, 20th Floor, San Francisco CA 94111. 415/954-6700. **Contact:** Sara Mayoux, Human Resources Department. **World Wide Web address:** http://www.ubspainewebber.com. **Description:** One of the world's largest investment services firms. UBS PaineWebber assists corporations, governments, and individuals in meeting their long-term financial needs. UBS PaineWebber also has operations in equity and fixed-income securities. Founded in 1879. **Corporate headquarters location:** New York NY. **Other U.S. locations:** Nationwide.

## FOOD AND BEVERAGES/ AGRICULTURE

**You can expect to find the following types of companies in this chapter:**
*Crop Services and Farm Supplies • Dairy Farms • Food Manufacturers/Processors and Agricultural Producers • Tobacco Products*

### BERINGER BLASS WINE ESTATES

P.O. Box 4500, Napa CA 94558. 707/259-4500. **Physical address:** 610 Air Park Road, Napa CA 94558. **Fax:** 707/259-4542. **Contact:** Human Resources. **E-mail address:** bwenet@bwecorp.com. **World Wide Web address:** http://www.beringerwineestates.com. **Description:** A leading producer and marketer of premium wines. In addition to operating their own local vineyards, Beringer Blass Wine Estates imports and markets wine from France, Italy, and Chile. Brands include Beringer Vineyards, Chateau St. Jean, Meridian Vineyards, St. Clement, Rivefort de France, and Campanile. **Positions advertised include:** Administrative Coordinator; Customer Service Specialist; Gardner; On-Call Server. **Corporate headquarters location:** This location. **Other area locations:** Cloverdale CA; Geyserville CA; Kenwood CA; Paso Robles CA; Santa Barbara CA; St. Helena CA. **Parent company:** Foster's Brewing Group Limited.

### BESTFOODS BAKING COMPANY

264 South Spruce Avenue, South San Francisco CA 94080. 650/875-3100. **Contact:** Human Resources. **World Wide Web address:** http://www.bestfoods.com. **Description:** Manufactures and distributes a line of cakes, cookies, doughnuts, and similar baked products. **Other U.S. locations:** Clinton CT; Greenwich CT; Trumbull CT; Chicago IL; Rolling Meadows IL; Edgewater NJ; Englewood Cliffs NJ; Saddle Brook NJ; New York NY; Cincinnati OH; Dallas TX. **International locations:** Worldwide. **Parent company:** Unilever Bestfoods, Inc. **Listed on:** New York Stock Exchange. **Stock exchange symbol:** UL.

### CAMPBELL SOUP COMPANY

6200 Franklin Boulevard, Sacramento CA 95824. 916/428-7890. **Contact:** Human Resources. **World Wide Web address:** http://www.campbellsoup.com. **Description:** Campbell Soup is a major producer of commercial soups, juices, pickles, frozen foods, canned beans and pasta products, spaghetti sauces, and baked goods. The company distributes its products worldwide. U.S. brands include Campbell's, Vlasic, V8, Chunky, Home Cookin', Prego, Pepperidge

Farm, Inc., LeMenu, and Swanson. European brand names include Pleybin, Biscuits Delacre, Freshbake, Groko, Godiva, and Betis. **Corporate headquarters location:** Camden NJ. **Other U.S. locations:** Nationwide. **International locations:** Worldwide. **Operations at this facility include:** This location makes a variety of soups. **Listed on:** New York Stock Exchange. **Stock exchange symbol:** CPB.

### CHALONE WINE GROUP, LTD.
621 Airpark Road, Napa CA 94558-6272. 707/254-4200. **Fax:** 707/254-4207. **Contact:** Human Resources. **E-mail address:** hr@ chalonewinegroup.com. **World Wide Web address:** http://www. chalonewinegroup.com. **Description:** Chalone Wine Group, Ltd. produces, markets, and sells premium white and red varietal table wines, primarily Chardonnay, Pinot Noir, Cabernet Sauvignon, and Sauvignon Blanc. **Corporate headquarters location:** This location. **Listed on:** NASDAQ. **Stock exchange symbol:** CHLN.

### DEL MONTE FOODS
P.O. Box 193757, San Francisco CA 94119. 415/247-3000. **Physical address:** The Landmark at One Market Street, San Francisco CA 94105. **Contact:** Human Resources. **World Wide Web address:** http://www.delmonte.com. **Description:** A producer of canned fruits and vegetables, tomato sauces, condiments, and dessert products for the consumer, institutional, and military markets. The company operates over 60 plants worldwide where it processes food and makes, labels, and packs its own cans. Brand names include Del Monte and Contadina. Founded in 1892. **Positions advertised include:** Product Manager; Customer Marketing Analyst. **Corporate headquarters location:** This location. **Listed on:** New York Stock Exchange. **Stock exchange symbol:** DLM.

### DREYER'S GRAND ICE CREAM, INC.
5929 College Avenue, Oakland CA 94618. 510/652-8187. **Contact:** Human Resources. **World Wide Web address:** http://www.dreyers. com. **Description:** Manufactures and distributes ice cream and other dairy dessert products under the Edy's Grand Ice Cream brand name. **Corporate headquarters location:** This location. **Listed on:** NASDAQ. **Stock exchange symbol:** DRYR. **Number of employees nationwide:** 1,150.

### GILROY FOODS
8180 Arroyo Circle, Gilroy CA 95020. 408/846-3200. **Fax:** 408/846-3529. **Contact:** Toni Rivera, Personnel Manager. **E-mail address:**

humanresources@gilroyfoods.com. **World Wide Web address:** http://www.gilroyfoods.com. **Description:** A dehydrator of vegetable products. Founded in 1959. **NOTE:** Second and third shifts are offered. **Special programs:** Internships; Summer Jobs. **Corporate headquarters location:** This location. **Parent company:** ConAgra, Inc. **Operations at this facility include:** Divisional Headquarters. **Listed on:** New York Stock Exchange. **Stock exchange symbol:** CAG. **President:** Randy Tognazzini. **Information Systems Manager:** Greg Cassalia. **Purchasing Manager:** Earl Pittman. **Annual sales/revenues:** More than $100 million. **Number of employees nationwide:** 2,000.

## KELLOGG COMPANY
## KELLOGG USA CONVENIENCE FOODS DIVISION
P.O. Box 5191, San Jose CA 95150. 408/295-8656. **Physical address:** 475 Eggo Way, San Jose CA 95116. **Contact:** Human Resources. **World Wide Web address:** http://www.kellogg.com. **Description:** Kellogg Company specializes in the manufacturing and marketing of ready-to-eat cereals, and other convenience foods. Kellogg products are manufactured in 18 countries in North America, Europe, Asia-Pacific, and Latin America, and are distributed in more than 150 countries. Founded in 1906. **Corporate headquarters location:** Battle Creek MI. **Other U.S. locations:** San Leandro CA; Atlanta GA; Omaha NE; Blue Anchor NJ; Lancaster PA; Muncy PA; Pottstown PA; Memphis TN; Rossville TN. **International locations:** Ontario, Canada. **Operations at this facility include:** This location manufactures products such as Kellogg's Pop-Tarts toaster pastries, Eggo waffles, Kellogg's Nutri-Grain bars, Kellogg's low-fat granola bars, Kellogg's Croutettes stuffing mix, and Kellogg's Corn Flake crumbs. **Listed on:** New York Stock Exchange. **Stock exchange symbol:** K.

## KRAFT FOODS, INC.
100 Halcyon Drive, San Leandro CA 94578. 510/639-5000. **Contact:** Human Resources. **World Wide Web address:** http://www.kraftfoods.com. **Description:** Overall, Kraft is one of the largest American-based packaged food companies. Other Kraft brands include DiGiorno, Maxwell House, Stove Top, and Oscar Mayer. **NOTE:** Resumes are accepted only via e-mail. Please e-mail your resume to the attention of the Human Resources representative listed in the job advertisement. **Corporate headquarters location:** Northfield IL. **Parent company:** Philip Morris Companies Inc. **Operations at this facility include:** This location is engaged in the

production of coffee, Jell-O, Log Cabin syrup, and Tang. **Listed on:** New York Stock Exchange. **Stock exchange symbol:** KFT.

## ODWALLA INC.
120 Stone Pine Road, Half Moon Bay Ca 94019. 650/726-1888. **Fax:** 650/712-5572. **Contact:** Human Resources. **E-mail address:** odwallajobs@odwalla.com. **World Wide Web address:** http://www. odwalla.com. **Description:** A juice company. **Positions advertised include:** District Sales Manager; Payroll Manager; QA Technician.

## PEPSI-COLA BOTTLING COMPANY
7550 Reese Road, Sacramento CA 95828. 916/423-1000. **Fax:** 916/423-0111. **Contact:** Human Resources. **World Wide Web address:** http://www.pepsico.com. **Description:** A bottling facility for the Pepsi-Cola Company. **Positions advertised include:** Sales Manager; Technical Manager; District Sales Leader. **Parent company:** PepsiCo, Inc. (Purchase NY) consists of Frito-Lay Company, Pepsi-Cola Company, and Tropicana Products, Inc. **Corporate headquarters location:** Purchase NY. **Listed on:** New York Stock Exchange. **Stock exchange symbol:** PBG.

## THE QUAKER OATS COMPANY
P.O. Box 2205, Oakland CA 94621. 510/261-5800. **Contact:** Human Resources Department. **E-mail address:** gorecruiting@ quakeroats.com. **World Wide Web address:** http://www.quakeroats. com. **Description:** The Quaker Oats Company is a leading manufacturer of sports beverages, cereals, snack foods, and pasta products. **NOTE:** Please include job code in subject line of e-mail. **Positions advertised include:** Production Supervisor. **Special programs:** Internships. **Corporate headquarters location:** Chicago IL. **Other U.S. locations:** Nationwide. **Parent company:** PepsiCo, Inc. **Operations at this facility include:** This location manufactures beverages and consumer food products. **Listed on:** New York Stock Exchange. **Stock exchange symbol:** PEP. **Operations at this facility include:** Manufacturing. **Number of employees at this location:** 200.

## SARA LEE
955 Kennedy Street, Oakland CA 94606. 510/436-5350. **Contact:** Personnel Department. **E-mail address:** recruiting@saralee.com. **World Wide Web address:** http://www.saralee.com. **Description:** An international producer and marketer of food and consumer products. **Corporate headquarters location:** Chicago IL. **Listed on:** New York Stock Exchange. **Stock exchange symbol:** SLE.

## SARA LEE

2411 Baumann Avenue, San Lorenzo CA 94580. 510/276-1300. **Contact:** Personnel. **World Wide Web address:** http://www. saralee.com. **Description:** An international producer and marketer of food and consumer products. **Corporate headquarters location:** Chicago IL. **Listed on:** New York Stock Exchange. **Stock exchange symbol:** SLE.

## SEE'S CANDIES

210 El Camino Real, South San Francisco CA 94080. 650/583-7307. **Contact:** Human Resources. **E-mail address:** resumes@sees.com. **World Wide Web address:** http://www.sees.com. **Description:** See's Candies manufactures candy. **Corporate headquarters location:** This location. **Operations at this facility include:** This location houses administrative offices.

## SHASTA BEVERAGES INC.
## BEVPAK MANUFACTURING

26901 Industrial Boulevard, Hayward CA 94545. 510/783-3200. **Contact:** Human Resources Director. **E-mail address:** humanresources@nationalbeverage.com. **World Wide Web address:** http://www.shastapop.com. **Description:** A producer of a variety of regular and diet soft drinks. Bevpak Manufacturing (also at this location) bottles beverages produced by Shasta. **Special programs:** Internships. **Corporate headquarters location:** This location. **Parent company:** National Beverage. **Listed on:** American Stock Exchange. **Stock exchange symbol:** FIZ.

## SNAPPLE

Oakland Army Base, Oakland CA 94601. 510/433-0900. **Contact:** Human Resources. **World Wide Web address:** http://www.snapple. com. **Description:** A beverage company. **NOTE:** Jobseekers should apply online. **Positions advertised include:** Director of National Accounts.

## SUN SEEDS

P.O. Box 2078, Morgan Hill CA 95038-2078. 408/776-1111. **Physical address:** 18640 Sutter Boulevard, Morgan Hill CA 95037-2825. **Contact:** Human Resources Department. **E-mail address:** resumes@sunseeds.com. **World Wide Web address:** http://www. sunseeds.com. **Description:** A producer of seeds and related products for the agricultural industry. **Corporate headquarters location:** This location. **Number of employees at this location:** 125.

**SYSCO FOOD SERVICES OF SAN FRANCISCO, INC.**
5900 Stewart Avenue, Fremont CA 94538. 510/226-3000. **Contact:** Elliott Levin, Vice President of Human Resources. **E-mail address:** levin.elliott.ro50@sysco.com. **World Wide Web address:** http://www.syscosf.com. **Description:** Distributes a wide variety of food and grocery products to businesses, hospitals, and school districts. **Positions advertised include:** Marketing Associate. **Corporate headquarters location:** Chicago IL. **Listed on:** New York Stock Exchange. **Stock exchange symbol:** SYY. **Number of employees at this location:** 1,100.

# GOVERNMENT

**You can expect to find the following types of agencies in this chapter:**
*Courts • Executive, Legislative, and General Government • Public Agencies
(Firefighters, Military, Police) • United States Postal Service*

## CALIFORNIA HIGHWAY PATROL
1551 Benecia Road, Vallejo CA 94591. 707/551-4100. **Toll-free phone:** 888/4A-CHP JOB. **Contact:** Recruitment Unit. **E-mail address:** recruiting@chp.ca.gov. **World Wide Web address:** http://www.chp.ca.gov. **Description:** Provides law enforcement services for the state of California. **Corporate headquarters location:** Sacramento CA. **Other area locations:** Statewide. **Number of employees nationwide:** 6,000.

## HAYWARD, CITY OF
777 B Street, Hayward CA 94541-5007. 510/583-4500. **Recorded jobline:** 510/583-4555. **Contact:** Personnel. **World Wide Web address:** http://www.ci.hayward.ca.us. **Description:** Government offices for the City of Hayward. **Positions advertised include:** Community Service Operator; Lateral Animal Control Officer; Lateral Communications Operator; Lateral Community Service Operator. **Special programs:** Internships. **Corporate headquarters location:** This location. **Operations at this facility include:** Administration. **Number of employees at this location:** 800.

## PORT OF SAN FRANCISCO
Pier One, San Francisco CA 94111. 415/274-0400. **Contact:** Kathy Mallegni, Personnel Manager. **World Wide Web address:** http://www.sfport.com. **Description:** Operates port facilities as an agency of both the City and County of San Francisco. **NOTE:** The San Francisco municipal employment application is available online at: http://www.sfgov.org.

## SAN FRANCISCO MEDICAL EXAMINER'S OFFICE
850 Bryant Street, San Francisco CA 94103. 415/553-1694. **Recorded jobline:** 415/557-4888. **Contact:** Human Resources. **World Wide Web address:** http://www.ci.sf.ca.us/dhr.com. **Description:** The medical examiner's office for the City of San Francisco.

## SANTA CLARA VALLEY TRANSPORTATION AUTHORITY

3331 North First Street, Building B, San Jose CA 95134. 408/321-5575. **Contact:** Personnel Director. **E-mail address:** personnel@ vta.org. **World Wide Web address:** http://www.vta.org. **Description:** Provides transportation services to the San Jose area. **Positions advertised include:** Community Outreach Manager.

## U.S. ENVIRONMENTAL PROTECTION AGENCY (EPA)

USEPA Region 9, PMD-12, 75 Hawthorne Street, San Francisco CA 94105. 415/947-8020. **Recorded jobline:** 415/947-8017. **Contact:** Human Resources. **World Wide Web address:** http://www.epa.gov. **Description:** The EPA is dedicated to improving and preserving the quality of the environment, both nationally and globally, and protecting human health and the productivity of natural resources. The agency is committed to ensuring that federal environmental laws are implemented and enforced effectively; U.S. policy, both foreign and domestic, encourages the integration of economic development and environmental protection so that economic growth can be sustained over the long term; and public and private decisions affecting energy, transportation, agriculture, industry, international trade, and natural resources fully integrate considerations of environmental quality. Founded in 1970. **Special programs:** Internships; Co-ops; Summer Jobs. **Office hours:** Monday - Friday, 8:00 a.m. - 4:30 p.m. **Corporate headquarters location:** Washington DC. **Number of employees nationwide:** 19,000.

# HEALTH CARE: SERVICES, EQUIPMENT, AND PRODUCTS

**You can expect to find the following types of companies in this chapter:**
*Dental Labs and Equipment • Home Health Care Agencies • Hospitals and Medical Centers • Medical Equipment Manufacturers and Wholesalers • Offices and Clinics of Health Practitioners • Residential Treatment Centers/Nursing Homes • Veterinary Services*

## ADOBE ANIMAL HOSPITAL

396 First Street, Los Altos CA 94022. 650/948-9661. **Contact:** Human Resources. **E-mail address:** adobe1@flash.net. **World Wide Web address:** http://www.adobe-animal.com. **Description:** A fully equipped animal hospital that provides surgical, pharmaceutical, intensive care, laboratory, and radiology services. The hospital also provides regular checkups and puppy training classes. **Positions advertised include:** Emergency Verterinarian; Registered Animal Health Technician.

## ALAMEDA COUNTY MEDICAL CENTER

1411 East 31st Street, Oakland CA 94602. 510/437-4108. **Fax:** 510/437-5197. **Contact:** Human Resources. **E-mail address:** resumes@acmedctr.org. **World Wide Web address:** http://www. acmedctr.org. **Description:** A 300-bed, adult, acute care teaching hospital. **Positions advertised include:** Clinical Clerk; Physician; Lab Manager; Food Service Worker; Risk Review Coordinator; Certified Nurses Aide; Secretary; Assistant Medical Records Director; Occupational Therapist. **Corporate headquarters location:** Oakland CA. **Other area locations:** San Leandro CA. **Operations at this facility include:** Service.

## ALTUS MEDICAL

821 Cowan Road, Burlingame CA 94010. 650/552-9700. **Fax:** 650/552-9787. **Contact:** Human Resources. **E-mail address:** rrodgers@altusmedical.com. **Description:** Develops, manufactures, and markets aesthetic laser systems for dermatologists. **Positions advertised include:** Mechanical Engineer; Senior Buyer/Planner; Director of Operations; Vice President of Japan.

## AMERICAN ACADEMY OF OPHTHALMOLOGY

P.O. Box 7274, San Francisco CA 94120-7424. 415/561-8500. **Physical address:** 655 Beach Street, San Francisco CA 94109. **Contact:** Human Resources. **E-mail address:** eyenet@aao.org. **World**

**Wide Web address:** http://www.aao.org/news/eyenet. **Description:** A lobbying group that focuses on all government legislation affecting the ophthalmology community. **Corporate headquarters location:** This location.

## AMERICAN SHARED HOSPITAL SERVICES
4 Embarcadero Center, Suite 3700, San Francisco CA 94111-3823. 415/788-5300. **Toll-free phone:** 800/735-0641. **Fax:** 415/788-5660. **Contact:** Human Resources. **World Wide Web address:** http://www.ashs.com. **Description:** Provides shared diagnostic imaging services and respiratory therapy contract management to several hospitals, medical centers, and medical offices worldwide. The four diagnostic imaging services provided by the company are Magnetic Resonance Imaging (MRI), Computed Axial Tomography Scanning (CT), Ultrasound, and Nuclear Medicine. **Corporate headquarters location:** This location. **Other U.S. locations:** AR; CT; IL; MA; MS; NV; NJ; TX; WI.

## ANESTHESIA PLUS, INC.
9255 Survey Road, Suite 1, Elk Grove CA 95624. 916/686-4480. **Toll-free phone:** 800/887-8161. **Fax:** 916/686-4311. **Contact:** Human Resources. **World Wide Web address:** http://www.anesplus.com. **Description:** Manufactures and markets new and refurbished O.R. equipment. The company specializes in anesthesia and related products.

## BAYSHORE ANIMAL HOSPITAL
233 North Amphlett Boulevard, San Mateo CA 94401. 650/342-7022. **Contact:** Human Resources. **World Wide Web address:** http://www.bahospital.com. **Description:** A full-service animal hospital that provides several specialty services including eye and tooth care, in-hospital consultation with outside specialists, pharmacy, and x-ray. The hospital also provides boarding facilities when required.

## BIGGS-GRIDLEY MEMORIAL HOSPITAL
P.O. Box 97, Gridley CA 95948. 530/846-5671. **Fax:** 530/846-9027. **Contact:** Personnel. **World Wide Web address:** http://www.frgh.org. **Description:** A hospital. **NOTE:** Please send resumes to: Rideout Memorial Hospital, 726 Fourth Street, Marysville CA 95901. **Parent company:** Freemont-Rideout Health Group. **Operations at this facility include:** Administration. **Listed on:** Privately held.

## BOSTON SCIENTIFIC EP TECHNOLOGIES

2710 Orchard Parkway, San Jose CA 95134. 408/895-3500. **Fax:** 408/895-2203. **Contact:** Human Resources. **World Wide Web address:** http://www.bsci.com. **Description:** A worldwide developer, manufacturer, and marketer of medical devices used in a broad range of interventional procedures including the fields of cardiology, gastroenterology, pulmonary medicine, and vascular surgery. **Positions advertised include:** Senior Regulatory Affairs Specialist; Product Manager; Principal Manufacturing Engineer; Senior Regulatory Compliance Specialist; Clinical Research Associate; Principal Clinical Data Specialist; Principal R&D Engineer; Project Manager. **Corporate headquarters location:** Natick MA. **Other area locations:** Fremont CA; Murietta CA; Santa Clara CA; San Diego CA. **International locations:** Worldwide. **Listed on:** New York Stock Exchange. **Stock exchange symbol:** BSX.

## BOSTON SCIENTIFIC TARGET

47900 Bayside Parkway, Fremont CA 94538. 510/440-7700. **Contact:** Human Resources Manager. **World Wide Web address:** http://www.bsci.com. **Description:** Manufactures specialized disposable microcatheters, guidewires, microcoils, and angioplasty products. **Positions advertised include:** Program Manager; Clinical Affairs Project Manager; Senior Quality Engineer; Program Manager, Meetings and Events; Clinical Affairs Project Manager; New Business Development Engineering Fellow; Senior Quality Engineer; Senior Software Quality Engineer. **Corporate headquarters location:** Natick MA. **Parent company:** Boston Scientific Corporation. **Listed on:** New York Stock Exchange. **Stock exchange symbol:** BSX.

## CALIFORNIA DENTAL ASSOCIATION

1201 K Street, Sacramento CA 95814. 916/443-0505. **Toll-free phone:** 800/736-7071. **Fax:** 916/444-0718. **Contact:** Brenda Dilchrist, Human Resources Director. **E-mail address:** billl@cda.org. **World Wide Web address:** http://www.cda.org. **Description:** A nonprofit dental association providing membership programs and services for California dentists. **Positions advertised include:** Associate; Dental Consultant. **Corporate headquarters location:** This location. **Operations at this facility include:** Administration; Sales; Service. **Listed on:** Privately held. **Number of employees at this location:** 200.

**DOCTORS MEDICAL CENTER**
2000 Vale Road, San Pablo CA 94806. 510/970-5000. **Contact:** Human Resources. **World Wide Web address:** http://www. tenethealth.com. **Description:** An acute care hospital. **Positions advertised include:** Respiratory Therapy Technician; Registered Nurse; Nursing Assistant; IT Contract Manager; Pharmacist; Contractor; Therapist; Secretary; Social Worker; Health Information Clerk; Clinical Nursing Manager. **Corporate headquarters location:** Santa Barbara CA. **Parent company:** Tenet Healthcare Corporation owns and operates, through its subsidiaries, 111 acute care hospitals and related businesses in 17 states. **Listed on:** New York Stock Exchange. **Stock exchange symbol:** THC. **Number of employees at this location:** 900.

**ENLOE MEDICAL CENTER**
1531 Esplanade, Chico CA 95926. 530/332-7300. **Toll-free phone:** 800/822-8102x7352. **Fax:** 530/899-2010. **Recorded jobline:** 530/892-6711. **Contact:** Charlene Davis, Recruiting Manager. **E-mail address:** recruiter@enloe.org. **World Wide Web address:** http:// www.enloe.org. **Description:** A nonprofit, 203-bed, regional, Level II trauma center. Enloe Medical Center offers a variety of services including breast cancer exams, cancer treatment, children's services, clinical laboratory services, educational programs, emergency/trauma services, gastroenterology, heart care, home care, hospice services, maternity care, neurological care, nutrition services, occupational health and risk assessment center, pharmacy, physical therapy, radiology, respiratory care, social services, stress management, surgery, and a trauma/surgical intensive care unit. Founded in 1913. **NOTE:** Entry-level positions and second and third shifts are offered. **Positions advertised include:** Physician Liaison; Applications Coordinator; Nurse Practitioner; RN; Support Group Facilitator; Orthopedic Technician; Monitor Technician; Unit Secretary; Nurse Assistant; Accounting Clerk; Administrative Assistant; Application Coordinator; Billing Clerk; Case Manager; Social Worker; Clinical Dietician. **Special programs:** Internships; Training. **Office hours:** Monday - Friday, 8:00 a.m. - 5:00 p.m. **CEO:** Phil Wolfe. **Number of employees at this location:** 1,800.

**FREMONT HOSPITAL**
39001 Sundale Drive, Fremont CA 94538. 510/796-1100x223. **Contact:** Human Resources. **World Wide Web address:** http://www. fremonthospital.com. **Description:** A psychiatric and chemical dependency treatment hospital. **Positions advertised include:** Chief

Financial Officer; Assessment and Referral Specialist; Registered Nurse. **Special programs:** Internships. **Office hours:** Monday - Friday, 9:00 a.m. - 4:00 p.m. **Parent company:** Arden Health Services. **Listed on:** Privately held. **CEO:** Terry Johnson.

## GE MEDICAL SYSTEMS
389 Oyster Point Boulevard, South San Francisco CA 94080. 650/583-9964. **Fax:** 650/827-7706. **Contact:** Human Resources. **World Wide Web address:** http://www.gemedicalsystems.com. **Description:** Designs, develops, manufactures, and markets medical diagnosis equipment. The company also offers healthcare management services. **NOTE:** Please send resumes to: Human Resources, 384 Wright Brothers Drive, Salt Lake City UT 84116. **Positions advertised include:** Global EBT Marketing Manager. **Corporate headquarters location:** Milwaukee WI. **Listed on:** New York Stock Exchange. **Stock exchange symbol:** GE.

## GN RESOUND CORPORATION
220 Saginaw Drive, Redwood City CA 94063. 650/780-7800. **Toll-free phone:** 800/582-4327. **Contact:** Human Resources. **E-mail address:** hr@gnresound.com. **Description:** Develops, manufactures, and markets hearing aids. Brand names include ReSound, Danavox, Viennatone. **Company slogan:** Partners in hearing innovation. **Corporate headquarters location:** Bloomington MN. **Other U.S. locations:** Minneapolis MN. **International locations:** Worldwide. **Annual sales/revenues:** More than $100 million. **Number of employees at this location:** 300. **Number of employees nationwide:** 500. **Number of employees worldwide:** 1,800.

## GUIDANT ENDOVASCULAR SOLUTIONS
1525 O'Brien Drive, Menlo Park CA 94025. 650/617-5000. **Toll-free phone:** 800/633-7970. **Fax:** 650/470-6320. **Contact:** Human Resources. **World Wide Web address:** http://www.guidant.com. **Description:** Designs, develops, manufactures, and markets a broad range of products for use in cardiac rhythm management, coronary artery disease intervention, and other forms of minimally invasive surgery. Founded in 1986. **NOTE:** Entry-level positions are offered. **Positions advertised include:** Clinical Research Associate; Clinical Research Manager; Corporate Pilot; Human Resources Representative; Regulatory Affairs Director; Regulatory Affairs Manager. **Office hours:** Monday - Friday, 8:00 a.m. - 5:00 p.m. **Corporate headquarters location:** Indianapolis IN. **International locations:** Brussels, Belgium. **Listed on:** New York Stock Exchange.

**Stock exchange symbol:** GDT. **Annual sales/revenues:** More than $100 million. **Number of employees at this location:** 350.

## GUIDANT VASCULAR INTERVENTION
## DEVICES FOR VASCULAR INTERVENTION, INC.
3200 Lakeside Drive, P.O. Box 58167, Santa Clara CA 95054-8167. 408/235-3000. **Toll-free phone:** 800/633-3375. **Fax:** 408/325-3702. **Contact:** Recruiting. **World Wide Web address:** http://www.guidant. com. **Description:** Develops and manufactures a broad line of specialized balloon catheters, guide wires, and accessories. Devices for Vascular Intervention, Inc. (also at this location) develops proprietary technologies that remove obstructive blockages from arteries. **Positions advertised include:** Principal Supplier Engineer; Collections Specialist; Clinical Research Associate; Corporate Pilot. **Parent company:** Guidant Corporation. **Corporate headquarters location:** Indianapolis IN. **Listed on:** New York Stock Exchange. **Stock exchange symbol:** GDT.

## INAMED AESTHETICS
48490 Milmont Drive, Fremont CA 94538. 510/683-6761. **Contact:** Human Resources. **World Wide Web address:** http://www.inamed. com. **Description:** Develops, manufactures, and markets products for breast and facial aesthetics and obesity intervention. **Positions advertised include:** Manufacturing Manager. **Corporate headquarters location:** Santa Barbara CA. **Listed on:** NASDAQ. **Stock exchange symbol:** IMDC.

## INHALE THERAPEUTIC SYSTEMS, INC.
150 Industrial Road, San Carlos CA 94070. 650/631-3100. **Fax:** 650/ 631-3150. **Contact:** Human Resources. **World Wide Web address:** http://www.inhale.com. **Description:** Researches, develops, and manufactures aerosol drug delivery systems for the treatment of lung diseases. The system allows macromolecules of drug powder particles to be absorbed by alveoli in the lungs. **Corporate headquarters location:** This location. **Listed on:** NASDAQ. **Stock exchange symbol:** INHL.

## JOMED INC.
2870 Kilgore Road, Rancho Cordova CA 95670. 916/638-8008. **Contact:** Human Resources. **E-mail address:** hr@jomed.com. **World Wide Web address:** http://www.jomed.com. **Description:** Develops, manufactures, and markets interventional catheter products such as balloon angioplasty catheters, ultrasound imaging, and site-specific

drug delivery catheters. These products target coronary angioplasty, peripheral vascular, neurointerventional, and drug delivery procedures. **Corporate headquarters location:** This location.

## LASERSCOPE
3070 Orchard Drive, San Jose CA 95134-2011. 408/943-0636. **Fax:** 408/944-9401. **Contact:** Human Resources. **E-mail address:** staffing@laserscope.com. **World Wide Web address:** http://www. laserscope.com. **Description:** Designs and markets an advanced line of medical laser systems and related energy delivery products. The company markets its products to hospitals, outpatient surgical centers, and physicians' offices worldwide. **Positions advertised include:** Director of Reimbursement; Regional Surgical Sales Manager. **Corporate headquarters location:** This location. **Operations at this facility include:** Administration; Manufacturing; Research and Development; Sales; Service. **Listed on:** NASDAQ. **Stock exchange symbol:** LSCP. **President/CEO:** Robert V. McCormick. **Annual sales/revenues:** $21 - $50 million. **Number of employees at this location:** 170. **Number of employees nationwide:** 220.

## LIFESCAN, INC.
1000 Gibraltar Drive, Milpitas CA 95035. 408/263-9789. **Contact:** Human Resources. **World Wide Web address:** http://www.lifescan. com. **Description:** Manufactures and markets a wide variety of diabetic devices designed to improve the lifestyles of people with diabetes. **Positions advertised include:** Executive Director of Operations; Receiving/Warehouse Supervisor; Senior Strategic Sourcing Manager; Compliance Officer; Director of Business Development; Scientist; Senior Regulatory Affairs Specialist. **Corporate headquarters location:** This location. **Parent company:** Johnson & Johnson (New Brunswick NJ). **Listed on:** New York Stock Exchange. **Stock exchange symbol:** JNJ.

## LUMENIS
2400 Condensa Street, Santa Clara CA 95051. 408/764-3000. **Toll-free phone:** 800/635-1313. **Fax:** 408/764-3948. **Contact:** Human Resources. **World Wide Web address:** http://www.lumenis.com. **Description:** Manufactures and markets a wide variety of specialty lasers for the medical, scientific, and commercial fields. **Positions advertised include:** Area Sales Manager; Senior Regulatory Affairs Associate; Regional Sales Manager; Senior Accountant. **Corporate headquarters location:** Yokneam, Israel. **Other U.S. locations:** New

York NY. **International locations:** Worldwide. **Operations at this facility include:** Administration; Research and Development; Sales; Service. **Listed on:** NASDAQ. **Stock exchange symbol:** LUME.

## McKESSON

One Post Street, 31st Floor, San Francisco CA 94104. 415/983-9087. **Fax:** 415/983-8900. **Contact:** Personnel. **E-mail address:** jobs. infosolutions@mckesson.com. **World Wide Web address:** http:// www.mckesson.com. **Description:** Provides information systems and technology to health care enterprises including hospitals, integrated delivery networks, and managed care organizations. McKessonHBOC's primary products are Pathways 2000, a family of client/server-based applications that allow the integration and uniting of health care providers; STAR, Series, and HealthQuest transaction systems; TRENDSTAR decision support system; and QUANTUM enterprise information system. The company also offers outsourcing services that include strategic information systems planning, data center operations, receivables management, business office administration, and major system conversions. Founded in 1833. **Positions advertised include:** Vice President, Enterprise Solutions; Director of Internal Communications; Human Resources Coordinator; Intranet Writer/Editor; Executive Assistant; Project Manager; Director of Transportation; Director of Analytic Services. **Corporate headquarters location:** Alpharetta GA. **Other U.S. locations:** Nationwide. **Subsidiaries include:** Automated Healthcare Inc.; Healthcare Delivery Systems, Inc.; McKesson BioServices Corporation; McKesson Pharmacy Systems; Medis Health and Pharmaceutical Services, Inc.; MedPath; U.S. Healthcare; Zee Medical, Inc. **Operations at this facility include:** Administration. **Listed on:** New York Stock Exchange. **Stock exchange symbol:** MCK. **Number of employees at this location:** 700. **Number of employees nationwide:** 14,000.

## McKESSON HEALTH SOLUTIONS

11020 White Rock Road, Rancho Cordova CA 95670. 916/576-4000. **Fax:** 916/576-4333. **Contact:** Human Resources. **E-mail address:** recruitingsac@mackesson.com. **World Wide Web address:** http://www.access-health.com. **Description:** Provides personal health management services to members and consumers through broadcast, telephone, and computer-based programs. Programs include health counseling and prevention services. **Corporate headquarters location:** San Francisco CA.

## MERCY HEALTHCARE NORTH

P.O. Box 496009, Redding CA 96049-6009. 530/246-2639. **Physical address:** 2175 Rosaline Avenue, Redding CA 96001. **Fax:** 530/225-6858. **Recorded jobline:** 530/243-2324. **Contact:** Human Resources Department. **World Wide Web address:** http://www. mercy.org. **Description:** A 256-bed hospital that provides comprehensive health care, acute care, and a variety of special programs to a six-county region. **Positions advertised include:** Air Ambulance Communication Specialist; Cardiac Eco Sonographer; Environmental Service Technician; Hospice RN; Medical Unit Staff RN; Pharmacist; Vascular Technologist. **Corporate headquarters location:** This location. **Parent company:** Catholic Healthcare West. **Number of employees at this location:** 1,455.

## METABOLEX, INC.

3876 Bay Center Place, Hayward CA 94545. 510/293-8800. **Fax:** 510/293-6857. **Contact:** Human Resources. **E-mail address:** jobs@ metaboles.com. **World Wide Web address:** http://www.metabolex. com. **Description:** Develops and markets drug treatments for type two Diabetes. **Positions advertised include:** Research Scientist, Insulin Resistance; Associate Director, Animal Physiology. **Corporate headquarters location:** This location.

## OPHTHALMIC IMAGING SYSTEMS

221 Lathrop Way, Suite I, Sacramento CA 95815. 916/646-2020. **Contact:** Human Resources. **World Wide Web address:** http://www. oisi.com. **Description:** Designs, manufactures, and markets ophthalmic digital imaging systems and other diagnostic imaging equipment used by eye care professionals. Ophthalmic Imaging Systems also develops image enhancement and analysis software. **Corporate headquarters location:** This location. **Number of employees at this location:** 25.

## PRACTICEWARES DENTAL SUPPLY

11291 Sunrise Park Drive, Rancho Cordova CA 95742. 916/638-8147. **Contact:** Human Resources. **World Wide Web address:** http:// www.practicewares.com. **Description:** Distributes professional and consumer dental products. Practicewares Dental Supply is also an authorized dealer for approximately 120 companies including 3M Dental Products, Eastman Kodak, and Premier. **Corporate headquarters location:** This location.

## REDDING MEDICAL CENTER
## REDDING SPECIALTY HOSPITAL

1100 Butte Street, Redding CA 96001. 530/244-5400. **Contact:** Brian Busk, Human Resources. **E-mail address:** brian.busk@ tenethealth.com. **World Wide Web address:** http://www.etenet.com. **Description:** Redding Medical Center is a regional health care provider operating the California Heart Institute, the Center for Neuroscience, the Cancer Care Professionals oncology unit, the Joint Care Center for knee and hip replacement, and the Baby Place for child birthing. Redding Specialty Hospital (also at this location) is a rehabilitation facility for alcohol and drug addictions; mental health problems; physical therapy needs following brain injury, neurological disorders, arthritis, amputation, major trauma, and spinal cord injury; and chronic pain. **NOTE:** Second and third shifts are offered. **Positions advertised include:** Case Manager; Medical Nursing Assistant; Surgical RN; Medical RN; Definitive Observation LVN. **Parent company:** Tenet Healthcare (Santa Barbara CA). **Listed on:** New York Stock Exchange. **Stock exchange symbol:** THC. **CEO:** Ken Rivers. **Annual sales/revenues:** More than $100 million. **Number of employees at this location:** 1,400.

## SANTA CLARA PET HOSPITAL

830 Kiely Boulevard, Suite 107, Santa Clara CA 95051. 408/296-5857. **Fax:** 408/243-5434. **Contact:** Human Resources Department. **World Wide Web address:** http://www.santaclarapethospital.com. **Description:** Provides general medical, surgical, dental, and radiological services to domestic and exotic animals. The hospital also provides cardiology services and avian intensive care. **Corporate headquarters location:** This location.

## SENECA DISTRICT HOSPITAL

P.O. Box 737, Chester CA 96020. 530/258-2159. **Physical address:** 130 Brentwood Drive, Chester CA 96020. **Fax:** 530/258-3595. **Contact:** Director of Human Resources. **Description:** Provides a variety of medical services including family centered birthing, obstetrical clinic, outpatient laboratory and X-ray services including mammography and sonography, in-house pharmacy, hospice, anesthesia, inpatient and outpatient surgical services, stress testing, respiratory care, nutritional counseling, EKG, Lifeline, and patient education. Founded in 1952. **NOTE:** Entry-level positions are offered. **Corporate headquarters location:** This location. **Administrator:** Bernard Hietpas. **Annual sales/revenues:** Less than $5 million. **Number of employees at this location:** 140.

## SIEMENS

1230 Shorebird Way, Mountain View CA 94304. 650/969-9112. **Toll-free phone:** 800/4AC-USON. **Fax:** 650/943-7006. **Recorded jobline:** 800/3AC-USON. **Contact:** Dean Hammer, Employment Programs Specialist. **World Wide Web address:** http://www. siemens.com. **Description:** A manufacturer, marketer, and service provider of diagnostic medical ultrasound systems and image management products for hospitals, clinics, and private practice physicians throughout the world. Founded in 1979. **NOTE:** Entry-level positions are offered. **Positions advertised include:** Accounting Manager; Business Development Direct Transducer; Reliability Engineer; Ultrasound Inventory Asset Analyst; Vice President of Sales, General Imaging. **Special programs:** Internships; Summer Jobs. **Corporate headquarters location:** Munich, Germany. **Other U.S. locations:** Nationwide. **International locations:** Worldwide. **Listed on:** New York Stock Exchange. **Stock exchange symbol:** XETRA. **CEO:** Samuel H. Maslak. **Facilities Manager:** Richard Sage. **Annual sales/revenues:** More than $100 million.

## STARLIGHT ADOLESCENT CENTER

455 Silicon Valley Boulevard, San Jose CA 95138. 408/284-9000. **Fax:** 408/284-9048. **Contact:** Human Resources. **E-mail address:** starlightjobs@starsinc.com. **World Wide Web address:** http://www. starsinc.com. **Description:** A mental health treatment and rehabilitation center. **Positions advertised include:** Recreation Therapist; Nurse; Youth Counselor; TBS Support Counselor; Occupational Therapist. **Corporate headquarters location:** Oakland CA.

## SUTTER ROSEVILLE MEDICAL CENTER

One Medical Plaza, Roseville CA 95661-3037. 916/781-1527. **Fax:** 916/781-1605. **Contact:** Human Resources. **E-mail address:** employment@sutterhealth.org. **World Wide Web address:** http:// www.sutterhealth.org. **Description:** A 205-bed, acute care hospital that serves the health care needs of the Roseville community and its outlying areas. **Positions advertised include:** Infusion Therapist; Health Record Analyst; Special Care Unit RN. **Corporate headquarters location:** Sacramento CA. **Other U.S. locations:** Honolulu HI. **Operations at this facility include:** Health Care; Service. **Number of employees at this location:** 1,250.

## TENDER LOVING CARE/STAFF BUILDERS

1190 South Bascom Avenue, #240, San Jose CA 95128. 408/271-1600. **Fax:** 916/372-8531. **Contact:** Anita Richard, Human Resources Manager. **World Wide Web address:** http://www.staffbuilders.com. **Description:** A home health care agency that provides services ranging from sitters and companions to 24-hour skilled nursing care. **Corporate headquarters location:** Lake Success NY. **Other U.S. locations:** Nationwide. **Number of employees nationwide:** 20,000.

## VISX, INCORPORATED

3400 Central Expressway, Santa Clara CA 95051. **Toll-free phone:** 800/246-VISX. **Fax:** 408/773-7200. **Contact:** Human Resources Department. **E-mail address:** greatcareers@visx.com. **World Wide Web address:** http://www.visx.com. **Description:** Designs, manufactures, and markets technologies and systems for laser vision correction. Founded in 1986. **Positions advertised include:** Programmer and Applications Specialist; Clinical Research Associate; Research Director; Senior Research Scientist; Optical Engineer. **Corporate headquarters location:** This location. **Listed on:** New York Stock Exchange. **Stock exchange symbol:** EYE. **Annual sales/revenues:** More than $100 million.

## WASHINGTON HOSPITAL

2000 Mowry Avenue, Fremont CA 94538. 510/791-3409. **Toll-free phone:** 800/963-7070. **Fax:** 510/745-6470. **Contact:** Personnel Services. **World Wide Web address:** http://www.whhs.com. **Description:** A general, acute care hospital that offers a community cancer program, health insurance information services, occupational medicine, and joint replacement services. **Positions advertised include:** Cardiac Rehabilitation Clinician; Health Information Technician; Clinical Nutrition Manager; Case Management Manager; Nursing Supervisor; Occupational Therapist; Staff Nurse; Transcription Coordinator; Unit Clerk, Emergency Room; Radiological Technologist; Physical Therapist; Diabetes Educator.

## HOTELS AND RESTAURANTS

**You can expect to find the following types of companies in this chapter:**
*Casinos • Dinner Theaters • Hotel/Motel Operators • Resorts • Restaurants*

### THE FAIRMONT HOTEL
650 California Street, 12th Floor, San Francisco CA 94108. 415/772-7800. **Fax:** 415/772-7805. **Contact:** Employment Manager. **E-mail address:** pathfinder@fairmont.com. **World Wide Web address:** http://www.fairmont.com. **Description:** A 591-room hotel. Founded in 1907. **NOTE:** Entry-level positions are offered. **Corporate headquarters location:** This location. **Other U.S. locations:** Los Angeles CA; San Jose CA; Chicago IL; New Orleans LA; Boston MA; Kansas City MO; New York NY; Dallas TX. **Operations at this facility include:** Regional Headquarters. **Listed on:** New York Stock Exchange. **Stock exchange symbol:** FHR. **Number of employees at this location:** 800.

### FRESH CHOICE, INC.
485 Cochrane Circle, Morgan Hill CA 95037. 408/776-0799. **Fax:** 408/986-8334. **Contact:** Human Resources. **E-mail address:** jobs@ reshchoice.com. **World Wide Web address:** http://www.freshchoice. com. **Description:** Operates 58 casual, self-service restaurants in Northern California, Washington, Texas, and Washington DC. **Special programs:** Internships. **Corporate headquarters location:** This location. **Listed on:** NASDAQ. **Stock exchange symbol:** SALD. **Number of employees at this location:** 60. **Number of employees nationwide:** 3,000.

### HILTON AT FISHERMAN'S WHARF
2620 Jones Street, San Francisco CA 94133. 415/885-4700. **Contact:** Personnel Department. **World Wide Web address:** http://www. hilton.com. **Description:** A 232-room hotel with a restaurant and lounge. **Positions advertised include:** Assistant Director of Revenue Management; Conference Sales Manager. **Corporate headquarters location:** Beverly Hills CA. **Parent company:** Hilton Group plc. **Listed on:** New York Stock Exchange. **Stock exchange symbol:** HLN.

### HILTON SAN FRANCISCO & TOWERS
333 O'Farrell Street, San Francisco CA 94102. 415/771-1400. **Contact:** Human Resources. **World Wide Web address:** http://www. hilton.com. **Description:** A 2,000-room hotel. **Special programs:** Internships. **Corporate headquarters location:** Beverly Hills CA.

**Other U.S. locations:** Nationwide. **Parent company:** Hilton Hotels Corporation. **Listed on:** New York Stock Exchange. **Stock exchange symbol:** HLT. **Number of employees at this location:** 1,200.

### HOLIDAY INN CIVIC CENTER
50 Eighth Street, San Francisco CA 94103. 415/626-6103. **Contact:** Director of Personnel. **World Wide Web address:** http://www. holiday-inn.com. **Description:** One location of the international hotel chain. Operations include the management of more than 1,750 company-owned and franchised hotels, gaming operations, restaurants, and a sea transportation subsidiary. **Corporate headquarters location:** Memphis TN. **Parent company:** Six Continents Hotels. **Listed on:** New York Stock Exchange. **Stock exchange symbol:** SXC.

### HYATT REGENCY SAN FRANCISCO
5 Embarcadero Center, San Francisco CA 94111. 415/788-1234. **Fax:** 415/291-6615. **Contact:** Human Resources. **World Wide Web address:** http://www.hyatt.com. **Description:** One location of the Hyatt chain of hotels, which operates hotel and recreational facilities throughout the world. **Corporate headquarters location:** Chicago IL.

### HYATT REGENCY SAN FRANCISCO AIRPORT
1333 Bayshore Highway, Burlingame CA 94010. 650/347-1234. **Fax:** 650/348-2541. **Recorded jobline:** 650/696-2625. **Contact:** Henry Augustus, Human Resources. **World Wide Web address:** http://www.hyatt.com. **Description:** Operates a full-service, four-star hotel complex offering restaurants, banquet rooms, and recreational and convention facilities. **Special programs:** Training. **Office hours:** Monday - Friday, 8:00 a.m. - 5:00 p.m. **Corporate headquarters location:** Chicago IL. **Other U.S. locations:** Nationwide. **Parent company:** Hyatt Corporation. **Listed on:** Privately held. **Number of employees at this location:** 500. **Number of employees nationwide:** 40,000.

### MARRIOTT SANTA CLARA
2700 Mission College Boulevard, Santa Clara CA 95054. 408/988-1500. **Contact:** Recruiter. **World Wide Web address:** http://www. marriott.com. **Description:** Operates a hotel with complete dining and recreational facilities. **Corporate headquarters location:** Washington DC. **Parent company:** Marriott International, Inc. **Listed on:** New York Stock Exchange. **Stock exchange symbol:** MAR.

## OAKLAND MARRIOTT CITY CENTER

1001 Broadway, Oakland CA 94607. 510/451-4000. **Fax:** 510/835-3460. **Recorded jobline:** 510/466-6440. **Contact:** Human Resources. **World Wide Web address:** http://www.marriott.com. **Description:** A full-service hotel and restaurant with over 400 rooms. Oakland Marriott City Center also has conference rooms and meeting space. This location also hires seasonally. **NOTE:** Entry-level positions and part-time jobs are offered. **Special programs:** Internships. **Office hours:** Monday - Friday, 9:00 a.m. - 5:00 p.m. **Corporate headquarters location:** San Francisco CA. **Parent company:** Park Lane Hotels International. **Listed on:** New York Stock Exchange. **Stock exchange symbol:** HMT. **Number of employees at this location:** 400.

## PANDA EXPRESS

255 Soscol Avenue, Napa CA 94559. 707/258-0202. **Toll-free phone:** 888/PANDA-XP. **Fax:** 888/PANDA-48. **Contact:** Human Resources. **E-mail address:** jobs@pandaarg.com. **World Wide Web address:** http://www.pandaexpress.com. **Description:** A quick service Chinese restaurant. **NOTE:** Jobseekers should apply online. **Positions advertised include:** Front Counter Helper; Cook; Kitchen Helper. **Other U.S. locations:** Nationwide.

## RAMADA PLAZA HOTEL

1231 Market Street, San Francisco CA 94103. 415/626-8000. **Toll-free phone:** 800/272-6232. **Contact:** Personnel Manager. **World Wide Web address:** http://www.ramada.com. **Description:** Operates a 458-room hotel with a variety of facilities including meeting rooms and restaurants.

## SHERATON FISHERMAN'S WHARF

2500 Mason Street, San Francisco CA 94133. 415/362-5500. **Fax:** 415/627-6529. **Recorded jobline:** 415/627-6567. **Contact:** Lisa Lucas-Yap, Human Resources Director. **World Wide Web address:** http://www.sheraton.com. **Description:** A 525-room hotel. Founded in 1998. **NOTE:** Part-time jobs are offered. **Corporate headquarters location:** Washington DC. **Parent company:** Starwood Hotels & Resorts Worldwide, Inc. **Listed on:** New York Stock Exchange. **Stock exchange symbol:** HOT. **Chairman and CEO:** Paul Whetsell. **Facilities Manager:** William Joe. **Information Systems Manager:** Christopher Kyle. **Sales Manager:** Frank Okun. **Annual sales/revenues:** $11 - $20 million. **Number of employees at this location:** 260. **Number of employees nationwide:** 27,000.

## WYNDHAM HOTEL SAN JOSE

1350 North First Street, San Jose CA 95112. 408/453-6200. **Contact:** Personnel Assistant. **World Wide Web address:** http://www. wyndham.com. **Description:** Operates a full-service hotel with a wide range of facilities including convention facilities, meeting rooms, suites, three lounges, two restaurants and an exercise room. **Positions advertised include:** Area Director of Sales; Executive Chef; Assistant Banquet Manager; Engineering Manager; Director of Financial Services; Director of Sales. **Corporate headquarters location:** Dallas TX. **Parent company:** Wyndham International. **Listed on:** New York Stock Exchange. **Stock exchange symbol:** WYN.

## INSURANCE

**You can expect to find the following types of companies in this chapter:**
*Commercial and Industrial Property/Casualty Insurers • Health Maintenance Organizations (HMOs) • Medical/Life Insurance Companies*

## AMERICAN INTERNATIONAL GROUP, INC. (AIG)
2 Rincon Center, 121 Spear Street, San Francisco CA 94105. 415/836-2700. **Contact:** Human Resources Manager. **World Wide Web address:** http://www.aig.com. **Description:** An international insurance firm that provides property and casualty coverage in 50 states and 130 jurisdictions. **NOTE:** Please use online form to submit resume. **Corporate headquarters location:** New York NY. **Other U.S. locations:** Phoenix AZ; Los Angeles CA; Chicago IL; Dallas TX; Seattle WA. **International locations:** Worldwide. **Operations at this facility include:** Administration; Sales; Service. **Listed on:** New York Stock Exchange. **Stock exchange symbol:** AIG.

## ANDREINI & COMPANY
220 West Twentieth Avenue, San Mateo CA 94403. 650/573-1111. **Fax:** 650/378-4330. **Contact:** Director of Human Resources. **E-mail address:** aheald@andreini.com. **World Wide Web address:** http://www.andreini.com. **Description:** A business insurance company. Founded in 1951. **Positions advertised include:** Account Manager; Marketing Executive; Producer.

## AON RISK SERVICES
199 Freemont Street, 14th Floor, San Francisco CA 94105. 415/486-7500. **Fax:** 415/486-7026. **Contact:** Human Resources Department. **World Wide Web address:** http://www.aon.com. **Description:** AON Risk Services specializes in property and casualty, marine, and public entities insurance. **Positions advertised include:** Manager Trainee; Senior Human Resources/Benefits Communications Counselor; Administrative Assistant; Consultant. **Operations at this facility include:** This location is a profit center for the large international insurance brokerage. **Listed on:** New York Stock Exchange. **Stock exchange symbol:** AOC.

## ARGONAUT GROUP, INC.
250 Middlefield Road, Menlo Park CA 94025. 650/326-0900. **Toll-free phone:** 800/222-7811. **Fax:** 650/858-6677. **Contact:** Jason F. Corbett, Corporate Recruiter. **E-mail address:** jcorbett@argonautgroup.com. **World Wide Web address:** http://www.

226/The San Francisco JobBank

argonautgroup.com. **Description:** Argonaut Group, Inc. is a holding company whose subsidiaries are mainly involved in the selling, underwriting, and servicing of workers' compensation and other lines of property and casualty insurance. **Office hours:** Monday - Friday, 8:00 a.m. - 5:00 p.m. **Corporate headquarters location:** This location. **Other area locations:** Fresno CA; San Francisco CA; San Jose CA. **Subsidiaries include:** Argonaut Great Central Insurance Company; Argonaut Insurance Company; Captive Advisory Services, Inc.; The Colony Insurance Group; The Redwoods Group; The Rockwood Insurance Group; Trident Insurance Services; Inc. **Listed on:** NASDAQ. **Stock exchange symbol:** AGII.

**BLUE SHIELD OF CALIFORNIA**
50 Beale Street, San Francisco CA 94120. 415/229-5000. **Toll-free phone:** 800/200-3242. **Fax:** 415/229-5070. **Contact:** Human Resources. **World Wide Web address:** http://www.blueshieldca. com. **Description:** A health maintenance organization that provides a variety of group and individual health plan coverage and professional medical services from doctors, dentists, psychiatrists, and other medical professionals. **Corporate headquarters location:** This location.

**CSE INSURANCE GROUP**
P.O. Box 7764, San Francisco CA 94120-7764. 415/274-7800. **Physical address:** 50 California Street, 25th Floor, San Francisco CA 94111. **Toll-free phone:** 800/282-6848. **Fax:** 415/274-7882. **Contact:** Sarah Brotman, Human Resources Representative. **E-mail address:** sbrotman@cse-insurance.com. **World Wide Web address:** http://www.cse-insurance.com. **Description:** Provides public employees and professionals in related fields with personal lines of insurance including homeowners, automobile, life and disability, and property insurance. **Positions advertised include:** Business Analyst. **Corporate headquarters location:** This location. **Other area locations:** Pasadena CA; Sacramento CA. **Other U.S. locations:** AZ; NV; UT.

**CALIFORNIA CASUALTY MANAGEMENT COMPANY**
P.O. Box M, San Mateo CA 94402. 650/574-4000. **Contact:** Human Resources. **World Wide Web address:** http://www.calcas.com. **Description:** A business and personal insurance firm. **Corporate headquarters location:** This location. **Operations at this facility include:** Administration; Sales; Service.

## CHICAGO TITLE INSURANCE COMPANY

388 Market Street, Suite 1300, San Francisco CA 94111. 415/788-0871. **Fax:** 415/781-4185. **Contact:** Human Resources. **World Wide Web address:** http://www.fntic.com. **Description:** Chicago Title Insurance Company writes title insurance policies and performs other title-related services such as escrow, collection, and trust activities in connection with real estate transactions. Founded in 1848. **Corporate headquarters location:** Santa Barbara CA. **Other U.S. locations:** Nationwide. **Subsidiaries include:** American Title Insurance; Fidelity National Title Insurance Company of New York; Fidelity National Title Insurance Company of Pennsylvania; Fidelity National Title Insurance Company of Texas; Security Title and Guaranty Company. **Parent company:** Fidelity National Financial, Inc. **Operations at this facility include:** This location houses administrative offices. **Listed on:** New York Stock Exchange. **Stock exchange symbol:** FNF. **Annual sales/revenues:** $51 - $100 million. **Number of employees nationwide:** 4,000.

## CHUBB GROUP OF INSURANCE COMPANIES

2 Embarcadero Center, Suite 1500, San Francisco CA 94111. 415/989-3000. **Contact:** Human Resources. **World Wide Web address:** http://www.chubb.com. **Description:** A multiple-line property and casualty insurance group that serves the public through independent agents and brokers. **Positions advertised include:** Claims Support Clerk; Underwriting Associate. **Corporate headquarters location:** Warren NJ. **Other area locations:** Fresno CA; Los Angeles CA; Newport Beach CA; Pleasanton CA; Sacramento CA; San Diego CA. **Other U.S. locations:** Nationwide. **International locations:** Worldwide. **Operations at this facility include:** Administration; Sales; Service. **Listed on:** New York Stock Exchange. **Stock exchange symbol:** CB. **Annual sales/revenues:** More than $100 million. **Number of employees worldwide:** 10,000.

## DELTA DENTAL PLAN OF CALIFORNIA

P.O. Box 7736, San Francisco CA 94120. 415/972-8300. **Contact:** Recruitment and Selection. **World Wide Web address:** http://www.deltadentalca.org. **Description:** A prepaid, dental insurance firm. **NOTE:** Entry-level positions are offered. **Positions advertised include:** Client Services Manager; Underwriter; Secretary; Compensation and Benefits Manager. **Corporate headquarters location:** This location. **Other U.S. locations:** Cerritos CA; Sacramento CA. **Subsidiaries include:** Delta Dental Insurance Company (DDIC); Private Medical Care, Inc. (PMI). **Operations at** this facility include: Administration; Sales; Service. **Annual sales/revenues:** More than $100 million. **Number of employees at this location:** 1,200.

### FIREMAN'S FUND INSURANCE COMPANY
777 San Marin Drive, Novato CA 94998. 415/899-2000. **Contact:** Personnel. **World Wide Web address:** http://www.the-fund.com. **Description:** An insurance company offering a wide range of coverage and policies. Founded in 1863. **Positions advertised include:** Accountant Consultant; Internal Auditor; Senior Research Accountant; Administrative Services Associate; Claims Service Specialist; Shared Services Director; Commercial Insurance Product Director. **Corporate headquarters location:** This location. **Other U.S. locations:** Nationwide. **Parent company:** Allianz A.G. (Munich, Germany). **Listed on:** New York Stock Exchange. **Stock exchange symbol:** AZ.

### FREMONT COMPENSATION INSURANCE GROUP
P.O. Box 29014, Glendale CA 91209. 415/627-5000. **Contact:** Personnel Director. **World Wide Web address:** http://www.eicn. com. **Description:** Provides workers' compensation insurance through more than 40 offices in 30 states. **Listed on:** New York Stock Exchange. **Stock exchange symbol:** FMT.

### GAB ROBINS
10989 Trade Center Drive, Rancho Cucamonga CA 95670. 916/ 853-8300. **Contact:** Frank Blaha, Branch Manager. **World Wide Web address:** http://www.gabrobins.com. **Description:** Provides adjustment, inspection, appraisal, and claims management services to 15,000 insurance industry customers through more than 550 branch offices. Specific services include the settlement of claims following major disasters; appraisal, investigation, and adjustment of auto insurance claims; casualty claims; and fire, marine, life, accident, health, and disability claims. **Corporate headquarters location:** Parsippany NJ. **Parent company:** SGS North America. **Number of employees nationwide:** 3,400.

### GREAT PACIFIC INSURANCE COMPANY
395 Oyster Point Boulevard, Suite 500, South San Francisco CA 94080. 650/872-6772. **Contact:** Human Resources. **World Wide Web address:** http://www.american-national.com. **Description:** A leading insurance company that, directly and through its subsidiaries, offers a broad line of insurance coverages including

individual life, health, and annuities; group life and health; and credit insurance. **Corporate headquarters location:** Galveston TX. **Parent company:** American National Insurance Company.

## HEALTH NET

3400 Data Drive, Rancho Cordova CA 95670. 916/631-5000. **Contact:** Human Resources. **E-mail address:** resume@healthnet.com. **World Wide Web address:** http://www.health.net. **Description:** Administers the delivery of managed care services to approximately 3.4 million individuals through its HMOs, government contracting, and specialty services managed care facilities. This location handles health plans for small businesses in Northern California. **Positions advertise include:** Help Desk Specialist; Membership Accounting Representative; Claims Adjuster; Clerical Specialist; Warehouse Clerk; Correspondence Representative; Senior Secretary; Finance Manager; Buyer. **Corporate headquarters location:** Woodland Hills CA. **Listed on:** New York Stock Exchange. **Stock exchange symbol:** HNT. **Number of employees at this location:** 15,000.

## KAISER PERMANENTE
## PEOPLE SOLUTIONS

P.O. Box 12916, Oakland CA 94604-2916. 916/973-6848. **Fax:** 888/499-1502. **Contact:** Personnel. **World Wide Web address:** http://www.kaiserpermanente.org. **Description:** Kaiser Permanente is a nonprofit, public-benefit, and charitable health care organization that enrolls members and arranges for their medical, hospital, and related services nationwide. **Positions advertised include:** Account Representative; Administrative Specialist; Analyst; Cashier; Clinical Coordinator; Consultant; Department Secretary; Health Information Coder; Home Care Nurse; Inpatient Case Manager; Laboratory Assistant; Licensed Vocational Nurse; Medical Assistant; New Member Outreach Assistant. **Corporate headquarters location:** This location. **Other U.S. locations:** Nationwide. **Operations at this facility include:** This location houses administrative offices.

## KEMPER INSURANCE COMPANIES

P.O. Box 7993, San Francisco CA 94120. 415/421-2400. **Physical address:** 475 Sansome Street, 6th Floor, San Francisco CA 94111. **Contact:** Human Resources Manager. **World Wide Web address:** http://www.kemperinsurance.com. **Description:** Provides property, casualty, and life insurance, reinsurance, and a wide range of diversified financial services operations. **Corporate headquarters**

**location:** Long Grove IL. **Other area locations:** City of Industry CA; Glendale CA; San Diego CA; Santa Ana CA; West Covina CA.

## MARSH RISK & INSURANCE SERVICES
One California Street, 5th Floor, San Francisco CA 94111. 415/743-8000. **Contact:** Human Resources. **E-mail address:** employment. jobs@marsh.com. **World Wide Web address:** http://www.marsh. com. **Description:** A professional firm that provides advice and services worldwide through an insurance brokerage and risk management firm, reinsurance intermediary facilities, and a consulting and financial services group to clients concerned with the management of assets and risks. Specific services include insurance and risk management services, reinsurance, consulting and financial services, consulting, merchandising, and investment management. **Corporate headquarters location:** New York NY. **Parent company:** Marsh & McLennan Companies, Inc.

## NORCAL MUTUAL INSURANCE COMPANY
560 Davis Street, 2nd Floor, San Francisco CA 94111. 415/397-9700. **Toll-free phone:** 800/652-1051. **Fax:** 415/835-9817. **Contact:** Human Resources Department. **E-mail address:** human_resources@ norcalmutual.com. **World Wide Web address:** http://www. norcalmutual.com. **Description:** Provides physicians with professional liability insurance. **Positions advertised include:** Finance Manager; Vice President of Sales and Marketing; Risk Management Specialist; Underwriting Supervisor; Senior Underwriter; Underwriter; Claims Receptionist; Underwriting Operations Analyst; QA Specialist; Risk Management Manager. **Special programs:** Internships. **Corporate headquarters location:** This location. **Other U.S. locations:** Anchorage AK; Pasadena CA. **Operations at this facility include:** Administration; Sales. **Listed on:** Privately held. **Number of employees at this location:** 165.

## PRUDENTIAL PREFERRED INSURANCE COMPANY
651 Gateway Boulevard, Suite 700, South San Francisco CA 94080. 650/952-1111. **Contact:** General Manager. **World Wide Web address:** http://www.prudential.com. **Description:** One of the largest multiline financial services organizations in the world, with offices throughout the United States and Canada. Prudential Preferred Insurance provides a wide range of financial services for individuals and groups including individual insurance, personal investments, group insurance, reinsurance, institutional investments, group pension, and health care programs. **Positions advertised include:**

Legal Assistant; Mortgage Origination; Sales Vice President. **Corporate headquarters location:** Newark NJ. **Other U.S. locations:** Westlake CA; Jacksonville FL; Chicago IL; Boston MA; Minneapolis MN; South Plainfield NJ; Philadelphia PA; Houston TX. **International locations:** Toronto, Canada. **Operations at this facility include:** Sales; Service. **Listed on:** New York Stock Exchange. **Stock exchange symbol:** PRU. **Number of employees at this location:** 65.

### STATE COMPENSATION INSURANCE FUND
P.O. Box 7455, San Francisco CA 94120. 415/565-1234. **Physical address:** 1275 Market Street, 9th Floor, San Francisco CA 94103. **Contact:** Ms. Terese Carter, Human Resources. **World Wide Web address:** http://www.scif.com. **Description:** One of California's largest writers of workers' compensation insurance through more than 20 district offices. **Corporate headquarters location:** This location.

### UNITED HEALTHCARE
425 Market Street, 13th Floor, San Francisco CA 94105. 415/546-3300. **Contact:** Human Resources Director. **E-mail address:** resume@uhc.com. **World Wide Web address:** http://www.uhc.com. **Description:** Offers group medical insurance. **Positions advertised include:** Director of Appeals and Complaints; Survey Administrator; Intake Supervisor; Data Analyst; EAP Specialist. **Corporate headquarters location:** Minneapolis MN. **Parent company:** United Health Group is a diversified health and well-being company. **Listed on:** New York Stock Exchange. **Stock exchange symbol:** UNH.

### VISION SERVICE PLAN
P.O. Box 997100, Sacramento CA 95899-7100. 916/851-5000. **Physical address:** 3333 Quality Drive, Rancho Cordova CA 95670. **Fax:** 916/851-4858. **Recorded jobline:** 916/851-4700. **Contact:** Corporate Recruiter. **E-mail address:** hreoc@vsp.com. **World Wide Web address:** http://www.vsp.com. **Description:** Sells and administers a prepaid vision care plan as an employee benefit. **Special programs:** Internships. **Corporate headquarters location:** This location. **Other U.S. locations:** Nationwide. **Subsidiaries include:** Altair Eyewear. **Operations at this facility include:** Administration; Research and Development; Sales; Service. **Listed on:** Privately held. **Number of employees at this location:** 1,000. **Number of employees nationwide:** 1,300.

## WEST COAST LIFE INSURANCE COMPANY

P.O. Box 193892, San Francisco CA 94119. 415/591-8383. **Physical address:** 343 Sansome Street, San Francisco CA 94104. **Toll-free phone:** 800/366-9378. **Contact:** Jamie Ferguson, Personnel Manager. **E-mail address:** jamie.ferguson@wclife.com. **World Wide Web address:** http://www.westcoastlife.com. **Description:** Offers a complete range of life insurance services. Founded in 1906. **Positions advertised include:** Reinsurance Manager; Assistant Actuary. **Office hours:** Monday - Friday, 7:30 a.m. - 4:30 p.m. **Corporate headquarters location:** This location. **Parent company:** Protective Life Insurance. **President/CEO/Owner:** Jim Massengale. **Facilities Manager:** George Tano. **Information Systems Manager:** Karl Snover. **Number of employees at this location:** 150.

## LEGAL SERVICES

**You can expect to find the following types of companies in this chapter:**
*Law Firms • Legal Service Agencies*

### BAKER & McKENZIE
2 Embarcadero Center, 24th Floor, San Francisco CA 94111-3909. 415/576-3000. **Contact:** Andrea Carr, Recruitment. **E-mail address:** andrea.l.carr@bakernet.com. **World Wide Web address:** http://www. bakerinfo.com. **Description:** An international law firm with more than 10 practice areas including banking and finance, e-commerce, intellectual property, labor and employment, tax, and U.S. litigation. **Other area locations:** Palo Alto CA; San Diego CA. **Other U.S. locations:** DC; FL; IL; NY; TX. **International locations:** Worldwide.

### BUCHALTER, NEMER, FIELDS & YOUNGER
333 Market Street, 29th Floor, San Francisco CA 94105-2130. 415/227-0900. **Contact:** Kristy Sessions, Recruitment. **World Wide Web address:** http://www.buchalter.com. **E-mail address:** recruting@ buchalter.com. **Description:** A law firm specializing in the area of business. Practice areas include corporate, real estate, real estate finance, general litigations, labor, financial institution litigation, and multimedia entertainment and communications. **Other area locations:** Los Angeles CA; Newport Beach CA.

### GUY KORNBLUM & ASSOCIATES
1388 Sutter Street, Suite 820, San Francisco CA 94109. 415/440-7800. **Toll-free phone:** 888/249-7800. **Fax:** 415/440-7898. **Contact:** Human Resources. **World Wide Web address:** http://www. kornblumlaw.com. **Description:** A law firm specializing in personal injury, wrongful death, malpractice, and class action suits. **Corporate headquarters location:** This location. **Other area locations:** Los Angeles CA. **U.S. locations:** Denver CO; Indianapolis IN.

### MORRISON & FOERSTER LLP
345 California Street, San Francisco CA 94104. 415/677-7000. **Contact:** Attorney Recruiting Coordinator. **E-mail address:** gchong@ mofo.com. **World Wide Web address:** http://www.mofo.com. **Description:** An international law firm specializing in corporate, financial, intellectual property, real estate, and tax law. **Corporate headquarters location:** This location. **Other area locations:** Los Angeles CA; Orange County CA; Palo Alto CA; Sacramento CA; Walnut Creek CA. **Other U.S. locations:** Denver CO; Washington

DC; New York NY. **International locations:** Beijing; Brussels; Hong Kong; London; Singapore; Tokyo.

## SACK, MILLER & ROSENDIN LLP

One Kaiser Plaza, Ordway Building, Suite 340, Oakland CA 94612. 510/286-2200. **Contact:** Human Resources. **World Wide Web address:** http://www.smrlaw.com. **Description:** A law firm specializing in a number of legal disciplines including personal and business injury, real estate, tax, and bankruptcy. **Office hours:** Monday - Friday, 9:00 a.m. - 5:00 p.m. **Corporate headquarters location:** This location.

## SIMONCINI & ASSOCIATES

1694 The Almenda, San Jose CA 95126. 408/280-7711. **Fax:** 408/280-1330. **Contact:** Kenneth Simoncini. **E-mail address:** kds@ simoncini-law.com. **World Wide Web address:** http://www. simoncini-law.com. **Description:** A law firm. **Positions advertised include:** Civil Litigation Attorney.

# MANUFACTURING: MISCELLANEOUS CONSUMER

**You can expect to find the following types of companies in this chapter:**
*Art Supplies • Batteries • Cosmetics and Related Products • Household Appliances and Audio/Video Equipment • Jewelry, Silverware, and Plated Ware • Miscellaneous Household Furniture and Fixtures • Musical Instruments • Tools • Toys and Sporting Goods*

## THE CLOROX COMPANY

P.O. Box 24305, Oakland CA 94623-1305. 510/271-7000. **Physical address:** 1221 Broadway, Oakland CA 94612. **Contact:** Corporate Staffing. **E-mail address:** corporate.staffing@clorox.com. **World Wide Web address:** http://www.clorox.com. **Description:** Clorox, a *Fortune* 500 company, is an international manufacturer and marketer of consumer food and cleaning products. Brand names include Clorox, 409, Hidden Valley Ranch, and KC Masterpiece. **Positions advertised include:** Accounts Payable Processor; A/P Supervisor; Senior Business Analyst. **Corporate headquarters location:** This location. **Operations at this facility include:** This location houses the executive offices. **Listed on:** New York Stock Exchange. **Listed on:** New York Stock Exchange. **Stock exchange symbol:** CLX.

## DEWALT CORPORATION

2512 Tripaldi Way, Hayward CA 94549. 510/783-3959. **Contact:** Human Resources Department. **E-mail address:** jobs@dewalt.com. **World Wide Web address:** http://www.dewalt.com. **Description:** A manufacturer of products used in and around the home and for commercial applications. The company is one of the world's largest manufacturers of power tools, power tool accessories, security hardware, and electric lawn and garden tools. **Corporate headquarters location:** Towson MO. **Other U.S. locations:** Baltimore MD; Mooresville NC; Bethlehem PA. **Parent company:** Black and Decker Corporation. **Listed on:** New York Stock Exchange. **Stock exchange symbol:** BDK.

## HUSSMANN CORPORATION

48438 Milmont Drive, Fremont CA 94538. 510/354-2040. **Contact:** Human Resources. **World Wide Web address:** http://www. hussmann.com. **Description:** A manufacturer of merchandising and refrigeration systems for the world's food industry. Products include refrigerated display cases, refrigeration systems, beverage coolers, walk-in coolers, and industrial refrigeration equipment. **Corporate**

**headquarters location:** Bridgeton MO. **International locations:** Canada; Mexico; United Kingdom. **Parent company:** Ingersoll-Rand. **Listed on:** New York Stock Exchange. **Stock exchange symbol:** IR.

## LASER EXCEL, INC.
3310 Coffey Lane, Santa Rosa CA 95403. 707/577-1301. **Toll-free phone:** 800/559-7965. **Contact:** Controller. **World Wide Web address:** http://www.laserexcel.com. **Description:** A manufacturer of laser-engraved wood and paper giftware including stationery and special occasion note cards. **Positions advertised include:** Marketing Coordinator. **Corporate headquarters location:** This location. **Other area locations:** Healdsburg CA. **Operations at this facility include:** Administration; Manufacturing; Research and Development; Sales.

## MEDIA ARTS GROUP, INC.
## LIGHTPOST PUBLISHING
900 Lightpost Way, Morgan Hill CA 95037. 408/201-5000. **Toll-free phone:** 800/366-3733. **Contact:** Human Resources. **E-mail address:** jobs@mediaarts.com. **World Wide Web address:** http://www. mediaarts.com. **Description:** Designs, manufactures, markets, and distributes fine-quality collectible, gift, and art products. **Positions advertised include:** Cost Accounting Manager; External Reporting Manager; Inside Sales Associate; Customer Care Representative; New Business Development Manager; Business Analyst for Sales and Creative Services. **Number of employees nationwide:** 580. **Corporate headquarters location:** This location. **Listed on:** New York Stock Exchange. **Stock exchange symbol:** MDA.

## THE NORTH FACE
2013 Farallon Drive, San Leandro CA 94577. 510/618-3500. **Fax:** 510/618-3531. **Contact:** Human Resources. **E-mail address:** tnf_hr@ vfc.com. **World Wide Web address:** http://www.thenorthface.com. **Description:** A manufacturer, wholesaler, and retailer of outdoor equipment and apparel including tents, backpacks, sleeping bags, outerwear, skiwear, and sportswear. **Positions advertised include:** Forecasting Analyst; Planner; Office Services Analyst; Sourcing Manager; Textile Color Technician; Sales and Merchandising Support Coordinator. **Corporate headquarters location:** This location. **Operations at this facility include:** Administration; Manufacturing; Research and Development; Sales; Service.

# MANUFACTURING: MISCELLANEOUS INDUSTRIAL

**You can expect to find the following types of companies in this chapter:**
*Ball and Roller Bearings • Commercial Furniture and Fixtures • Fans, Blowers, and Purification Equipment • Industrial Machinery and Equipment • Motors and Generators/Compressors and Engine Parts • Vending Machines*

## ATMI, INC.
617 River Oaks Parkway, San Jose CA 95134. 408/262-1631. **Toll-free phone:** 800/886-1968. **Fax:** 408/526-1651. **Contact:** Glenda Edwards, Human Resources Manager. **World Wide Web address:** http://www.atmi.com. **Description:** Manufactures gas exhaust conditioning systems used in the semiconductor industry. **Corporate headquarters location:** Danbury CT. **Other U.S. locations:** Tempe AZ; Brookfield CT; Austin TX. **Listed on:** Privately held. **Annual sales/revenues:** $21 - $50 million. **Number of employees at this location:** 95.

## ANDROS INC.
870 Harbour Way South, Richmond CA 94804. 510/837-3500. **Fax:** 510/837-3600. **Contact:** Human Resources. **E-mail address:** careers@andros.com. **World Wide Web address:** http://www.andros.com. **Description:** A supplier of instrumentation and a leading worldwide designer and supplier to original equipment manufacturers of nondispersive infrared gas analyzers. These devices measure concentrations of carbon dioxide, carbon monoxide, and hydrocarbons. Andros also manufactures medical products that measure gases in human breath including carbon dioxide, halogenated hydrocarbon gases, and nitrous oxide. **Corporate headquarters location:** This location.

## BOC COATING TECHNOLOGY
2700 Maxwell Way, Fairfield CA 94533. 707/423-2100. **Contact:** Eileen Graham-Klotz, Human Resources. **Fax:** 707/425-1706. **World Wide Web address:** http://www.boc.com. **Description:** Manufactures vacuum systems and equipment for industrial applications. **Corporate headquarters location:** Murray Hill NJ. **Other area locations:** Concord, CA. **Parent company:** The BOC Group, Inc. **Operations at this facility include:** Administration; Divisional Headquarters; Manufacturing; Sales. **Listed on:** London Stock Exchange. **Number of employees at this location:** 170. **Number of**

**employees nationwide:** 250. **Listed on:** New York Stock Exchange. **Stock exchange symbol:** BOX.

## BECKMAN COULTER, INC.

1050 Page Mill Road, Palo Alto CA 94304. 650/857-1150. **Fax:** 650/859-1526. **Contact:** Human Resources. **E-mail address:** palo_ alto_jobs@beckman.com. **World Wide Web address:** http://www. beckman.com. **Description:** Sells and services a diverse range of scientific instruments, reagents, and related equipment. Products include DNA synthesizers, robotic workstations, centrifuges, electrophoresis systems, detection and measurement equipment, data processing software, and specialty chemical and automated general chemical systems. Many of the company's products are used in research, development and diagnostic analysis. **NOTE:** Second and third shifts are offered. **Other area locations:** Brea CA; Carlsbad CA; Fullerton CA; Porterville CA; San Diego CA. **Other U.S. locations:** Nationwide. **International locations:** Worldwide. **Parent company:** Beckman Instruments, Inc. **Listed on:** New York Stock Exchange. **Stock exchange symbol:** BEC.

## BEMIS COMPANY INC.

3030 Union City Boulevard, Union City CA 94587. 510/471-2811. **Contact:** Human Resources. **World Wide Web address:** http://www. bemis.com. **Description:** A diversified producer of consumer and industrial packaging materials, film products, and business products. Packaging products include tapes, paper bags, and packaging for pharmaceuticals, candy, toilet paper, and detergents. The company also produces sheetprint stock, roll labels, laminates, and adhesive products. **Corporate headquarters location:** Minneapolis MN. **Listed on:** New York Stock Exchange. **Stock exchange symbol:** BMS.

## COOPER ENERGY SERVICES

14796 Wicks Boulevard, San Leandro CA 94577. 510/614-1151. **Contact:** Personnel. **World Wide Web address:** http://www. cooperenergy.com. **Description:** Cooper Energy Services is a leading provider of power and compression equipment. **Corporate headquarters location:** Houston TX. **Other area locations:** Bakersfield CA; Corona CA; Garden Grove CA; Rio Vista CA; Taft CA; Yuba City CA. **Other U.S. locations:** Nationwide. **International locations:** Worldwide. **Parent company:** Cooper Cameron. **Operations at this facility include:** This location is a sales and service office for industrial power plant engines. **Listed on:** New York Stock Exchange. **Stock exchange symbol:** CAM.

## DIONEX CORPORATION

1228 Titan Way, P.O. Box 3606, Sunnyvale CA 94088-3606. 408/737-0700. **Fax:** 408/739-8015. **Contact:** Human Resources. **E-mail address:** jobs@dionex.com. **World Wide Web address:** http://www.dionex.com. **Description:** Develops, manufactures, sells, and services systems and related products that isolate and identify the components of chemical mixtures. The company's products are used extensively for environmental analysis by the pharmaceutical, life science, biotechnology, chemical, petrochemical, power generation, and electronics industries. Customers include industrial companies, government agencies, research institutions, and universities. The company's research and development teams explore new technologies in order to enhance the performance of ion technology, high-performance liquid chromatography, capillary electrophoresis, and supercritical fluid extraction and chromatography technologies. **Positions advertised include:** Staff Chemist; Senior Web Developer; Project Manager. **Corporate headquarters location:** This location. **Other U.S. locations:** Atlanta GA; Salt Lake City UT. **Operations at this facility include:** Administration; Manufacturing; Research and Development; Sales; Service. **Listed on:** NASDAQ. **Stock exchange symbol:** DNEX. **Number of employees nationwide:** 565.

## FLOWSERVE CORPORATION

6077 Egret Court, Benicia CA 94510. 707/745-3773. **Contact:** Human Resources. **World Wide Web address:** http://www.flowserve.com. **Description:** Manufactures and supplies pumps, valves, seals, and services to the process industries. **Corporate headquarters location:** Dallas TX. **Listed on:** New York Stock Exchange. **Stock exchange symbol:** FLS. **Number of employees worldwide:** 7,000.

## HUSSMANN CORPORATION

4244 South Market Street, Sacramento CA 95834. 916/920-4993. **Contact:** Human Resources. **World Wide Web address:** http://www.hussmann.com. **Description:** A manufacturer of merchandising and refrigeration systems for the world's food industry. Products include refrigerated display cases, refrigeration systems, beverage coolers, walk-in coolers, and industrial refrigeration equipment. **Corporate headquarters location:** Bridgeton MO. **International locations:** Canada; Mexico; United Kingdom. **Parent company:** Ingersoll-Rand. **Listed on:** New York Stock Exchange. **Stock exchange symbol:** IR.

## INGERSOLL-RAND EQUIPMENT SALES
1944 Marina Boulevard, San Leandro CA 94577. 510/357-9131. **Contact:** Human Resources. **World Wide Web address:** http://www. ingersoll-rand.com. **Description:** Manufactures compressors, pumps, and other nonelectrical industrial equipment and machinery. Products include air compression systems, antifriction systems, construction equipment, air tools, bearings, locks, tools, and pumps. The company operates more than 90 production facilities worldwide. **Corporate headquarters location:** Woodcliff Lake NJ. **International locations:** Worldwide. **Listed on:** New York Stock Exchange. **Stock exchange symbol:** IR.

## KONICA BUSINESS TECHNOLOGIES, INC.
44 Montgomery Street, Suite 1010, San Francisco CA 94104. 415/ 398-4141. **Toll-free phone:** 800/926-7616. **Contact:** Human Resources. **E-mail address:** philbins@konicabt.com. **World Wide Web address:** http://www.konicabt.com. **Description:** Manufactures and distributes high-technology business equipment. **NOTE:** Entry-level positions are offered. **Positions advertised include:** Information Processing Specialist; Key Accounts Manager; Color Sales Executive; Major Account Sales Representative; Technician. **Special programs:** Training. **Corporate headquarters location:** Windsor CT. **Other U.S. locations:** Nationwide. **International locations:** Worldwide. **Listed on:** Privately held. **Annual sales/revenues:** More than $100 million. **Number of employees at this location:** 50. **Number of employees nationwide:** 4,000.

## OPTICAL COATING LABORATORY, INC.
2789 North Point Parkway, Santa Rosa CA 95407-7397. 707/545-6440. **Contact:** Human Resources. **E-mail address:** resumes@ocli. com. **World Wide Web address:** http://www.ocli.com. **Description:** Manufactures thin film-coated components that are used in the manufacture of photographic products, office equipment, and computers. **Positions advertised include:** Electrical Engineering Manager; Mechanical Development Engineer; Optical Development Engineer; Business Manager; Product Marketing Manager; National Account Manager; Electrical Development Engineer; Lasers Manufacturing Engineer; Engineering Technician. **Corporate headquarters location:** This location. **Parent company:** JDS Uniphase Corporation. **Listed on:** NASDAQ. **Stock exchange symbol:** JDSU. **Number of employees at this location:** 900.

## PACIFIC LUMBER COMPANY
P.O. Box 565, Scotia CA 95565. 707/764-2222. **Contact:** Personnel Department. **World Wide Web address:** http://www.palco.com. **Description:** Manufactures redwood and Douglas fir lumber. **Corporate headquarters location:** This location.

## PACIFIC ROLLER DIE COMPANY INC.
P.O. Box 3398, Hayward CA 94540. 510/782-7242. **Fax:** 510/887-5639. **Contact:** Human Resources. **World Wide Web address:** http://www.prdcompany.com. **Description:** Designs, manufactures, and supports a full range of systems to produce spiral weldseam pipe, corrugated metal pipe and building panels, and duct products. **Corporate headquarters location:** This location.

## PERKINELMER
399 West Java Drive, Sunnyvale CA 94089. 408/745-7900. **Contact:** Human Resources. **World Wide Web address:** http://www.perkinelmer.com. **Description:** Manufactures specialty lamps and equipment for laser pump, medical, industrial, and aerospace applications. The company is a leading designer and supplier of arc lamps for optical pumping of solid waste, other lasers, and specialty equipment. **Corporate headquarters location:** Wellesley MA. **Operations at this facility include:** Administration; Manufacturing; Research and Development; Sales; Service. **Listed on:** New York Stock Exchange. **Stock exchange symbol:** PKI. **Number of employees at this location:** 365.

## RAY BURNER COMPANY
401 Parr Boulevard, Richmond CA 94801. 415/333-5800. **Toll-free phone:** 800/RAY-BURNxER. **Contact:** Human Resources Department. **World Wide Web address:** http://www.rayburner.com. **Description:** Manufactures and distributes boilers and gas burners. Founded in 1872. **Corporate headquarters location:** This location.

## SAVIN CORPORATION
850 Dubuque Avenue, South San Francisco CA 94080-1804. 650/952-8214. **Contact:** Human Resources. **World Wide Web address:** http://www.savin.com. **Description:** Manufactures and markets a wide range of large- and small-scale electronic calculators, programmable calculators, electronic accounting machines, facsimiles, shredders, and copy machines. Products are used in a wide range of business, governmental, medical, and educational applications. Products are sold through company-owned branches in

the United States and Canada. **Positions advertised include:** Branch General Manager. **Corporate headquarters location:** Stamford CT.

## SCHINDLER ELEVATOR CORPORATION
500 Carlton Court, South San Francisco CA 94080. 650/873-8222. **Contact:** Human Resources. **World Wide Web address:** http://www. schindler.com. **Description:** Repairs, services, and renovates elevators and escalators produced by various manufacturers. **Corporate headquarters location:** Ebikon, Switzerland.

## SIEMENS POWER TRANSMISSION AND DISTRIBUTION
1730 Technology Drive, San Jose CA 95110. 408/453-5222. **Contact:** Human Resources. **World Wide Web address:** http://www. siemenstd.com. **Description:** Manufactures supervisory control and energy management equipment for the power and utility industries. **Corporate headquarters location:** This location. **Parent company:** Siemens. **Listed on:** New York Stock Exchange. **Stock exchange symbol:** SI.

## SILICON MICROSTRUCTURES, INC.
1701 McCarthy Boulevard, Milpitas CA 95035. 408/557-0100. **Contact:** Human Resources. **E-mail address:** hr@si-micro.com. **World Wide Web address:** http://www.si-micro.com. **Description:** A CPA firm specializing in attest services. Founded in 1954. **Positions advertised include:** Staff Auditor.

## USFILTER
960 Ames Avenue, Milpitas CA 95035. 408/946-1520. **Contact:** Human Resources Department. **E-mail address:** corpstaff@ usfilter.com. **World Wide Web address:** http://www.usfilter.com. **Description:** Manufactures and services water purification and treatment equipment. Primary customers are entities with the need for highly purified water including the electronic, utility, and pharmaceutical industries. **Corporate headquarters location:** Palm Desert CA. **Parent company:** Vivendi. **Operations at this facility include:** Administration; Marketing; Sales; Service. **Listed on:** New York Stock Exchange. **Stock exchange symbol:** V.

## ULTRATECH STEPPER, INC.
3050 Zanker Road, San Jose CA 95134. 408/321-8835. **Fax:** 408/ 577-3378. **Contact:** Human Resources. **World Wide Web address:** http://www.ultratech.com. **Description:** Develops, manufactures, and markets photolithography equipment designed to reduce the

cost of ownership for manufacturers of integrated circuits and thin-film head magnetic recording devices. Founded in 1979. **Positions advertised include:** Mechanical Design Engineer; Product Safety Engineer; Program Manager; Technical Account Manager. **Corporate headquarters location:** This location. **Listed on:** NASDAQ. **Stock exchange symbol:** UTEK.

## VARIAN MEDICAL SYSTEMS

3100 Hansen Way, Mail Stop E-140, Palo Alto CA 94304. 650/493-4000. **Contact:** Human Resources. **World Wide Web address:** http://www.varian.com. **Description:** A diversified, international manufacturing company. Varian operates manufacturing facilities in seven countries and sales and service offices worldwide. The company is organized around the following core businesses: Health Care Systems, Instruments, Electronic Devices, and Semiconductor Equipment. Varian provides medical linear accelerators, treatment stimulators, and information management systems to hospitals and clinics worldwide. The company is a leading supplier of X-ray tubes for imaging systems of all types, as well as instruments that help in the treatment of diseases such as AIDS. Varian instruments also regulate the quality of a wide range of products, including petroleum, pharmaceuticals, ice cream, and champagne, and its vacuum pumps and leak detectors are used to create a vacuum environment. Varian is a worldwide leader in the manufacture of devices that generate, amplify, and define signals for radio and television broadcasting and satellite communications. They are also used in air traffic control, navigation, radar, fusion energy, and other scientific research applications. **Positions advertised include:** Senior Accountant; Office Administrator; Software Engineer; Test Technician; Program Manager; Customer Support Representative; Regional Sales Manager; Product Manager; Product Training Specialist. **Special programs:** Internships. **Corporate headquarters location:** This location. **Other U.S. locations:** AZ; MA; UT. **Listed on:** New York Stock Exchange. **Stock exchange symbol:** VAR. **Number of employees at this location:** 3,000. **Number of employees nationwide:** 6,500.

## WEIGH-TRONIX, INC.

3990 Brickway Boulevard, Santa Rosa CA 95403-1098. 707/527-5555. **Fax:** 707/579-1655. **Contact:** Human Resources Manager. **E-mail address:** employment@weigh-tronix.com. **World Wide Web address:** http://www.weigh-tronix.com. **Description:** Manufactures electronic weighing systems, thermal and impact printers, POS scales, mailing systems, and related products. **Corporate headquarters location:** Norwalk CT. **Other U.S. locations:** Nationwide. **Parent company:** Staveley. **Operations at this facility include:** Administration; Divisional Headquarters; Manufacturing; Research and Development; Sales; Service. **Listed on:** Privately held. **Number of employees at this location:** 85. **Number of employees nationwide:** 1,000.

**WIEGMANN & ROSE**
P.O. Box 4187, Oakland CA 94614. 510/632-8828. **Fax:** 510/632-8920. **Contact:** John Gasparini, Vice President of Human Resources. **World Wide Web address:** http://www.wiegmannandrose.com. **Description:** Manufactures fabricated heat exchangers. **Corporate headquarters location:** This location.

## MINING/GAS/PETROLEUM/ENERGY RELATED

You can expect to find the following types of companies in this chapter:
*Anthracite, Coal, and Ore Mining • Mining Machinery and Equipment •*
*Oil and Gas Field Services • Petroleum and Natural Gas*

### AIR LIQUIDE AMERICA CORPORATION

700 Decoto Road, Union City CA 94587. 510/429-4200. **Contact:** Human Resources. **World Wide Web address:** http://www. airliquide.com. **Description:** Air Liquide America Corporation is a diversified manufacturer engaged primarily in the recovery and sale of atmospheric industrial gases, the manufacture and sale of oil field equipment and supplies, and the distribution of welding and industrial equipment and supplies. The company operates several business segments. The Gas Group produces and sells oxygen, nitrogen, and argon in liquid and gaseous forms at approximately 20 locations in Texas, Louisiana, Florida, California, and Hawaii, operating more than 2,200 miles of pipeline. The Energy Group operates under two names (Bowen Tools and Dia-Log Companies) and manufactures and sells equipment to petroleum and natural gas companies. The Welding Group distributes electric arc welding equipment and supplies in Texas, Louisiana, California, and Hawaii for Lincoln Electric Company. **NOTE:** Please send resumes to Kristy Carlson, Human Resources, 12800 West Little York Road, Houston TX 77041. 713/624-8000. **Corporate headquarters location:** Houston TX. **International locations:** Worldwide. **Operations at this facility include:** This location houses administrative offices. **Number of employees nationwide:** 2,300.

### CALPINE CORPORATION

50 West San Fernando Street, Suite 500, San Jose CA 95113. 408/995-5115. **Contact:** Human Resources. **E-mail address:** jobs@calpine.com. **World Wide Web address:** http://www.calpine. com. **Description:** Sells steam and electricity to electric utilities, industrial companies, and government institutions. The company develops, owns, and operates independent power projects, including three geothermal and two natural gas-fired plants. Calpine Corporation is one of the largest producers of geothermal energy in the United States. **Corporate headquarters location:** This location. **Other area locations:** Dublin CA; Middletown CA; Walnut Creek CA. **Other U.S. locations:** Nationwide. **Listed on:** New York Stock Exchange. **Stock exchange symbol:** CPN. **Annual sales/revenues:** More than $100 million.

## ELECTRIC POWER RESEARCH INSTITUTE (EPRI)

3412 Hillview Avenue, Palo Alto CA 94304. 650/855-2000. **Contact:** Human Resources. **World Wide Web address:** http://www. epri.com. **Description:** A nonprofit research management firm specializing in all areas of electric power production, origin, transmission, distribution, storage, and end use. Founded in 1972. **Positions advertised include:** Area Manager. **Corporate headquarters location:** This location. **Annual sales/revenues:** $21 - $50 million. **Number of employees at this location:** 500. **Number of employees nationwide:** 850.

## HOMESTAKE MINING COMPANY

1600 Riviera Avenue, Suite 200, Walnut Creek CA 94596. 415/981-8150. **Contact:** Vice President of Human Resources. **World Wide Web address:** http://www.homestake.com. **Description:** One of the largest gold mining companies in the world. Homestake Mining has production facilities in the United States, Canada, and Australia, with minor interests in Chile, Mexico, and Venezuela. **Corporate headquarters location:** This location. **Other U.S. locations:** SD. **Operations at this facility include:** Administration. **Number of employees at this location:** 70. **Number of employees nationwide:** 2,100.

## OLYMPIAN

260 Michelle Court, South San Francisco CA 94080. 650/873-8200. **Toll-free phone:** 800/899-4659. **Contact:** Human Resources. **E-mail address:** jobs@oly.com. **World Wide Web address:** http://www.oly. com. **Description:** Distributes a wide variety of petroleum products. Founded in 1954. **NOTE:** Entry-level positions and second and third shifts are offered. **Positions advertised include:** Cashier; Gulf Transportation Driver. **Special programs:** Summer Jobs. **Corporate headquarters location:** This location. **Listed on:** Privately held. **Number of employees at this location:** 80.

## PAPER AND WOOD PRODUCTS

**You can expect to find the following types of companies in this chapter:**
*Forest and Wood Products and Services • Lumber and Wood Wholesale •*
*Millwork, Plywood, and Structural Members • Paper and Wood Mills*

### GEORGIA-PACIFIC CORPORATION

P.O. Box 2407, South San Francisco CA 94083. 650/873-7800. **Physical address:** 249 East Grand Avenue, South San Francisco CA 94080. **Contact:** Human Resources Manager. **World Wide Web address:** http://www.gp.com. **Description:** Georgia-Pacific Corporation is a manufacturer, wholesaler, and distributor of building products, industrial wood products, pulp, paper, packaging, and related chemicals. The company is one of the world's largest manufacturers of forest products, with facilities in 48 states and overseas. Georgia-Pacific owns 6 million acres of forestland in North America. **Corporate headquarters location:** Atlanta GA. **Operations at this facility include:** This location produces corrugated containers. **Listed on:** New York Stock Exchange. **Stock exchange symbol:** GP. **Number of employees at this location:** 220.

### SAMOA PACIFIC CELLULOSE

P.O. Box 218, Samoa CA 95564. 707/443-7511. **Contact:** Human Resources. **Description:** A forest products firm that harvests timber and converts it into a wide range of wood products including lumber, panel products, doors, and other goods. Louisiana-Pacific Corporation operates more than 100 manufacturing facilities and 20 distribution centers in the United States and Canada. **Corporate headquarters location:** This location.

### SMURFIT-STONE CONTAINER CORPORATION

201 South Hillview Drive, Milpitas CA 95035. 408/946-3600. **Toll-free phone:** 877/772-2932. **Contact:** Human Resources. **World Wide Web address:** http://www.smurfit-stone.com. **Description:** Smurfit-Stone Container Corporation is one of the world's leading paper-based packaging companies. The company's main products include corrugated containers, folding cartons, and multiwall industrial bags. The company is also one of the world's largest collectors and processors of recycled products that are then sold to a worldwide customer base. Smurfit-Stone Container Corporation also operates several paper tube, market pulp, and newsprint production facilities. **Corporate headquarters location:** Chicago IL. **Operations**

**advertised include:** This location manufactures corrugated containers. **Listed on:** NASDAQ. **Stock exchange symbol:** SSCC.

## SMURFIT-STONE CONTAINER CORPORATION
2600 De La Cruz Boulevard, Santa Clara CA 95050. 408/496-5118. **Contact:** Human Resources. **World Wide Web address:** http://www. smurfit-stone.com. **Description:** Smurfit-Stone Container Corporation is one of the world's leading paper-based packaging companies. The company's main products include corrugated containers, folding cartons, and multiwall industrial bags. The company is also one of the world's largest collectors and processors of recycled products that are then sold to a worldwide customer base. **Corporate headquarters location:** Chicago IL. **Operations advertised include:** This location is a paper mill. **Listed on:** NASDAQ. **Stock exchange symbol:** SSCC.

## WEYERHAEUSER COMPANY
P.O. Box 1878, San Leandro CA 94577. 510/357-5400. **Physical address:** 2800 Alvardo, San Leandro CA 94577. **Contact:** Human Resources. **World Wide Web address:** http://www.weyerhaeuser. com. **Description:** A forest management and manufacturing company. The company recycles pulp, paper, and packaging products; manufactures wood products; manages timberland; and develops real estate. **Corporate headquarters location:** Tacoma WA. **Other U.S. locations:** Nationwide. **Operations at this facility include:** Manufacturing; Sales. **Listed on:** New York Stock Exchange. **Stock exchange symbol:** WY.

## XPEDX
1381 North 10th Street, San Jose CA 95112. 408/435-8200. **Contact:** Human Resources. **World Wide Web address:** http://www. xpedx.com. **Description:** Distributes paper and paper products; office supplies and equipment; packaging supplies and equipment; and consumables. **Other area locations:** Hayward CA.

## PRINTING AND PUBLISHING

**You can expect to find the following types of companies in this chapter:**
*Book, Newspaper, and Periodical Publishers • Commercial Photographers •*
*Commercial Printing Services • Graphic Designers*

### ALAMEDA NEWSPAPER GROUP
401 13th Street, Oakland CA 94612. 510/208-6300. **Contact:** Human Resources Department. **E-mail address:** hr@angnewspapers. com. **World Wide Web address:** http://www.insidebayarea.com. **Description:** Publishes six daily newspapers with a combined daily circulation of more than 232,000. **Parent company:** Garden State Newspapers. **Operations at this facility include:** Administration; Manufacturing; Regional Headquarters; Sales; Service. **Number of employees nationwide:** 1,000.

### BROWNTROUT PUBLISHERS INC.
P.O. Box 280070, San Francisco CA 94128-0070. 650/340-9800. **Toll-free phone:** 877/950-7812. **Contact:** Human Resources. **World Wide Web address:** http://www.browntrout.com. **Description:** Publishes desk calendars and gift books on subjects including art, history, animals, sports, and travel. The company also customizes calendars for corporations and private businesses. **Corporate headquarters location:** This location. **International locations:** Australia; Canada; Mexico; United Kingdom.

### DELUXE FINANCIAL SERVICES
1551 Dell Avenue, Campbell CA 95008. 408/370-8801. **Contact:** Personnel. **World Wide Web address:** http://www.deluxe.com. **Description:** Provides check printing, electronic funds transfer processing services, and related services to the financial industry; check authorization and collection services to retailers; and electronic benefit transfer services to state governments. Deluxe also produces forms, specialty papers, and other products for small businesses, professional practices, and medical/dental offices; and provides tax forms and electronic tax filing services to tax preparers. Through the direct mail channel, Deluxe sells greeting cards, gift wrapping, and related products to households. The company entered the lithographic ink market in 1994 as a result of developing a breakthrough water-washable ink. Deluxe is a *Fortune* 500 company with facilities located in the United States, Canada, and the United Kingdom. **Corporate headquarters location:** Shoreview MN. **Other U.S. locations:** Nationwide. **Listed on:** New York Stock Exchange.

**Stock exchange symbol:** DLX. **Number of employees nationwide:** 15,000.

## FUJICOLOR PROCESSING INC.

27105 Industrial Boulevard, Hayward CA 94545. 510/783-7000. **Toll-free phone:** 800/999-4686. **Fax:** 510/783-0535. **Contact:** Leah Mollat, Human Resources Manager. **World Wide Web address:** http://www.fujifilm.com. **Description:** Provides wholesale photofinishing services and related sales and service activities. **NOTE:** Entry-level positions, part-time jobs, and second and third shifts are offered. **Positions advertised include:** Production Manager; Production Supervisor. **Special programs:** Training; Summer Jobs. **Corporate headquarters location:** Elmsford NY. **Other U.S. locations:** Nationwide. **International locations:** Worldwide. **Parent company:** Fuji Film Ltd. **CEO:** Hank Hyyashi. **Facilities Manager:** M. Merryfield. **Purchasing Manager:** David Trujillo. **Annual sales/revenues:** More than $100 million. **Number of employees at this location:** 225. **Number of employees nationwide:** 8,000.

## HARPERCOLLINS SAN FRANCISCO

353 Sacramento Street, Suite 500, San Francisco CA 94111. 415/477-4400. **Contact:** Human Resources. **E-mail address:** jobs@ harpercollins.com. **World Wide Web address:** http://www. harpercollins.com. **Description:** HarperCollins is a leading book publisher. **Positions advertised include:** Assistant Art Director; Interior Design Manager; Business Manager; Senior Production Editor; Rotational Associate; Senior Sales Director, Special Markets. **Special programs:** Internships. **Corporate headquarters location:** New York NY. **Other U.S. locations:** Glenview IL; Scranton PA. **Subsidiaries include:** Scott Foresman; Zondervan. **Parent company:** News Corporation. **Operations at this facility include:** This location publishes religious, academic, and psychology titles, as well as visual books such as cookbooks and gift books. **Listed on:** New York Stock Exchange. **Stock exchange symbol:** NWS. **Number of employees at this location:** 135. **Number of employees nationwide:** 3,000.

## HOUGHTON MIFFLIN COMPANY

2001 Gateway Place, Suite 750, San Jose CA 95110. 408/392-3100. **Contact:** Human Resources. **E-mail address:** hrassist@hmco.com. **World Wide Web address:** http://www.hmco.com. **Description:** Houghton Mifflin Company is a publisher of school textbooks, fiction, nonfiction, reference books, educational software, and related multimedia products. **Corporate headquarters location:** Boston MA. **Operations at this facility include:** This location is a sales office for the Western Elementary School Division. **Listed on:** New York Stock Exchange. **Stock exchange symbol:** HTN. **Number of employees at this location:** 40.

## K.P. CORPORATION

428 South Abbott Avenue, Milpitas CA 93505. 408/934-8600. **Contact:** Human Resources. **E-mail address:** jobs@kpcorp.com. **World Wide Web address:** http://www.kpcorp.com. **Description:** A commercial lithographic printer. **Corporate headquarters location:** San Ramon CA.

## KNIGHT-RIDDER

50 West San Fernando Street, Suite 1500, San Jose CA 95113. 408/938-7700. **Fax:** 408/938-7758. **Contact:** Human Resources. **World Wide Web address:** http://www.kri.com. **Description:** A major newspaper publishing company that owns 28 dailies in 15 states and 3 nondailies in suburban areas. The company also produces niche publications such as Myrtle Beach's *Golf, CubaNews* newsletter in Miami, and *Northland Outdoors* in Grand Forks. The larger papers include the *Miami Herald, Philadelphia Inquirer, Philadelphia Daily News, Detroit Free Press,* and *San Jose Mercury News.* **Positions advertised include:** Business Analyst; Database Analyst; Team Member; Financial Analyst; Outside Sales Representative. **Corporate headquarters location:** This location. **Subsidiaries include:** Knight-Ridder also has interests in the information distribution market through Knight-Ridder Information, Inc.; Knight-Ridder Financial; and Technimetrics. Knight-Ridder's online information retrieval serves the business, scientific, technology, medical, and education communities in more than 100 countries. Knight-Ridder Financial provides real-time financial news and pricing information through products such as MoneyCenter, Digital Datafeed, ProfitCenter, and TradeCenter. Knight-Ridder also has interests in cable television and other businesses. TKR Cable, a 50-50 joint venture with Liberty Media Corporation, serves 344,000 basic subscribers in New Jersey and New York and manages Kentucky systems with 277,000 subscribers. Through TKR Cable Partners, Knight-Ridder owns a 15 percent share of TCI/TKR L.P. Cable Systems with 867,000 subscribers in five states. Other interests include partial ownership of the Seattle Times Company, two paper mills, a newspaper advertising sales company, and SCI Holdings.

**Listed on:** New York Stock Exchange. **Stock exchange symbol:** KRI. **Annual sales/revenues:** More than $100 million.

## THE McCLATCHY COMPANY
P.O. Box 15779, Sacramento CA 95852. 916/321-1846. **Physical address:** 2100 Q Street, Sacramento CA 95816. **Contact:** Human Resources. **World Wide Web address:** http://www.mcclatchy.com. **Description:** Publishes 12 daily and 8 community newspapers in California, Washington, Alaska, and South Carolina. The combined average circulation is 825,800 daily and 977,200 Sunday. **Positions advertised include:** Disposition Clerk. **Corporate headquarters location:** This location. **Listed on:** New York Stock Exchange. **Stock exchange symbol:** MNI.

## McGRAW-HILL COMPANY
55 Francisco Street, Suite 200, San Francisco CA 94133. 415/433-2821. **Contact:** Personnel. **E-mail address:** career_ops@mcgraw-hill.com. **World Wide Web address:** http://www.mcgraw-hill.com. **Description:** McGraw-Hill is a provider of information and services through books, magazines, newsletters, software, CD-ROMs, and online data, fax, and TV broadcasting services. The company operates four network-affiliated TV stations and also publishes *Business Week* magazine and books for college, medical, international, legal, and professional markets. McGraw-Hill also offers financial services including Standard & Poor's, commodity items, and international and logistics management products and services. **Positions advertised include:** Account Manager. **Corporate headquarters location:** New York NY. **Operations at this facility include:** This location publishes college textbooks. **Listed on:** New York Stock Exchange. **Stock exchange symbol:** MHP.

## OAKLAND TRIBUNE, INC.
401 13th Street, Oakland CA 94612. 510/208-6300. **Contact:** Bob Jendusa, Vice President of Human Resources. **E-mail address:** bjendusa@angnewspapers.com. **World Wide Web address:** http://www.insidebayarea.com. **Description:** Publishes a daily metropolitan newspaper with a circulation of approximately 155,000. **Positions advertised include:** Graphic Artist; Pressperson Trainee. **Corporate headquarters location:** This location. **Parent company:** ANG Newspapers.

## PEARSON EDUCATION

1301 Sansome Street, San Francisco CA 94111. 415/402-2500. **Contact:** Kelly Ripplone, Personnel Manager. **E-mail address:** staffing@pearsoned.com. **World Wide Web address:** http://www. pearsoned.com. **Description:** Pearson Education is one of the world's largest publishers and distributors of educational materials for use in elementary and high schools, universities, and businesses. **Positions advertised include:** Assistant Editor; Editorial Assistant; Copywriter; Managing Editor; Project Editor. **Office hours:** Monday - Friday, 8:30 a.m. - 5:00 p.m. **Corporate headquarters location:** Upper Saddle River NJ. **Other U.S. locations:** Glenview IL; New York NY; White Plains NY. **Parent company:** Pearson plc. **Operations at this facility include:** This location primarily publishes higher education computer science and engineering materials. **Listed on:** New York Stock Exchange. **Stock exchange symbol:** PSO.

## PORTAL PUBLICATIONS

201 Alameda Del Prado, Novato CA 94949. 415/884-6200. **Fax:** 415/382-3377. **Contact:** Human Resources. **E-mail address:** recruiter@portalpub.com. **World Wide Web address:** http://www.p ortalpub.com. **Description:** One of the world's largest publishers of original artwork, posters, prints, cards, calendars, and related products. **Positions advertised include:** Art Director; Inside Sales Representative; Chain Sales Service Representative; Sales Representative; Graphic Designer. **Corporate headquarters location:** Stamford CT. **Subsidiaries include:** Aird Imports Pty. Ltd., Australia; Regency House Pictures and Frames, Inc., Decatur GA; The Winn Devon Art Group, Ltd., Seattle WA. **Parent company:** Applied Graphics Technology. **Listed on:** American Stock Exchange. **Stock exchange symbol:** AGD.

## REDDING RECORD SEARCHLIGHT

P.O. Box 492397, Redding CA 96049-2397. 530/243-2424. **Physical address:** 1101 Twin View Boulevard, Redding CA 96003. **Contact:** Bonnie Salyer, Human Resources Director. **E-mail address:** sayler@redding.com. **World Wide Web address:** http://www. redding.com. **Description:** Publishes a daily newspaper with a circulation of approximately 40,000. **Positions advertised include:** outside Classified Multi-Media Sales Representative; Features Reporter; Inserter. **Special programs:** Internships. **Corporate headquarters location:** Cincinnati OH. **Other U.S. locations:** Nationwide. **Parent company:** The E.W. Scripps Company. **Operations at this facility include:** Administration; Sales; Service.

**Listed on:** New York Stock Exchange. **Stock exchange symbol:** SSP. **Number of employees at this location:** 190.

## SKC AMERICA, INC.
307 North Pastoria Avenue, Sunnyvale CA 94085. 408/739-4170. **Fax:** 408/720-0947. **Contact:** Human Resources/Administration Manager. **E-mail address:** resumes@skcam.com. **Description:** Develops, manufactures, and markets various imaging products used for data storage, PCB, and graphic arts applications. Products include duplicate microfilm and polyester-based media for ink-jet printers. **Office hours:** Monday - Friday, 8:00 a.m. - 5:00 p.m. **Operations at this facility include:** Manufacturing; Sales.

## SAN FRANCISCO CHRONICLE
901 Mission Street, San Francisco CA 94103. 415/777-7000. **Contact:** Adrianne Cabanatuan, Director of Recruitment. **World Wide Web address:** http://www.sfchron.com. **Description:** A daily newspaper with a circulation of 530,000. **Positions advertised include:** Payroll and Administrative Clerk; Customer Sales Representative; Tractor/Trailer Driver; Disability Management Specialist; Assistant Operations Manager; National Advertising Sales Manager. **Parent company:** Hearst Communications, Inc.

## SAN JOSE MERCURY NEWS WEST
750 Ridder Park Drive, Boca CA 95190. 408/920-5725. **Contact:** Human Resources. **World Wide Web address:** http://www. mercurycenter.com. **Description:** An office of the *San Jose Mercury News*, which publishes a daily newspaper with a circulation of 320,000. **NOTE:** Interested applicants should send resumes to Employment Manager, San Jose Mercury News, 750 Ridder Park Drive, San Jose CA 95190. **Parent company:** Knight-Ridder, Inc. (Miami FL). **Listed on:** New York Stock Exchange.

## SAN JOSE MERCURY NEWS, INC.
750 Ridder Park Drive, San Jose CA 95190. 408/920-5000. **Contact:** Employment Manager. **World Wide Web address:** http://www. bayarea.com. **Description:** Publishes a daily newspaper with a circulation of 320,000. **Parent company:** Knight-Ridder, Inc. (Miami FL). **Listed on:** New York Stock Exchange.

## TIMES-HERALD, INC.

P.O. Box 3188, Vallejo CA 94590. 707/644-1141. **Contact:** Joan Rondoni, Personnel Secretary. **World Wide Web address:** http://www.timesheraldonline.com. **Description:** Publishes a daily newspaper with a circulation of more than 25,000. **Parent company:** MediaNews Group.

## WEST GROUP

50 California Street, 19th Floor, San Francisco CA 94111. 415/732-8500. **Fax:** 415/732-8874. **Contact:** Human Resources Manager. **World Wide Web address:** http://www.westgroup.com. **Description:** Publishes legal research information in CD-ROM and book formats for law practitioners and the judiciary. **Positions advertised include:** Finance Manager. **Corporate headquarters location:** Eagan MN. **Other U.S. locations:** Stamford CT. **Parent company:** Thomson Corporation. **Number of employees at this location:** 200.

## REAL ESTATE

You can expect to find the following types of companies in this chapter:
*Land Subdividers and Developers • Real Estate Agents, Managers,
and Operators • Real Estate Investment Trusts*

### BRE PROPERTIES, INC.
44 Montgomery Street, 36th Floor, San Francisco CA 94104. 415/445-6530. **Fax:** 415/449-6505. **Contact:** Louisa Fassett, Vice President. **E-mail address:** humanresources@breproperties.com. **World Wide Web address:** http://www.breproperties.com. **Description:** A real estate investment trust. **Corporate headquarters location:** This location. **Listed on:** New York Stock Exchange. **Stock exchange symbol:** BRE.

### BAY MEADOWS COMPANY
P.O. Box 5050, San Mateo CA 94402. 650/574-7223. **Physical address:** 2600 South Delaware Street, San Mateo CA 94403. **Fax:** 650/349-5884. **Contact:** Human Resources. **World Wide Web address:** http://www.baymeadows.com. **Description:** Operates Bay Meadows Race Track on the San Francisco Peninsula, and California Jockey Club, an equity real estate investment trust whose principal asset is Bay Meadows Race Track. **Corporate headquarters location:** This location.

### BELMONT VILLAGE
500 South Winchester Boulevard, San Jose CA 95128. 408/984-4767. **Contact:** Human Resources. **E-mail address:** jobs4u@belmontvillage.com. **World Wide Web address:** http://www.belmontvillage.com. **Description:** A senior citizens assisted living community. **Positions advertised include:** Activities Director; Concierge; Driver; Administrative Assistant; Chef Manager; Building Engineer.

### CB RICHARD ELLIS
275 Battery Street, Suite 1300, San Francisco CA 94111. 415/772-0123. **Contact:** Human Resources. **E-mail address:** opps@cbre.com. **World Wide Web address:** http://www.cbrichardellis.com. **Description:** A fully integrated commercial real estate services company offering property sales and leasing, property and facility management, mortgage banking, and investment management services. **Corporate headquarters location:** Los Angeles CA. **Other U.S. locations:** Nationwide. **International locations:** Worldwide.

## CATELLUS DEVELOPMENT CORPORATION

201 Mission Street, Suite 200, San Francisco CA 94105. 415/974-4500. **Contact:** Human Resources. **E-mail address:** human-resources@catellus.com. **World Wide Web address:** http://www.catellus.com. **Description:** Owns, develops, and manages industrial, retail, and office buildings. The company's properties, land holdings, and joint-venture interests are located in major markets in California and 11 other states. **Corporate headquarters location:** This location. **Other area locations:** Los Angeles CA; Newport Beach CA; Norwalk CA; Oakland CA; San Diego CA; San Jose CA. **Other U.S. locations:** Lakewood CO; Woodridge IL; Dallas TX; Seattle WA. **Listed on:** New York Stock Exchange. **Stock exchange symbol:** CDX.

## COLDWELL BANKER

2633 Ocean Avenue, San Francisco CA 94132. 415/334-1880. **Contact:** Human Resources. **World Wide Web address:** http://www.coldwellbanker.com. **Description:** One of the largest residential real estate companies in the United States and Canada. **Corporate headquarters location:** Parsippany NJ. **Parent company:** Cendant Corporation. **Listed on:** New York Stock Exchange. **Stock exchange symbol:** CD.

## COLDWELL BANKER

350 Bon Aire Center, Suite 100, Greenbrae CA 94904. 415/461-3220. **Contact:** Human Resources. **World Wide Web address:** http://www.coldwellbanker.com. **Description:** One of the largest residential real estate companies in the United States and Canada. **Corporate headquarters location:** Parsippany NJ. **Parent company:** Cendant Corporation. **Listed on:** New York Stock Exchange. **Stock exchange symbol:** CD.

## CUSHMAN & WAKEFIELD

One Maritime Plaza, Suite 900, San Francisco CA 94111. 415/397-1700. **Contact:** Jill Campbell, Human Resources. **World Wide Web address:** http://www.cushwake.com. **Description:** An international commercial and industrial real estate services firm. The company is engaged in appraisals, financial services, project development, research services, and the management and leasing of commercial office space. **Corporate headquarters location:** New York NY.

## LINCOLN PROPERTY COMPANY

1700 Montgomery Street, Suite 209, San Francisco CA 94111. 415/788-3000. **Contact:** Human Resources. **World Wide Web address:**

http://www.lincolnproperty.com. **Description:** A property management and development company. Founded in 1965. **Corporate headquarters location:** Dallas TX.

## RETAIL

**You can expect to find the following types of companies in this chapter:**
*Catalog Retailers • Department Stores; Specialty Stores •*
*Retail Bakeries • Supermarkets*

### ALBERTSON'S
1150 East 14th Street, San Leandro CA 94577. 510/483-0881. **Contact:** Human Resources. **E-mail address:** employment@ albertsons.com. **World Wide Web address:** http://www.albertsons. com. **Description:** Operates a nationwide chain of food and drug stores. **Corporate headquarters location:** Boise ID. **Listed on:** New York Stock Exchange. **Stock exchange symbol:** ABS.

### ANDRONICO'S MARKET
1109 Washington Avenue, Albany CA 94706. **Recorded jobline:** 510/287-5978. **Contact:** Human Resources Department. **E-mail address:** human.resources@andronicos.com. **World Wide Web address:** http://www.andronicos.com. **Description:** Operates a chain of retail grocery stores. Founded in 1929. **NOTE:** Entry-level positions and part-time jobs are offered. **Special programs:** Training. **Corporate headquarters location:** This location. **Other area locations:** Berkeley CA; Danville CA; Emeryville CA; Los Altos CA; Palo Alto CA; San Anselmo CA; San Francisco CA. **Operations at this facility include:** Administration. **Listed on:** Privately held. **COO:** William J. Andronico. **Information Systems Manager:** Michael Miller. **Number of employees at this location:** 800.

### BROOKS BROTHERS
150 Post Street, San Francisco CA 94108. 415/397-4500. **Contact:** Human Resources Department. **E-mail address:** hr@brooksbrothers. com. **World Wide Web address:** http://www.brooksbrothers.com. **Description:** One location of the specialty clothing store chain. Brooks Brothers operates 80 retail and 72 factory stores in the United States. **Corporate headquarters location:** New York NY. **International locations:** China; Japan; Taiwan.

### BROOKS CAMERA
125 Kearney Street, San Francisco CA 94108. 415/362-4708. **Contact:** Don Boyle, Manager. **Description:** A retailer of photography equipment. **Corporate headquarters location:** This location. **Parent company:** Inventory Supply Company, Inc.

**Operations at this facility include:** Administration; Sales. **Number of employees at this location:** 10.

### COLDWATER CREEK
850 Stanford Shopping Center, Palo Alto CA 94304. 650/321-4112. **Fax:** 650/321-9909. **Recorded jobline:** 888/729-9909. **Contact:** Human Resources. **E-mail address:** retailjobs3@thecreek.com. **World Wide Web address:** http://www.coldwatercreek.com. **Description:** A retail chain. **Positions advertised include:** Assistant Manager. **Corporate headquarters location:** Sandpoint ID. **Listed on:** NASDAQ. **Stock exchange symbol:** CWTR.

### DUNN-EDWARDS CORPORATION
2201 Junipero Serra Boulevard, Davis City CA 94015. 650/992-9660. **Toll-free phone:** 888/DE-PAINT. **Contact:** Human Resources Manager. **World Wide Web address:** http://www.dunnedwards.com. **Description:** Dunn-Edwards Corporation manufactures paint. **Corporate headquarters location:** Los Angeles CA. **operations at this facility include:** This location is a retail store.

### eBAY, INC.
2145 Hamilton Avenue, San Jose CA 95125. 408/558-7400. **Contact:** Human Resources. **World Wide Web address:** http://www.ebay.com. **Description:** An online auction site that offers items such as antiques, coins, computers, stamps, and toys. **Positions advertised include:** Senior UNIX Systems Administrator; Senior Software Engineer; Associate Manager; Senior Finance Manager; Java Development Manager; Director, Indirect Taxes; Staff Software Engineer. **Corporate headquarters location:** This location. **Listed on:** NASDAQ. **Stock exchange symbol:** EBAY.

### GAP INC.
900 Cherry Avenue, San Bruno CA 94066. 650/952-4400. **Contact:** Personnel. **World Wide Web address:** http://www.gap.com. **Description:** A nationwide retailer of moderately priced casual apparel for men, women, and children. The company operates over 1,800 stores under the names Gap, GapKids, BabyGap, Banana Republic, and Old Navy Clothing Company. **Positions advertised include:** Treasury Director; Account Manager; Director of Finance; Strategic Sourcing Manager; Legal Assistant; Project Manager; Proposal Analyst; Administrative Assistant; Senior Account Analyst; Estimator; Finance Manager; Engineering Project Manager. **Corporate headquarters location:** This location. **Other U.S.**

**locations:** Nationwide. **International locations:** Canada; France; Germany; Japan; United Kingdom. **Listed on:** New York Stock Exchange. **Stock exchange symbol:** GPS.

## THE GOOD GUYS!
1600 Harbor Bay Parkway, Suite 200, Alameda CA 94502. 510/747-6000. **Contact:** Human Resources. **E-mail address:** jobs@goodguys.com (no attachments, please). **World Wide Web address:** http://www.thegoodguys.com. **Description:** Owns a chain of retail consumer electronic products stores specializing in televisions, videos, home audio systems, telephones, home office systems, car audio systems and cellular phones, photographic equipment, and other related electronic products. **Positions advertised include:** Extended Service Product Program Manager; Senior Installation Technician. **Corporate headquarters location:** This location. **Listed on:** NASDAQ. **Stock exchange symbol:** GGUY.

## GYMBOREE
700 Airport Boulevard, Suite 200, Burlingame CA 94010. 650/579-0600. **Contact:** Human Resources. **World Wide Web address:** http://www.gymboree.com. **Description:** Operates a chain of retail stores that sell children's active wear and accessories. The company also franchises Gymboree Play and Music Programs for children and their parents. **Positions advertised include:** Designer; Fabric Technician Manager; Business Systems Analyst; Textile Graphic Designer; Senior Manager of Store Maintenance and Repair; Transportation Manager; Regional Loss Prevention Manager; Oracle Database Distributor; Franchise Development Director. **Corporate headquarters location:** This location. **Listed on:** NASDAQ. **Stock exchange symbol:** GYMB. **Number of employees at this location:** 100. **Number of employees nationwide:** 3,700.

## HELLO-DIRECT
5893 Rue Ferrari, San Jose CA 95138-1857. 408/972-1990. **Toll-free phone:** 800/444-3556. **Contact:** Human Resources. **E-mail address:** resumes@hello-direct.com. **World Wide Web address:** http://www.hellodirect.com. **Description:** A catalog retailer of telephone productivity items including headsets, cordless phones, line switches, digital adapters, and call recording devices. **Corporate headquarters location:** This location.

## KRIEGAN
4240 International Boulevard, Oakland CA 94621. 510/532-1240. Contact: Regional Recruiter. Description: A retailer and distributor of automotive aftermarket products. Company slogan: Whatever it takes. Operations at this facility include: Sales; Service.

## MACY'S
1 Stonestown Mall, San Francisco CA 94132. 415/753-4000. Contact: Human Resources. World Wide Web address: http://www.macys.com. Description: A location of the retail department store chain. Corporate headquarters location: New York NY.

## MACY'S UNION SQUARE
170 O'Farrell Street, San Francisco CA 94102. 415/397-3333. Contact: Human Resources. World Wide Web address: http://www. macys.com. Description: One of three divisions of R.H. Macy Company (New York NY). Macy's Union Square operates 50 stores regionally as part of the full-line department store chain. Corporate headquarters location: New York NY. Operations at this facility include: Divisional Headquarters.

## MARSHALL'S OF SAN FRANCISCO
901 Market Street, San Francisco CA 94103. 415/974-5368. Contact: Human Resources. World Wide Web address: http://www. marshallsonline.com. Description: An off-price retail organization providing wide assortments of men's, women's, and children's apparel, footwear, accessories, and selected home furnishings at over 500 locations nationwide. Positions advertised include: Cashier; Merchandise Associate; Processor. Corporate headquarters location: Framingham MA. Parent company: TJX. Listed on: New York Stock Exchange. Stock exchange symbol: TJX.

## NORDSTROM, INC.
285 Winston Drive, San Francisco CA 94132. 415/753-1344. Toll-free phone: 888/282-6060. Contact: Human Resources Department. World Wide Web address: http://www.nordstrom.com. Description: A specialty retailer that sells apparel, shoes, and accessories. Nordstrom operates more than 60 stores, with over 20 clearance, boutique, and leased shoe departments in 12 department stores in Hawaii and Guam. Founded in 1901. Positions advertised include: Cosmetics Counter Manager; Cosmetics Sales Representative; Restaurant Chef. Corporate headquarters location: Seattle WA. Listed on: New York Stock Exchange. Stock exchange symbol: JWN.

## NORDSTROM, INC.
865 Market Street, San Francisco CA 94103. 415/243-8500. **Toll-free phone:** 888/282-6060. **Contact:** Human Resources Department. **World Wide Web address:** http://www.nordstrom.com. **Description:** A specialty retailer that sells apparel, shoes, and accessories. Nordstrom operates more than 60 stores, with over 20 clearance, boutique, and leased shoe departments in 12 department stores in Hawaii and Guam. **Corporate headquarters location:** Seattle WA. **Listed on:** New York Stock Exchange. **Stock exchange symbol:** JWN.

## ORCHARD SUPPLY HARDWARE
## SEARS HARDWARE STORES
6450 Via Del Oro, San Jose CA 95119. 408/281-3500. **Fax:** 408/365-2690. **Contact:** Human Resources. **World Wide Web address:** http://www.osh.com. **Description:** Operates more than 250 retail stores nationwide. Products are primarily geared toward home repair and maintenance projects. Founded in 1931. **NOTE:** Entry-level positions and part-time jobs are offered. **Company slogan:** We are committed to providing our customers with legendary customer service. **Positions advertised include:** Assistant Store Manager. **Special programs:** Internships; Training; Summer Jobs. **Corporate headquarters location:** This location. **Other U.S. locations:** Nationwide. **Parent company:** Sears, Roebuck and Company. **Number of employees at this location:** 300. **Number of employees nationwide:** 13,000.

## RALEY'S & BEL AIR
P.O. Box 15618, Sacramento CA 95852. 916/373-6300. **Contact:** Ronnie Cobb, Corporate Recruiter. **E-mail address:** jobs@raleys.com. **World Wide Web address:** http://www.raleys.com. **Description:** A large supermarket chain with more than 145 locations in Northern California and Nevada. Raley's owns and operates Bel Air Markets (also at this location) a supermarket chain in San Francisco. **NOTE:** Entry-level positions are offered. **Positions advertised include:** Food Service Technician; Loss Prevention Agent. **Special programs:** Internships. **Corporate headquarters location:** This location. **Subsidiaries include:** Food Source; Nob Hill Foods. **Operations at this facility include:** Divisional Headquarters.

## SAKS FIFTH AVENUE
384 Post Street, San Francisco CA 94108. 415/986-4300. **Contact:** Ms. Bobi Eisenberg, Director of Human Resources Department. **World Wide Web address:** http://www.saksincorporated.com.

**Description:** Saks Fifth Avenue is a 62-store chain emphasizing soft-goods products, primarily apparel for men, women, and children. **Corporate headquarters location:** New York NY. **Other area locations:** Palo Alto CA. **Parent company:** Saks Incorporated is a department store holding company that operates approximately 360 stores in 36 states. The company's stores include Saks Fifth Avenue, Parisian, Proffit's, Younker's, Herberger's, Carson Pirie Scott, Boston Store, Bergner's, and Off 5th, the company's outlet store. Saks Incorporated also operates two retail catalogs and several retail Internet sites. **Operations at this facility include:** This location is a part of the nationwide specialty department store chain. **Listed on:** New York Stock Exchange. **Stock exchange symbol:** SKS.

## SHARPER IMAGE CORPORATION
650 Davis Street, San Francisco CA 94111. 415/445-6000. **Contact:** Deborah Baker-Reyes, Human Resources. **World Wide Web address:** http://www.sharperimage.com. **Description:** A retailer of a wide variety of gifts in the following categories: automotive, outdoor and garden, travel and luggage, electronics, health and fitness, personal care, and home and safety. **Corporate headquarters location:** This location. **Listed on:** NASDAQ. **Stock exchange symbol:** SHRP.

## THE SHERWIN-WILLIAMS COMPANY INC.
320 Fourth Street, San Francisco CA 94107. 415/495-5720. **Contact:** Human Resources. **World Wide Web address:** http://www.sherwin. com. **Description:** Sherwin-Williams manufactures, sells, and distributes coatings and related products. Coatings are produced for original equipment manufacturers in various industries, as well as for the automotive aftermarket, the industrial maintenance market, and the traffic paint market. Sherwin-Williams labeled architectural and industrial coatings are sold through company-owned specialty paint and wall covering stores. The Sherwin-Williams Company also manufactures paint under the Acme, Dutch Boy, Kem-Tone, Lucas, Martin-Senour, Minwax, Pratt & Lambert, Rogers, and Thompson brand names, as well as private labels, and markets its products to independent dealers, mass merchandisers, and home improvement centers. **Corporate headquarters location:** Cleveland OH. **Other U.S. locations:** Nationwide. **Operations at this facility include:** This location is a retail paint and wall covering store. **Listed on:** New York Stock Exchange. **Stock exchange symbol:** SHW.

## THE SHERWIN-WILLIAMS COMPANY INC.

1525 Rollins Road, Suite A, Burlingame CA 94010. 650/697-2595. **Contact:** Human Resources. **World Wide Web address:** http://www. sherwin.com. **Description:** Sherwin-Williams manufactures, sells, and distributes coatings and related products. Coatings are produced for original equipment manufacturers in various industries, as well as for the automotive aftermarket, the industrial maintenance market, and the traffic paint market. Sherwin-Williams labeled architectural and industrial coatings are sold through company-owned specialty paint and wall covering stores. The Sherwin-Williams Company also manufactures paint under the Acme, Dutch Boy, Kem-Tone, Lucas, Martin-Senour, Minwax, Pratt & Lambert, Rogers, and Thompson brand names, as well as private labels, and markets its products to independent dealers, mass merchandisers, and home improvement centers. **Corporate headquarters location:** Cleveland OH. **Other U.S. locations:** Nationwide. **Operations at this facility include:** This location is a retail paint and wall covering store. **Listed on:** New York Stock Exchange. **Stock exchange symbol:** SHW.

## WILLIAMS-SONOMA, INC.

3250 Van Nass Avenue, San Francisco CA 94109. 415/421-7900. **Fax:** 415/616-8462. **Contact:** Human Resources. **World Wide Web address:** http://www.williams-sonomainc.com. **Description:** A retailer of cookware, serving equipment, and other specialty items. Products are sold both through retail stores and mail order catalogs with the following brand names: Williams-Sonoma, Hold Everything, Gardener's Eden, Pottery Barn, and Chambers. **Positions advertised include:** Pottery Barn Kids, Senior Manager; Visual Merchandising; Retail Inventory Manager; Project Manager, Retail Operations; Store Construction Director; Marketing Decision Support Manager; Design Manager; Lighting Control Buyer; Direct Marketing Assistant Planner. **Corporate headquarters location:** This location. **Listed on:** New York Stock Exchange. **Stock exchange symbol:** WSM.

# STONE, CLAY, GLASS, AND CONCRETE PRODUCTS

**You can expect to find the following types of companies in this chapter:**
*Cement, Tile, Sand, and Gravel • Crushed and Broken Stone •*
*Glass and Glass Products • Mineral Products*

## CENTRAL CONCRETE INC.
755 Stockton Avenue, San Jose CA 95126. 408/293-6272. **Contact:** Human Resources. **World Wide Web address:** http://www. centralconcrete.com. **Description:** A producer of ready-mixed concrete and concrete products. **Corporate headquarters location:** This location. **Parent company:** US Concrete. **Listed on:** NASDAQ. **Stock exchange symbol:** RMIX.

## NEWBASIS
156 Center Street, Auburn CA 95603. 530/885-2465. **Contact:** Human Resources. **World Wide Web address:** http://www.newbasis. com. **Description:** Manufactures concrete, polymer, fiberglass, and plastics products. **Corporate headquarters location:** Auburn CA. **Other U.S. locations:** AR; FL; TX. **International locations:** Chile; Mexico.

## OWENS-BROCKWAY
22302 Hathaway Avenue, Hayward CA 94541. 510/784-0881. **Fax:** 419/247-7107. **Contact:** Human Resources Department. **E-mail address:** resumes.oi@owens-ill.com (no attachments, please). **World Wide Web address:** http://www.o-i.com. **Description:** Owens-Brockway produces glass containers and also produces and sells containerboard, corrugated containers, printing plates and ink, plywood and dimension lumber, blown plastic containers, plastic beverage bottles, plastic drums, metal and plastic closures, tamper-resistant closures, plastic and glass prescription containers, pharmaceutical items, labels, and multipack plastic carriers for containers. **Corporate headquarters location:** Toledo OH. **Parent company:** Owens-Illinois, Inc. **Operations at this facility include:** This location manufactures glass. **Listed on:** New York Stock Exchange. **Stock exchange symbol:** OI.

## OWENS-BROCKWAY GLASS CONTAINER PLANT
3600 Alameda Avenue, Oakland CA 94601. 510/436-2000. **Contact:** Personnel Director. **E-mail address:** resumes.oi@owens-ill.com (no attachments, please). **World Wide Web address:** http://

www.o-i.com. **Description:** Owens-Brockway produces glass containers and also produces and sells containerboard, corrugated containers, printing plates and ink, plywood and dimension lumber, blown plastic containers, plastic beverage bottles, plastic drums, metal and plastic closures, tamper-resistant closures, plastic and glass prescription containers, pharmaceutical items, labels and multipack plastic carriers for containers. **Corporate headquarters location:** Toledo OH. **Parent company:** Owens-Illinois, Inc. **Operations at this facility include:** This location is a diversified manufacturer of packaging products including glass containers. **Listed on:** New York Stock Exchange. **Stock exchange symbol:** OI.

## OWENS-CORNING FIBERGLAS CORPORATION
960 Central Expressway, Santa Clara CA 95050. 408/727-3535. **Toll-free phone:** 800/GET-PINK. **Contact:** Personnel. **E-mail address:** resume@owenscorning.com. **World Wide Web address:** http://www.owenscorning.com. **Description:** Manufactures and sells thermal and acoustical insulation products including insulation for appliances, glass fiber roofing shingles, and roof insulation and industrial asphalt. Other products of the company include windows, glass fiber textile yarns, wet process chopped strands and specialty mats, and polyester resins. **Corporate headquarters location:** Toledo OH. **Other U.S. locations:** Nationwide. **Subsidiaries include:** Barbcorp, Inc.; Dansk-Svensk Glasfiber AS; Eric Co.; European Owens-Corning Fiberglas SA; IPM Inc.; Kitsons Insulations Products Ltd.; Owens-Corning AS; Owens-Corning Building Products; Owens-Corning Finance; Owens-Corning FSC, Inc. Illinois, Inc. **Listed on:** New York Stock Exchange. **Stock exchange symbol:** OWC.

## SYAR INDUSTRIES INC.
P.O. Box 2540, Napa CA 94558-0524. 707/252-8711. **Fax:** 707/254-3007. **Contact:** Human Resources. **Description:** Produces high-quality rock products and asphaltic paving materials. Founded in 1938. **NOTE:** Entry-level positions and second and third shifts are offered. **Special programs:** Summer Jobs. **Corporate headquarters location:** This location. **Listed on:** Privately held. **Number of employees at this location:** 50. **Number of employees nationwide:** 375.

## TRANSPORTATION/TRAVEL

**You can expect to find the following types of companies in this chapter:**
*Air, Railroad, and Water Transportation Services • Courier Services • Local and Interurban Passenger Transit • Ship Building and Repair • Transportation Equipment Travel Agencies • Trucking • Warehousing and Storage*

**CNF TRANSPORTATION CORPORATION**
3240 Hillview Avenue, Palo Alto CA 94304. 650/494-2900. **Contact:** Personnel. **E-mail address:** jobs@cnf.com. **World Wide Web address:** http://www.cnf.com. **Description:** A motor freight carrier and air freight forwarder operating in all 50 states. Operations include import/export brokerage, overseas forwarding, and warehousing and distribution services. **Positions advertised include:** Executive Administrative Assistant. **Corporate headquarters location:** This location. **Other U.S. locations:** Portland OR. **Listed on:** New York Stock Exchange. **Stock exchange symbol:** CNF. **Number of employees nationwide:** 33,700.

**CHIPMAN CORPORATION**
1521 Buena Vista Avenue, Alameda CA 94501. 510/748-8700. **Toll-free phone:** 800/755-0661. **Contact:** Personnel. **E-mail address:** chipman@chipmancorp.com. **World Wide Web address:** http://www.chipmancorp.com. **Description:** Provides moving and storage services both domestically and internationally. **Corporate headquarters location:** This location. **Other area locations:** Concord CA; Long Beach CA; Sacramento CA; San Jose CA; Valejo CA. **Other U.S. locations:** Portland OR; Seattle WA.

**CROWLEY MARITIME CORPORATION**
155 Grand Avenue, Oakland CA 94612. 510/251-7500. **Recorded jobline:** 904/727-4287. **Contact:** Personnel. **World Wide Web address:** http://www.crowley.com. **Description:** Provides marine transportation and construction services. **NOTE:** Jobseekers should send resumes to: Crowley Liner Services Human Resources, P.O. Box 2110, Jacksonville FL 32203. **Corporate headquarters location:** This location.

**DHL WORLDWIDE EXPRESS**
50 California Street, San Francisco CA 94111. 415/677-6100. **Contact:** Human Resources. **E-mail address:** hr_jobs@us.dhl.com. **World Wide Web address:** http://www.dhl.com. **Description:** An air

express network that, through its subsidiaries, services national and foreign markets in over 190 countries. **Subsidiaries include:** DHL Airways Inc.; DHL International Ltd.

### DISALVO TRUCKING COMPANY
859 Harrison Street, San Francisco CA 94107. 415/495-1800. **Contact:** Janet Mayer, Personnel Director. **E-mail address:** trucking@ disalvo.com. **World Wide Web address:** http://www.disalvo.com. **Description:** Operates an area trucking and trucking terminal services firm. **Corporate headquarters location:** This location.

### EAGLE GLOBAL LOGISTICS
385 Valley Drive, Brisbane CA 94005. 415/657-5200. **Contact:** Manager of Human Resources. **World Wide Web address:** http://www.eagleusa.com. **Description:** Provides international air and ocean freight forwarding services. **Positions advertised include:** Global Account Director. **Other area locations:** Sacramento CA; San Diego CA; San Jose CA. **Other U.S. locations:** Nationwide. **International locations:** Worldwide. **Listed on:** NASDAQ. **Stock exchange symbol:** EGL.

### FEDERAL EXPRESS CORPORATION (FEDEX)
950 Tower Lane, Suite 770, Foster City CA 94404. 650/578-5100. **Fax:** 650/866-2235. **Recorded jobline:** 888/513-2294. **Contact:** Jon Phillips, Senior Recruitment Specialist. **World Wide Web address:** http://www.fedex.com. **Description:** One of the world's largest express transportation companies serving 212 countries worldwide. FedEx ships approximately 3.2 million packages daily. FedEx operates more than 45,000 drop-off locations, and has a fleet that consists of more than 640 aircraft and 44,5000 vehicles. Founded in 1973. **Corporate headquarters location:** Memphis TN. **Listed on:** New York Stock Exchange. **Stock exchange symbol:** FDX. **Number of employees at this location:** 100. **Number of employees nationwide:** 148,000.

### FRITZ COMPANIES, INC.
706 Mission Street, San Francisco CA 94105. 415/904-8360. **Fax:** 415/904-8373. **Contact:** Human Resources. **World Wide Web address:** http://www.fritz.com. **Description:** A leader in global transportation and logistics. The company's services range from integrated logistics programs to traditional freight forwarding and customs brokerage. Fritz develops, implements, and delivers worldwide supply chain solutions for its clients. Founded in 1933.

**NOTE:** Entry-level positions are offered. **Special programs:** Internships. **Internship information:** Fritz Companies has an internship program with fall, winter, spring, and summer internships available in over 70 U.S. locations. All information concerning the internship program is available on the company's Website. **Corporate headquarters location:** This location. **Other U.S. locations:** Nationwide. **International locations:** Worldwide. **Parent company:** UPS. **Listed on:** New York Stock Exchange. **Stock exchange symbol:** UPS. **Annual sales/revenues:** More than $100 million. **Number of employees at this location:** 4,500. **Number of employees nationwide:** 8,000.

### GENERAL STEAMSHIP AGENCIES, INC.
575 Redwood Highway, Suite 200, Mill Valley CA 94941-3007. 415/389-5200. **Contact:** Janis Mahoney, Vice President of Human Resources. **E-mail address:** hr@gensteam.com. **World Wide Web address:** http://www.gensteam.com. **Description:** Operates a shipping agency. **Corporate headquarters location:** This location.

### PORT OF OAKLAND
530 Water Street, Oakland CA 94607. 510/627-1100. **Contact:** Manager of Personnel and Employee Services. **E-mail address:** perstech@portofoakland.com. **World Wide Web address:** http://www.portofoakland.com. **Description:** Operates Oakland International Airport, maritime facilities, and commercial real estate properties. **NOTE:** The above e-mail address may be used to request an application. **Special programs:** Internships. **Corporate headquarters location:** This location. **Operations at this facility include:** Administration; Service. **Number of employees at this location:** 600.

### SAN JOSE INTERNATIONAL AIRPORT
801 North First Street, Room 207, San Jose CA 95110. 408/277-4205. **Recorded jobline:** 408/277-5627. **Contact:** Human Resources. **World Wide Web address:** http://www.sjc.org. **Description:** Operates and manages the city's airport facilities. The airport is a city-funded department, and all airport staff are City of San Jose employees. **NOTE:** Employment applications must be obtained from the City of San Jose's Human Resources Department. **Positions advertised include:** Class Instructor; Firefighter; Heavy Diesel Equipment Operator; Lifeguard Instructor; Plant Operator; School Crossing Guard; Swimming Pool Aide.

## SHELL VACATIONS CLUB

The Cannery, 2801 Leavenworth Street, San Francisco CA 94133. 415/775-9601. **Fax:** 415/775-7928. **Contact:** Melanie Ignacio, Human Resources. **E-mail address:** resumes@shellvacationsllc.com. **World Wide Web address:** http://www.shellvacationsclub.com. **Description:** A vacation agency. **Positions advertised include:** Front Desk Agent; OPC Agent; Senior Tour Guide; Vacation Sales Representative; Vacation Loan Officer. **Corporate headquarters location:** Northbrooks IL.

## VIKING FREIGHT SYSTEM, INC.

P.O. Box 649002, San Jose CA 95164. 408/268-9600. **Contact:** Human Resources Department. **E-mail address:** hr@vikingfreight. com. **World Wide Web address:** http://www.vikingfreight.com. **Description:** A trucking company. **Corporate headquarters location:** This location. **Parent company:** FedEx. **Listed on:** New York Stock Exchange. **Stock exchange symbol:** FDX.

## UTILITIES: ELECTRIC/GAS/WATER

You can expect to find the following types of companies in this chapter:
*Gas, Electric, and Fuel Companies; Other Energy-Producing Companies •
• Public Utility Holding Companies • Water Utilities*

### AMERIGAS
4240 Rocklin Road, Suite 6, Rocklin CA 95677. 916/630-1588. **Fax:**
916/630-4279. **Contact:** Jim Stein, Employee Relations Manager. **E-mail address:** steinj@amerigas.com. **World Wide Web address:**
http://www.amerigas.com. **Description:** One of the nation's leading
suppliers of propane to various residential and commercial
customers. **Corporate headquarters location:** Valley Forge PA.
**Parent company:** UGI Corporation is a holding company whose
additional businesses include UGI Utilities, Inc. and UGI Enterprises,
Inc. **Operations at this facility include:** Regional Headquarters.
**Listed on:** New York Stock Exchange. **Stock exchange symbol:** APU.

### CALIFORNIA WATER SERVICE COMPANY
1720 North First Street, San Jose CA 95112. 408/367-8200. **Contact:**
Human Resources. **E-mail address:** employment@calwater.com.
**World Wide Web address:** http://www.calwater.com. **Description:** A
public utility supplying water service through 20 separate water
systems to 365,000 customers living in 38 California communities.
**Corporate headquarters location:** This location. **Other area
locations:** Statewide. **Parent company:** California Water Service
Group. **Listed on:** New York Stock Exchange. **Stock exchange
symbol:** CWT.

### PACIFIC GAS & ELECTRIC COMPANY (PG&E)
P.O. Box 770000, San Francisco CA 94177. 415/973-7000. **Fax:**
415/972-5972. **Contact:** Human Resources. **World Wide Web
address:** http://www.pgecorp.com. **Description:** An investor-owned
utility that supplies electric and natural gas service throughout
northern and central California. **Positions advertised include:** Senior
Financial Reporting Analyst; Accounting Analyst; Document
Production Specialist; Regulatory Analyst. **Corporate headquarters
location:** This location. **Listed on:** New York Stock Exchange. **Stock
exchange symbol:** PCG. **Number of employees nationwide:** 23,000.

### REDWOOD OIL COMPANY
P.O. Box 428, Santa Rosa CA 95402. 707/546-0766. **Physical
address:** 455 Yolanda Avenue, Santa Rosa 95404. **Fax:** 707/526-

4954. **Contact:** Human Resources Manager. **World Wide Web address:** http://redwoodoil.com. **Description:** Distributes and carries various brand name petroleum products throughout northern California. Redwood Oil Company also sells, installs, and services a variety of petroleum storage and dispensing equipment. **Corporate headquarters location:** This location.

## MISCELLANEOUS WHOLESALING

**You can expect to find the following types of companies in this chapter:**
*Exporters and Importers • General Wholesale Distribution Companies*

### ABATIX ENVIRONMENTAL CORPORATION
14068 Catalina Street, San Leandro CA 94577. 510/614-2340. **Contact:** Andrea Staub, Director of Human Resources. **E-mail address:** hr@abatix.com. **World Wide Web address:** http://www.abatix.com. **Description:** A full-line distributor of durable and nondurable supplies to the following industry segments: asbestos and lead abatement, hazardous material remediation, and construction. Products include industrial safety supplies, construction tools, general safety products such as protective clothing and eyewear, and clean-up equipment. Abatix Environmental Corporation has seven distribution centers serving customers throughout the Southwest, the Midwest, and the Pacific Coast. **Corporate headquarters location:** Dallas TX. **Other U.S. locations:** Phoenix AZ; Las Vegas NV; Houston TX; Seattle WA. **Listed on:** NASDAQ. **Stock exchange symbol:** ABIX.

### THE COAST DISTRIBUTION SYSTEM
16725 Condit Road, Morgan Hill CA 95037. 408/782-6686. **Contact:** Human Resources. **World Wide Web address:** http://www.go-rv.com. **Description:** One of North America's largest distributors of parts and accessories to the recreational vehicle and boating industries. Products include awnings, electrical and plumbing items, towing equipment and hitches, appliances, marine electronics and safety equipment, and various accessories and consumables. The company distributes its products to an active customer base of over 15,000 retailers through 19 distribution centers located throughout the United States and Canada. **Corporate headquarters location:** This location.

### DO ALL BAY AREA
330 Commerce Circle, Sacramento CA 95815. 510/887-1331. **Toll-free phone:** 800/92-DOALL. **Contact:** Personnel. **E-mail address:** info@doall.com. **World Wide Web address:** http://www.doall.com. **Description:** A distributor of machine tools and other industrial supplies. **Corporate headquarters location:** Hartford CT.

## ITOCHU INTERNATIONAL INC.

50 California Street, Suite 2500, San Francisco CA 94111. 415/399-3700. **Contact:** General Manager. **E-mail address:** recruiting@itochu.com. **World Wide Web address:** http://www.itochu.com. **Description:** An international, multibusiness trading and investment company. Itochu International specializes in developing and sponsoring profitable opportunities in international and domestic commerce, industry, and finance, both as a principal and as an agent. **Corporate headquarters location:** New York NY. **Parent company:** Itochu Corporation.

## PETERSON TRACTOR COMPANY

P.O. Box 5258, San Leandro CA 94577. 510/357-6200. **Physical address:** 955 Marina Boulevard, San Leandro CA 94577. **Contact:** Rich Hasper, Director of Human Resources. **E-mail address:** rhasper@petersontractor.com. **World Wide Web address:** http://www.petersontractor.com. **Description:** A wholesaler of Caterpillar heavy construction equipment and diesel engines. Peterson also has retail locations. **Positions advertised include:** Utility Person; Technician/Welder; Heavy Duty Repairman; Steam Cleaner; Senior Accountant. **Corporate headquarters location:** This location. **Operations at this facility include:** Administration; Sales; Service.

## QUADREP

2635 North First Street, Suite 116, San Jose CA 95134. 408/432-3300. **Contact:** Personnel. **World Wide Web address:** http://www.quadrep.com. **Description:** Distributes connectors, cable assemblies, and other products manufactured by a variety of manufacturers. **Corporate headquarters location:** This location.

## WILBUR-ELLIS COMPANY
## CONNELL BROS. COMPANY

345 California Street, 27th Floor, San Francisco CA 94104. 415/772-4000. **Contact:** Human Resources. **World Wide Web address:** http://www.wilburellis.com. **Description:** International merchants and distributors involved in importing and exporting goods. Wilbur-Ellis trades agricultural feed and chemical products. **Corporate headquarters location:** This location. **Operations at this facility include:** Administration.

## ACCOUNTING & MANAGEMENT CONSULTING

AON Consulting/50
Bain & Company/51
Benson & Neff/51
Crawford Pimentel & Company,
  Inc./51
Deloitte & Touche/51
Ernst & Young LLP/52
Grant Thorton/52
H&R Block/52
KPMG Consulting/53
Arthur D. Little, Inc./ 53
PricewaterhouseCoopers/53, 54

## ADVERTISING, MARKETING, AND PUBLIC RELATIONS

A&R Partners/55
Access Communications/55
Aviso Inc./ 55
BBDO West/55
Blanc & Otus/56
Burson-Marsteller/56
Citigate Cunningham/56
Edelman Public Relations
  Worldwide/56
The Financial Relations Board
  Inc./57
Foote, Cone & Belding/57
GCI Group/57
Gartner Group/57
Golin Harris International/58
Hill and Knowlton Inc./58
The Horn Group Inc./58
Mackenzie Communications,
  Inc./58
Porter Novelli Convergence
  Group/59
Solem & Associates/59
Sterling Communications, Inc./59
TBWA/Chiat/Day/59
TMP Worldwide/59
J. Walter Thompson Company/60
UpStart Communications/60
Wilson McHenry Company/60
Young & Rubicam West/60

## AEROSPACE

Aerojet/61
Invision Technologies/61
Kaiser Electronics/61
Lockheed Martin Space Systems/62
Pacific Scientific Quantic/62
Rolls Royce Engine Services/62
Sanmina-Sci Corporation/63
Universal Propulsion Company/64
Wyman-Gordon Company/64

## APPAREL, FASHION, AND TEXTILES

Byer California/65
Koret of California, Inc./65
Levi Strauss & Company/65
The Tom James Company/66
Unifirst Corporation/66

## ARCHITECTURE/ CONSTRUCTION/ ENGINEERING (MISC.)

Bechtel Corporation/67
Burke Mercer/67
CH2M Hill California Inc./67
Cal-Air Conditioning/68
The Clark Construction Group,
  Inc./68
Exponent, Inc./68
Gensler/69
Hathaway Dinwiddie Construction
  Company/69
Lathrop Construction Company/70
Locus Technologies/70
Parsons Brinckerhoff Inc./70
Swinerton and Walberg Builders/70
Thomas Outdoor Lighting/71
URS Corporation/71
Wentz Group/71

## ARTS, ENTERTAINMENT, SPORTS, AND RECREATION

Allied Vaughn/73
Lucas Digital Ltd. LLC/73
Lucasfilm Ltd./73
The Oakland Athletics (A's)/74
Pixar Animation Studios/74
San Francisco Opera/74

San Jose Sharks/74

## AUTOMOTIVE

Conexant Systems Inc./75
Cummins West Inc./75
Custom Chrome, Inc./75
Firestone Tire & Service Center/76
Honeywell/76
New United Motor Manufacturing
  Inc./76

## BANKING/SAVINGS & LOANS/ OTHER DEPOSITORY INSTITUTIONS (MISC.)

Bank of America/77
Bay Bank of Commerce/77
Bay View Bank/77, 78
City National Bank/78
Comerica Bank California/78
Cupertino National Bank &
  Trust/79
Federal Home Loan Bank of San
  Francisco/79
First Bank and Trust/79
First Republic Bancorp Inc./79
Golden State Bancorp/California
  Federal Bank/79
Greater Bay Bancorp/80
Patelco Credit Union/80
U.S. Bank/80
U.S. Federal Reserve Bank of San
  Francisco/81
Union Banks of California/81
Wells Fargo & Company/81
Westamerica Bank/82
World Savings & Loan
  Association/82

## BIOTECHNOLOGY/ PHARMACEUTICALS/ SCIENTIFIC R&D (MISC.)

A.P. Pharma/83
Abaxis, Inc./83
ALZA Corporation/83
Applied Biosystems/84
Aradigm /84
BD Biosciences/84
Bayer Corporation/85
Bio-Rad Laboratories/85

BioTime, Inc./86
Calgene, Inc./86
Celera/86
Cell Genesys, Inc./86
Chiron Corporation/87
Cholestech Corporation/87
Cygnus, Inc./87
DNA PLant Technology
  Corporation/88
Dade Behring, Inc./88
Elan Pharmaceuticals, Inc./88
Genelabs Technologies, Inc./88
Genentech, Inc./89
Gilead Sciences/89
Insite Vision Incorporated/90
Northview Pacific Laboratories/90
Oncology Therapeutics Network/90
Onyx Pharmaceuticals, Inc./90
Protein Design Labs, Inc./91
SRI International/91
SangStat Medical Corporation/91
Scios Inc./91
Thermo Finnigan/92
Unilab Corporation/92
Xenogen Corporation/92

## BUSINESS SERVICES/ NON-SCIENTIFIC RESEARCH

ABM Industries Incorporated/93
Automatic Data Processing
  (ADP)/93
Buck Consultants/93
CJ Laser Business Services/93
Computer Horizons Corporation/94
Copart, Inc./94
Fair, Isaac and Co., Inc./94
Jetro San Francisco/95
Quest Discovery Services, Inc./95
Underwriters Laboratories Inc./95

## CHARITIES/SOCIAL SERVICES

American Cancer Society/96
Boy Scouts of America/96
Catholic Charities/96
Filipinos For Affirmative Action/96
Integrated Community Services/97
The Salvation Army/97
San Jose Job Corps Center/97
Sierra Club/97
YMCA of the East Bay/98

## CHEMICALS/RUBBER AND PLASTICS

BOC Gases/99
Cargill Salt Company/99
Flint Ink/100
Kelly-Moore Paint Company, Inc./100
The Sherwin-Williams Company Inc./100

## COMMUNICATIONS: TELECOMMUNICATIONS/ BROADCASTING

ABC7/KGO-TV/102
AT&T Media Services/102
Accom, Inc./102
Allied Telesyn, Inc./102
Applied Signal Technology/103
Aspect Telecommunications/103
CNet Networks, Inc./103
CopperCom/104
Cylink Corporation/104
CXR Telcom/104
Earthlink/105
Grass Valley Group/105
JDS Uniphase Corporation/105
KCRA-TV/105
L3 Communications, Inc./106
Lucent Technologies Internetworking System/106
Metro Tel Corporation/106
NextiraOne/107
RFI Enterprises/107
SS8 Networks/107
Siemens ICN/108
Stratex Networks/108
TCI (Technology for Communications International)/108
Tropian/108

## COMPUTERS (MISC.)

ADI Systems, Inc./110
Acma Computers/110
Actel Corporation/110
Acer America Corporation/111
Adobe Systems, Inc./111
Advent Software, Inc./111
Agilent Technologies/112
Alcatel/113

Aligo, Inc./113
Alldata Corporation/113
Amdahl Corporation/113
Amdocs Limited/114
Ampro Computers Inc./114
Anacomp, Inc./114
Apple Computer, Inc./115
Applied Imaging/115
Applied Materials, Inc./115
Asante Technologies/116
Auspex Systems, Inc./116
Autodesk, Inc./117
BMC Software, Inc./117
BARRA, Inc./117
Bell Microproducts Inc./118
Blue Coat Systems/118
BlueDot Software/118
Broderbund LLC/119
Cadence Design Systems, Inc./119
California Digital/119
Chrontel, Inc./120
Ciber Enterprise Solutions/120
Cisco Systems, Inc./120
Clarinet Systems, Inc./120
Communication Intelligence Corporation (CIC)/121
Computer Associates International, Inc./121
Compuware Corporation/122
Comsys/122
Consilium, Inc./122, 123
Cornerstone Peripherals Technology, Inc./123
Creative Labs, Inc./123, 124
Data Technology Corporation (DTC)/124
DecisionOne/124
DisCopyLabs/125
E*Trade/125
Edify Corporation/126
Electronic Arts, Inc./126
Electronic Data Systems Corporation (EDS)/126
Elevon, Inc./126
Engage-Adknowledge Technologies/127
ePlus, Inc./127
Everex Systems Inc./127
Excite Inc./127
Exodus Communications/128
Filemaker Inc./128
Force Computers, Inc./128
Fortel Corporation/128
Fujitsu Computer Products of America, Inc./129
Fujitsu Microelectronics, Inc./129
General Magic, Inc./129

## EDUCATIONAL SERVICES

## ELECTRONIC/INDUSTRIAL ELECTRICAL EQUIPMENT AND COMPONENTS

## ENVIRONMENTAL & WASTE MANAGEMENT SERVICES

## FABRICATED METAL PRODUCTS AND PRIMARY METALS

## FINANCIAL SERVICES (MISC.)

## FOOD AND BEVERAGES/ AGRICULTURE

## GOVERNMENT

## HEALTH CARE: SERVICES, EQUIPMENT, AND PRODUCTS (MISC.)

## HOTELS AND RESTAURANTS

## INSURANCE